# KINDERGARTEN LANGUAGE ARTS
# Teacher's Guide

## CONTENTS

| | |
|---|---|
| **Author:** | Mary Ellen Quint, M.A. |
| Editor: | Alan Christopherson, M.S. |
| Graphic Design: | Marybeth D. Graville |

Alpha Omega Publications®

804 N. 2nd Ave. E., Rock Rapids, IA 51246-1759

# OVERVIEW

# LANGUAGE ARTS

## Curriculum Overview
## Grades K-12

■————————————————————————————————————————————■

## Kindergarten

### Language Arts Lessons

| 1-40 | 41-80 | 81-120 | 121-160 |
|---|---|---|---|
| **Alphabet-**say the alphabet<br>**Colors-**recognize colors<br>**Directions-**left to right<br>**Following directions-**given once<br>**Grammar-**form simple sentences<br>**Listening skills**<br>**Personal recognition-**read and write first name<br>-know age and address<br>-recognize names of family members<br>**Phonics-**short *a, e, i* vowels<br>-initial: *b, t, m, r, s, n, d, p, l*<br>-form and read simple words<br>-form rhyming words<br>**Shapes-**circle, square, triangle, and rectangle<br>-recognize shapes in objects<br>**Stories and Poems-**create simple stories and poems<br>**Writing-**form circle and lines<br>-*Aa, Bb, Dd, Ee, Ii, Ll, Mm, Nn, Pp, Rr, Ss,* and *Tt* | **Grammar-**sentences begin with capital, end with period<br>**Patterns-**simple shape, color patterns<br>**Personal recognition-**read and write first and last name<br>**Phonics-**short *a, e, i, o,* and *u* vowels<br>-initial: *k, c, ck, f, h, g, j, v, w, y, z, qu,* and *x*<br>-read simple sentences<br>**Position/direction concepts-**in/out, in front of/behind, up/down, on/off, open/closed, over/under<br>**Sequencing-**alphabetical order<br>-simple story<br>**Shapes-**oval<br>**Size concepts-**big/little, large/small<br>**Writing-***Kk, Cc, Ff, Hh, Oo, Gg, Jj, Vv, Ww, Uu, Yy, Zz, Qq,* and *Xx* | **Phonics-**recognize the short vowel sounds<br>-recognize all initial consonant sounds<br>-recognize long *a, e, i, o,* and *u* sounds<br>-silent *e*<br>-initial consonant digraphs: *sh, ch,* both soft and hard *th*<br>-final consonant sounds: *_b, _ck, _k, _l*<br>**Word recognition-**color words, number words & shape words<br>**Writing-**name<br>-complete alphabet, capital and small letters<br>-all color words<br>-number words: *one, two, three, four, five, six*<br>-shape words: *circle, square, triangle* | **Phonics-**recognize the long vowel sounds<br>-initial consonant digraphs: *wh;* review *ch, sh, th*<br>-recognize all final consonant sounds:<br>**Stories and poems-**create, tell, and recite stories and poems<br>**Word recognition-**position/direction words: *up/down, high/low, in, inside, out, outside, top/bottom*<br>-number words: *seven, eight, nine, ten*<br>-shape words: *rectangle, oval, star*<br>**Writing-**number words: *seven, eight, nine, ten*<br>-shape words: *rectangle, oval, star*<br>-position/direction words: *up/down, high/low, in, inside, out, outside, top/bottom* |

# Language Arts LIFEPAC Overview

| | Grade 1 | Grade 2 | Grade 3 |
|---|---|---|---|
| **LIFEPAC 1** | **FUN WITH PHONICS**<br>• Short vowel sounds<br>• Consonants<br>• Main ideas<br>• Rhyming words | **KNOW YOUR NOUNS**<br>• Review vowels & consonants<br>• Beginning, middle, ending sounds<br>• Singular & plural nouns<br>• Common & proper nouns | **OLD AND NEW SKILLS**<br>• Vowels • Consonants<br>• Sentences phrases<br>• Capital letters<br>• Reading skills |
| **LIFEPAC 2** | **FUN WITH PHONICS**<br>• Kinds of sentences<br>• Cardinal • Ordinal numbers<br>• Suffixes • Plurals<br>• Classifying | **ACTION VERBS**<br>• Vowel digraphs<br>• Action words – verbs<br>• Following directions<br>• The dictionary • ABC order | **BUILDING WORDS • SENTENCES**<br>• Vowels - long, short<br>• Questions<br>• ABC order<br>• Capital letters |
| **LIFEPAC 3** | **FUN WITH PHONICS**<br>• Consonant digraphs<br>• Compounds • Syllables<br>• Possessives • Contractions<br>• Soft c and g | **SIMPLE SENTENCES**<br>• r-controlled vowels<br>• Consonant blends<br>• Using capital letters<br>• Subjects & verbs in sentences | **WORDS • GETTING TO THE ROOTS**<br>• Root words<br>• Dictionary Guide Words<br>• Synonyms • Antonyms<br>• Capital letters |
| **LIFEPAC 4** | **FUN WITH PHONICS**<br>• Paragraphs<br>• Silent letters<br>• Sequencing<br>• Subject-verb agreement | **TYPES OF SENTENCES**<br>• Consonant digraphs<br>• Statement, question, exclamation sentences<br>• Using capital letters • The library | **WORDS • HOW TO USE THEM**<br>• Noun • Verb<br>• Adjective •Adverb<br>• Irregular vowels<br>• Composition |
| **LIFEPAC 5** | **FUN WITH PHONICS**<br>• Long vowels • Homonyms<br>• Poetry • Syllables<br>• Possessives • Contractions<br>• Plurals • Suffixes | **USING PUNCTUATION**<br>• Diphthongs • Punctuation review<br>• Using a comma<br>• Rules for making words plural<br>• Writing a biography • Contractions | **SENTENCE • START TO FINISH**<br>• Main idea<br>• Capital letters and punctuation<br>• Paragraphs<br>• Making words plural |
| **LIFEPAC 6** | **FUN WITH PHONICS**<br>• R-controlled vowels<br>• Writing stories<br>• Pronouns<br>• Following directions | **ADJECTIVES**<br>• Rhyming words • Biblical poetry<br>• Adjectives in sentences<br>• Synonyms, antonyms • Thesaurus<br>• Comparative, superlative adjectives | **ALL ABOUT BOOKS**<br>• Main idea<br>• Books<br>• Stories • Poems<br>• Critical thinking |
| **LIFEPAC 7** | **FUN WITH PHONICS**<br>• Vowel digraphs<br>• Letters - business, friendly, invitations<br>• Syllables | **POSSESSIVE NOUNS**<br>• Introduction to letter writing<br>• Pronunciation key<br>• Possessive nouns<br>• Silent consonants • Homonyms | **READING AND WRITING**<br>• For directions<br>• Friendly letters<br>• Pronouns<br>• Fact • Fiction |
| **LIFEPAC 8** | **FUN WITH PHONICS**<br>• Vowel digraphs<br>• Subject-verb agreement<br>• Compounds • Contractions<br>• Possessives •Pronouns | **PRONOUNS**<br>• Author's intent & use of titles<br>• Predicting content • Suffixes<br>• Character, setting, & plot<br>• Analogies • Writing in cursive | **READING SKILLS**<br>• For sequence<br>• For detail<br>• Verbs – being, compound<br>• Drama |
| **LIFEPAC 9** | **FUN WITH PHONICS**<br>• Vowel digraphs<br>• Titles • Main ideas<br>• Sentences • Paragraphs<br>• Proper nouns | **VERB TYPES AND TENSES**<br>• Review action verbs<br>• Dividing words into syllables<br>• State of being verbs<br>• Past & present verb tenses | **MORE READING & WRITING**<br>• For information<br>• Thank you letters<br>• Book reports<br>• Reference books |
| **LIFEPAC 10** | **LOOKING BACK**<br>• Letters and sounds<br>• Contractions<br>• Plurals • Possessives<br>• Sentences • Stories | **LOOKING BACK**<br>• Nouns & verbs • Word division<br>• Consonant blends, digraphs<br>• Prefixes, suffixes, root words<br>• Possessives • Pronouns, adjectives | **LOOKING BACK**<br>• Reading for comprehension<br>• Sentence punctuation<br>• Writing letters<br>• Parts of Speech |

| Grade 4 | Grade 5 | Grade 6 |
|---------|---------|---------|
| **WRITTEN COMMUNICATION**<br>• Word derivations<br>• Story sequence<br>• Writing an outline<br>• Writing a report | **STORY MESSAGES**<br>• Main idea • Plot<br>• Character • Setting<br>• Dialogue<br>• Diphthong • Digraph | **READING FOR A PURPOSE**<br>• Critical thinking<br>• Research data<br>• Parables<br>• Synonyms | LIFEPAC 1 |
| **SOUNDS TO WORDS**<br>• Hard and soft – c and g<br>• Parts of dictionary<br>• Accented syllables<br>• Haiku Poetry | **MAIN IDEAS**<br>• Poetry • Story<br>• Synonyms • Compounds<br>• Topic sentence<br>• Adjectives • Nouns | **FORMING NEW WORDS**<br>• Prefixes • Suffixes<br>• Synonyms • Antonyms<br>• Adjectives • Adverbs<br>• Critical thinking | LIFEPAC 2 |
| **WORDS • HOW TO USE THEM**<br>• Prefixes • Suffixes<br>• Homonyms • Antonyms<br>• Poetry • Stories<br>• Writing an outline | **WORDS TO STORIES**<br>• Subject • Predicate<br>• Adverbs • Idioms<br>• Critical thinking<br>• Writing a short story | **BETTER READING**<br>• Story elements<br>• Author's purpose<br>• Information sources<br>• Outline | LIFEPAC 3 |
| **MORE WORDS • HOW TO USE THEM**<br>• Parts of speech<br>• Possession<br>• Written directions<br>• Verb tenses | **WRITTEN REPORT**<br>• Outline<br>• Four types of sentences<br>• Metaphor • Simile<br>• Writing the report | **SENTENCES**<br>• Capitals • Punctuation<br>• Four types of sentences<br>• Author's purpose<br>• Propaganda | LIFEPAC 4 |
| **WRITING FOR CLARITY**<br>• Figures of Speech<br>• Capital letters<br>• Punctuation marks<br>• Writing stories | **STORY ELEMENTS**<br>• Legend • Implied meaning<br>• Dialogue • Quotations<br>• Word order • Usage<br>• Story elements | **READING SKILLS**<br>• Following directions<br>• Literary forms<br>• Phrases • Nouns • Verbs<br>• Paragraph structure | LIFEPAC 5 |
| **FUN WITH FICTION**<br>• Book reports<br>• Fiction • Nonfiction<br>• Parables • Fables<br>• Poetry | **POETRY**<br>• Rhythm • Stanza<br>• Symbolism<br>• Personification<br>• Irregular plurals | **POETRY**<br>• Similes • Metaphors<br>• Alliteration • Homonyms<br>• Palindromes • Acronyms<br>• Figures of speech | LIFEPAC 6 |
| **FACT AND FICTION**<br>• Nouns • Verbs<br>• Contractions<br>• Biography • Fables<br>• Tall Tales | **WORD USAGE**<br>• Nouns - common, plural, possessive<br>• Fact • Opinion<br>• Story • Main idea | **STORIES**<br>• Story elements<br>• Nouns • Pronouns<br>• Vowel digraphs<br>• Business letter | LIFEPAC 7 |
| **GRAMMAR AND WRITING**<br>• Adjectives to compare<br>• Adverbs<br>• Figurative language<br>• Paragraphs | **ALL ABOUT VERBS**<br>• Tense • Action<br>• Participles • Of being<br>• Regular • Irregular<br>• Singular • Plural | **NEWSPAPERS**<br>• Propaganda<br>• News stories<br>• Verbs – auxiliary, tenses<br>• Adverbs | LIFEPAC 8 |
| **THE WRITTEN REPORT**<br>• Planning a report<br>• Finding information<br>• Outline<br>• Writing a report | **READING FLUENCY**<br>• Speed reading<br>• Graphic aids<br>• Study skills<br>• Literary forms | **READING THE BIBLE**<br>• Parables • Proverbs<br>• Hebrew - poetry, prophecy<br>• Bible History<br>• Old Testament Law | LIFEPAC 9 |
| **LOOKING BACK**<br>• Reading skills<br>• Nouns • Adverbs<br>• Written communication<br>• Literary forms | **LOOKING BACK**<br>• Literary forms<br>• Parts of speech<br>• Writing skills<br>• Study skills | **LOOKING BACK**<br>• Literary forms<br>• Writing letters<br>• Parts of speech<br>• Punctuation | LIFEPAC 10 |

# Language Arts LIFEPAC Overview

| | Grade 7 | Grade 8 | Grade 9 |
|---|---|---|---|
| **LIFEPAC 1** | **WORD USAGE**<br>• Nouns – proper, common<br>• Pronouns<br>• Prefixes • Suffixes<br>• Synonyms • Antonyms | **IMPROVE COMMUNICATION**<br>• Roots • Inflections<br>• Affixes • Interjections<br>• Directions – oral, written<br>• Non-verbal communication | **STRUCTURE OF LANGUAGE**<br>• Nouns • Adjectives<br>• Verbs • Prepositions<br>• Adverbs • Conjunctions<br>• Sentence parts |
| **LIFEPAC 2** | **MORE WORD USAGE**<br>• Speech – stress, pitch<br>• Verbs – tenses<br>• Principle parts<br>• Story telling | **ALL ABOUT ENGLISH**<br>• Origin of language<br>• Classification–<br>  nouns, pronouns, verbs,<br>  adjectives, adverbs | **NATURE OF LANGUAGE**<br>• Origin of language<br>• Use – oral and written<br>• Dictionary<br>• Writing a paper |
| **LIFEPAC 3** | **BIOGRAPHIES**<br>• Biography as a form<br>• Flashback technique<br>• Deductive reasoning<br>• Words – base, root | **PUNCTUATION AND WRITING**<br>• Connecting and<br>  interrupting<br>• The Essay<br>• Thesis Statement | **PRACTICAL ENGLISH**<br>• Dictionary use<br>• Mnemonics<br>• Writing a paper<br>• Five minute speech |
| **LIFEPAC 4** | **LANGUAGE STRUCTURE**<br>• Verbs – tenses<br>• Principle parts<br>• Sentence creativity<br>• Speech – pitch, accent | **WORDS • HOW TO USE THEM**<br>• Dictionary<br>• Thesaurus<br>• Accent • Diacritical mark<br>• Standard • Nonstandard | **SHORT STORY FUNDAMENTALS**<br>• Plot • Setting<br>• Characterization<br>• Conflict<br>• Symbolism |
| **LIFEPAC 5** | **NATURE OF ENGLISH**<br>• Formal • Informal<br>• Redundant expressions<br>• Verb tenses<br>• Subject–verb agreement | **CORRECT LANGUAGE**<br>• Using good form<br>• Synonyms • Antonyms<br>• Homonyms<br>• Good speaking qualities | **LANGUAGE IN LITERATURE**<br>• Collective Nouns • Verbs<br>• Use of comparisons<br>• Gerunds • Participles<br>• Literary genres |
| **LIFEPAC 6** | **MECHANICS OF ENGLISH**<br>• Punctuation<br>• Complements • Modifiers<br>• Clauses – subordinate,<br>  coordinate | **LANGUAGE AND LITERATURE**<br>• History of English<br>• Coordination and<br>  Subordination<br>• Autobiography | **STRUCTURE AND MEANING IN LITERATURE**<br>• Reading for purpose<br>• Reading for meaning<br>• Reading persuasion<br>• Understanding poetry |
| **LIFEPAC 7** | **THE NOVEL**<br>• The Hiding Place<br>• Sequence of Events<br>• Author's purpose<br>• Character sketch | **CRITICAL THINKING**<br>• Word evaluation<br>• The Paragraph –<br>  structure, coherence,<br>  introductory, concluding | **COMMUNICATION**<br>• Planning a speech<br>• Listening comprehension<br>• Letters – business,<br>  informal, social |
| **LIFEPAC 8** | **LITERATURE**<br>• Nonfiction<br>• Listening skills<br>• Commas • Semicolons<br>• Nonverbal communications | **WRITE • LISTEN • READ**<br>• Business letters<br>• Personal letters<br>• Four steps to listen<br>• Nonfiction | **LIBRARY AND DRAMA**<br>• Library resources<br>• Drama – history,<br>  elements, reading<br>• The Miracle Worker |
| **LIFEPAC 9** | **COMPOSITIONS**<br>• Sentence types<br>• Quality of paragraph<br>• Pronunciation<br>• Nonsense literature | **SPEAK AND WRITE**<br>• Etymology<br>• Modifiers • Person<br>• Number • Tense<br>• Oral report | **STUDIES IN THE NOVEL**<br>• History • Define • Write<br>• Critical essay<br>• Twenty Thousand Leagues<br>  Under the Sea |
| **LIFEPAC 10** | **LOOKING BACK**<br>• Parts of speech<br>• Sentence structure<br>• Punctuation<br>• How to communicate | **LOOKING BACK**<br>• Composition structure<br>• Parts of speech<br>• Critical thinking<br>• Literary forms | **LOOKING BACK**<br>• Communication – writing<br>  speaking, listening<br>• Using resources<br>• Literature review |

| Grade 10 | Grade 11 | Grade 12 | |
|---|---|---|---|
| EVOLUTION OF ENGLISH<br>• Historical development<br>• Varieties of English<br>• Substandard & standard<br>• Changes in English | STANDARD ENGLISH<br>• Need for standard English<br>• Guardians of the standard<br>• Dictionaries<br>• Types of standard English texts | THE WORTH OF WORDS<br>• Word categories<br>• Expository writing<br>• Sentence structure<br>• Diction | LIFEPAC 1 |
| LISTENING AND SPEAKING<br>• Noun plurals<br>• Suffixes<br>• Creating a speech<br>• Nature of listening | EFFECTIVE SENTENCES<br>• Subordinate – clauses,<br>  conjunctions<br>• Relative pronouns<br>• Verbals • Appositives | STRUCTURE OF LANGUAGE<br>• Parts of speech<br>• Sentence structure<br>• Subordinate phrases<br>• Subordinate clauses | LIFEPAC 2 |
| EFFECTIVE SENTENCES<br>• Participles • Infinitives<br>• Prepositions • Gerunds<br>• Sentences – simple,<br>  compound, complex | SENTENCE WORKSHOP<br>• Understanding pronouns<br>• Using pronouns correctly<br>• Using modifiers correctly<br>• Parallel sentence structures | READ, RESEARCH, LISTEN<br>• Reading skills<br>• Resources for research<br>• Taking notes<br>• Drawing conclusions | LIFEPAC 3 |
| POWER OF WORDS<br>• Etymology • Connotations<br>• Poetic devices<br>• Poetry – literal,<br>  figurative, symbolic | WHY STUDY READING?<br>• Greek and Latin roots<br>• Diacritical markings<br>• Finding the main idea<br>• Analyzing a textbook | GIFT OF LANGUAGE<br>• Origin–Biblical,<br>  Koine Greek<br>• Purpose of Grammar<br>• Semantics | LIFEPAC 4 |
| ELEMENTS OF COMPOSITION<br>• Paragraphs<br>• Connectives • Transitions<br>• Expository writing –<br>  elements, ideas | POETRY<br>• Metrical feet • Sets<br>• Musical effects<br>• Universality<br>• Imagery • Connotation | ENGLISH LITERATURE<br>• Early England<br>• Medieval England<br>• Fourteenth century<br>• Chaucer | LIFEPAC 5 |
| STRUCTURE AND READING<br>• Subordinate clauses<br>• Pronouns – gender,<br>  case, agreement<br>• Reading for recognition | NONFICTION<br>• Elements<br>• Types – essays, diaries,<br>  newspaper, biography<br>• Composition | ELIZABETHAN LITERATURE<br>• Poetry<br>• Prose<br>• Drama<br>• Essay | LIFEPAC 6 |
| ORAL READING AND DRAMA<br>• Skills of oral reading<br>• Drama – history, irony<br>  elements, allegory<br>• Everyman | AMERICAN DRAMA<br>• Development • History<br>• Structure<br>• Purpose<br>• Our Town | 17TH—18TH CENTURY LITERATURE<br>• Historical background<br>• Puritan Literature<br>• Common sense – satire<br>• Sensibility | LIFEPAC 7 |
| THE SHORT STORY<br>• Elements<br>• Enjoying<br>• Writing<br>• The Literary Critique | AMERICAN NOVEL<br>• Eighteenth, nineteenth<br>  twentieth Century<br>• The Old Man and the Sea<br>• The Critical Essay | WRITING • SHORT STORY, POETRY<br>• Fundamentals<br>• Inspiration<br>• Technique and style<br>• Form and process | LIFEPAC 8 |
| THE NOVEL<br>• Elements<br>• In His Steps<br>• The Critical Essay<br>• The Book Review | COMPOSITION<br>• Stating the thesis<br>• Research<br>• Outline<br>• Writing the paper | POETRY • ROMANTIC , VICTORIAN<br>• Wordsworth • Coleridge<br>• Gordon • Byron • Shelley<br>• Keats • Tennyson • Hopkins<br>• Robert and Elizabeth B Browning | LIFEPAC 9 |
| LOOKING BACK<br>• Writing skills<br>• Speech skills<br>• Poetry • Drama<br>• Short stories • Novel | LOOKING BACK<br>• Analyzing written word<br>• Effective sentences<br>• Expository prose<br>• Genres of American literature | LOOKING BACK<br>• Creative writing<br>• English literature –<br>  Medieval to<br>  Victorian | LIFEPAC 10 |

# MANAGEMENT

*STRUCTURE OF THE KINDERGARTEN CURRICULUM*

The Kindergarten *Learning to Read* program provides language readiness activities to support the LIFEPAC Language Arts curriculum. Students move from very basic skills of size, shape, colors, to learning recognition of capital and small letters of the alphabet, initial and final consonant sounds, short and long vowel sounds, and consonant digraphs.

*Kindergarten Language Arts* is conveniently structured to provide two student workbooks and one Teacher's Guide. The Teacher's Guide is designed to provide a step-by-step procedure that will help the teacher prepare for and present each lesson effectively. It is suggested that the 160 lessons be completed in a nine month program.

A thorough study of the Curriculum Overview and teacher materials by the teacher before instruction begins is essential to the success of the student. The teacher should become familiar with expected skill mastery and understand how these grade level skills fit into the overall skill development of the curriculum.

*EVALUATION*

Kindergarten students are generally not ready for formal test situations; however, some type of assessment of student progress is both appropriate and necessary. Although student evaluation may be done at any time, a thorough assessment should be done at the completion of each quarter's work (40 lessons). The results of the assessment will provide the teacher with a guide to the student's progress and an analysis of any of the student's weak areas. Student evaluation information is provided in Part IV of the Teacher's Guide. Remember, the evaluation is *not* a test. The procedure is meant to help identify weaknesses before they become too great to overcome. Several days may be set aside for assessment or it may be integrated with regular daily work. Do not allow the student to tire of the activity or you will not achieve accurate results. Review is essential to success. Time invested in review where review is suggested will be time saved in correcting errors later.

## GOAL SETTING AND SCHEDULES

Each school must develop its own schedule, because no one set of procedures will fit every situation. The following is an example of a daily schedule that gives an overall view of a typical day for a kindergarten student.

Possible Daily Schedule

| | | | |
|---|---|---|---|
| 8:30 | - | 8:40 | Pledges, songs, devotions, etc. |
| 8:40 | - | 9:00 | Bible Reading, Memory Time, etc. |
| 9:00 | - | 10:00 | Language Arts - *Learning to Read* |
| 10:00 | - | 10:15 | Break |
| 10:15 | - | 11:00 | Mathematics |
| 11:00 | - | 11:10 | Review and Drill Assignments |
| 11:10 | - | 11:15 | Washroom Break |
| 11:15 | - | 11:30 | Activity (art, music, science, etc.) |
| 11:30 | - | 11:45 | Story Time |
| 11:45 | - | 12:00 | Clean Up |
| 12:00 | | | Dismissal |

A key concept here is to be structured (have a plan), but be flexible enough to realize that some days will need to be adjusted to better fit the lesson and rate of learning. If more time is needed on a particular day to teach concepts, omit the noncritical activities and abbreviate each individual lesson while being careful that the concept is still covered. But be sure to leave in singing, story time and other fun activities for transition between the more mentally taxing subjects. Because of the varying levels of maturity of children, they will grasp and retain the material at various times.

Long range planning requires some organization. Because the traditional school year originates in the early fall of one year and continues to late spring of the following year, a calendar should be devised that covers this period of time. Approximate beginning and completion dates can be noted on the calendar as well as special occasions such as holidays, vacations, and birthdays. The 160 lessons in the kindergarten curriculum may be divided into four quarters of 40 lessons each. Starting at the beginning school date, mark off forty school days on the calendar and that will become the targeted completion date for the first quarter. Continue marking the calendar until you have established dates for the following three quarters or 120 lessons making adjustments for previously noted holidays and vacations.

# WEEKLY LESSON PLANNER

**Week of:**

| | Subject | Subject | Subject | Subject |
|---|---|---|---|---|
| **Monday** | | | | |
| **Tuesday** | Subject | Subject | Subject | Subject |
| | | | | |
| **Wednesday** | Subject | Subject | Subject | Subject |
| | | | | |
| **Thursday** | Subject | Subject | Subject | Subject |
| | | | | |
| **Friday** | Subject | Subject | Subject | Subject |
| | | | | |

# WEEKLY LESSON PLANNER

**Week of:**

| Subject | Subject | Subject | Subject |
|---|---|---|---|
| **Monday** | | | |

| Subject | Subject | Subject | Subject |
|---|---|---|---|
| **Tuesday** | | | |

| Subject | Subject | Subject | Subject |
|---|---|---|---|
| **Wednesday** | | | |

| Subject | Subject | Subject | Subject |
|---|---|---|---|
| **Thursday** | | | |

| Subject | Subject | Subject | Subject |
|---|---|---|---|
| **Friday** | | | |

NOTES

## INTRODUCTION TO KINDERGARTEN LANGUAGE

This Language Arts Kindergarten Reading Readiness Program is meant to bridge the gap between the *Preschool Readiness* program and the LA 100 series of LIFEPACs. It is geared to children of Kindergarten age (usually five year olds) and is meant to lead them gradually to reading. It provides the basis from which more advanced children can move into reading at any time while moving children who simply are not yet ready to read gradually into the reading process.

Each Volume of 80 lessons is divided into four sections: the main lessons; a writing practice section; a story log section; and a story book section. The last three sections are intended for use along with the main lessons throughout the year.

The *Writing Practice* section in Volume One gives additional space to practice each letter of the alphabet as it is presented in the lessons. In Volume Two, this section gives additional practice space for name, address, color, number, and shape words as well as position and direction words. This section is to be used in "small doses" according to the child's abilities and individual needs. Correct letter formation and word spacing are the goal, not completion of a large number of pages in a short space of time. If a child forms some letters easily and well very quickly, additional practice for those particular letters may not be needed. Other letters, however, may cause more difficulty and need practice.

The *Story Log* section provides space for teacher, parent, or both to record the titles of stories and poems read aloud to the child, as well as stories read by the child as abilities increase. Reading aloud to children has been found, in several studies, to be one of the most important factors in successful learning for children. Reading aloud to children from an early age promotes vocabulary understanding and development; increases attention span; develops imagination; helps the child not only gain an interest in reading , but actually read more quickly; and establishes a bond between child and reader which is very important for learning and growth. A key to this program is spending at least 15 to 30 minutes a day, every day, reading to the children. Trips to the library which allow the children to select the books to be read and to choose the books they are able to read are also suggested.

The *Story Book* section of the children's book provides space for stories *created by the children* but *scripted by teacher, older child, or other adult*. Telling and writing stories, reciting and creating poems are another key to developing the vocabulary and skills needed for reading. This program contains many activities, both within the lessons and supplementary to the lessons, for creating stories and poems. Children should not be expected to write out all of the stories and poems created. This can be handled in several ways:
1. Write group stories or poems on chart paper and save them like a "big book."
2. Write stories or poems on the board copying them later and reproducing them to be made into booklets for the children to review and reread.
3. Have parents, aides, or older children who write legibly script the stories and poems for the children in the back of their book, or in a notebook.

Later in the year, depending on the children's abilities, they can begin to write short stories and poems on their own.

The *Lessons* are structured in such a way that the primary instruction is phonetic, that the children will learn to build words as they learn the sounds needed for those words. In addition to the phonetic approach, however, the children are exposed to words that they see and use daily. In Volume One, these words are printed in the lessons, not as words which must be read at the time, but as words that, when introduced in later lessons, will be recognized. Color words, number words, words for pictures on vowel and initial sound pages all fall into this category. This is done to encourage those children who are able to read these words to increase their skills. Those who are not ready to read them initially, should be able to when all sounds have been taught.

Most lessons encourage finding and listing words and names from the Bible which relate to the sound or lesson being taught. This is done to build understanding and familiarity with the Bible. Many of the words will be too difficult for the children to actually read and they should not be required to do so. Hearing and seeing these words, however will benefit their learning both to read and to understand the word of God.

Listening is a very important skill for everyone. Small children often do not listen carefully to directions. Reading to the children, giving them simple directions, listening to music, and learning songs and nursery rhymes help to build listening skills. The following activities should be apart of the children's experience from birth. In preparation for kindergarten, some specific listening activities can be introduced.

1. When giving a direction to children, keep it simple and do not repeat it. This will teach them to listen the first time and to ask questions only if the direction is not clearly understood.
2. Do some simple pattern drills with the children.
   - Say a set of three words and have the children repeat them. Increase the number of words as the children are able.
   - Read a simple sentence and ask the children to repeat. Make the sentences longer as they are able to repeat them correctly.
   - Clap or snap a pattern for the children to repeat. Clap the syllables in each child's name and ask them to repeat it.
   - Play musical games such as "musical chairs."
   - Have the children clap to the rhythm of music.
   - Listen for sounds in words. Have a "b" day in which the children become conscious of the times they hear the "b" sound.
   - Have the children close their eyes and listen to the sounds around them: inside the room, outside the room, and so on.

This section of the teacher handbook includes the following teacher aids: 1) Index of Concepts 2) Phonics/Spelling/Syllable Guidelines 3) Teacher Instruction Pages.

The Index of Concepts is a quick reference guide for the teacher who may be looking for a rule or explanation that applies to a particular concept. It does not identify each use of the concept in the various LIFEPACs. The Phonics/Spelling/Syllable Guidelines are another convenient reference guide.

Materials needed are usually items such as pencils and crayons which are readily available. Additional items that may be required are Alphabet-Penmanship Charts (available for purchase through the catalog ), writing tablets or any lined paper, alphabet cards, color and number charts, and flash cards for vocabulary words.

# PHONICS for Language Arts Kindergarten

The following letter and letter combinations are introduced in Language Arts Kindergarten. They may be put on cards for drilling purposes.

a  e  i  o  u

b  c  d  f  g  h  j  k  l  m  n  p  q  r  s  t  v  w  x  y  z

th  wh  sh  ch,  ng  nk,  ck  mb  lk  gn  kn  gh

ar  er  ir  or  ur,  ai  ay,  au  aw,  ei  ey,  ea  ee,  ie

oa,  oo,  ew,  ou,  ow,  oi,  oy

gh  ph,  igh

| | | | |
|---|---|---|---|
| 1. | short vowels | - | a (bat)  e (bet)  i (bit)  o (cot)  u (but) |
| 2. | long vowels | - | a (bait)  e (beat)  i (bite)  o (coat)  u (use) |
| 3. | consonants | - | b  d  f  h  j  k  l  m  n  p  r  s  t  v  w  x  z |
| 4. | c and g | - | hard sound before a, o, u |
| | | - | soft sound before e, i |
| 5. | q (qu) | - | always has the sound of kw |
| 6. | y | - | as y  (yard) |
| | | - | as e  (baby) |
| | | - | as i  (cry) |
| 7. | consonant digraphs | - | th,  wh,  sh,  ch |
| 8. | special blends | - | ng (sing)  nk (sank) |
| 9. | silent consonants | - | ck (lock) |
| | | - | mb (lamb)  lk (talk)  gn (sign) |
| | | - | kn (know)  gh (though)  t (often) |
| 10. | r-controlled vowels | - | ar (car)  or (for) |
| | | - | er (her)  ir (sir)  ur (fur) |
| 11. | vowel digraphs | - | ai,  ay  as long a  (pail) (pay) |
| | | - | au,  aw  (Paul) (paw) |
| | | - | ei,  ey as long a  (veil) (they) |
| | | - | ea,  ee as long e  (beat) (feet) |
| | | - | ie as long e  (piece) |
| | | - | as long i  (pie) |
| | | - | oa as long o  (boat) |
| | | - | oo long sound  (boot) |
| | | | short sound  (book) |
| | | - | ew as long u  (few) |
| | | - | ou as long u  (soup) |
| | | - | as `ow'  (cloud)* |
| | | - | ow as long  o (slow) |
| | | | as `ow'  (clown)* |
| | | - | oi, oy  (boil) (boy)* |
| 12. | letter groups | - | gh  ph  as f (laugh) (phone) |
| | | - | igh as long i (sigh) |
| | | | *sometimes referred to as diphthongs |

## SPELLING RULES for Language Arts Kindergarten

1. Double the final consonant of a short vowel word before adding *er, ed* and *ing,* and drop the final *e* in long vowel words and some short vowel words before adding *er, ed* and *ing.*
2. Even though the sound is the same, some words with the *ch* sound are spelled *tch* . In *ch* words, if the letter right after the *h* is an *l* or *r,* the *ch* will usually have the sound of *k* as in *Christmas* or *chlorine.*
3. Words ending in *s, x, sh* or *ch* must have the *es* ending to make them plural.
4. *Y* is used at the end of short words to make the sound of *i. Y* is used at the end of long words (those with two or more syllables) to make the sound of *e.*
5. A word that has a long vowel sound may have a silent *e* at the end of the word.
6. Because *er, ir, ur* and sometimes *or* all have the same sound, it becomes necessary to remember how the word is spelled.
7. Words that end in *y,* change the *y* to *i* before adding *es.* Words that end in *f,* change the *f* to *v* before adding *es.*

## THE SYLLABLE RULE  for Language Arts Kindergarten

There are as many syllables in a word as the number of vowels you can hear.

Example:     boat:     One vowel is heard.  (*oa* is a vowel digraph)
This is a one syllable word.

basket:     Two vowels are heard - *a* and *e.*
This is a two syllable word.

difference:     Three vowels are heard - *i, e, e.*
(The final *e* simply makes the *c* a soft sound.)
This is a three syllable word.

# INVENTORY OF SKILLS – LESSONS 1 - 40

**Address:**          Lesson 2

**Age:**              Lesson 1

**Alphabetical order:**
                      Lessons 4, 6, 22, 39

**Individual letter recognition:**
                      Lessons 7, 10, 13, 15, 18, 21, 24, 25,  27, 29, 31, 34, 37, 40

**Colors:**           Lessons 9, 11, 12, 14, 23, 36, 38

**Following Directions/Listening:**
                      Lessons 2, 3, 14, 17, 20, 26, 36

**Name:**             Lessons 1, 26, 39

**Numbers:**
  **Counting:**       Lessons 11, 16, 20, 23

**Patterns:**         Lesson 5

**Phonics**
  **Initial sounds:**
    Bb:               Lessons 10, 11, 17, 20, 40
    Tt:               Lessons 13, 14, 17, 20, 40
    Mm:               Lessons 15, 16, 20, 40
    Rr:               Lessons 18, 19, 20, 39
    Ss:               Lessons 24, 25, 33, 39
    Nn:               Lessons 27, 28, 33, 39
    Dd:               Lessons 29, 30, 33, 39
    Pp:               Lessons 31, 32, 33, 39

  **Vowels- short:**
    Aa:               Lessons 7, 8, 17, 40
    Ee:               Lessons 21, 22, 33, 40
    Ii:               Lessons 34, 35, 40

**Position and Direction:**
  **Left to Right:**  Lessons 5, 8, 9

**Sentences:**        Lessons 26, 30, 33

**Sequence:**
  **Stories:**        Lesson 36

**Shapes:**           Lessons 9, 11, 12, 14, 16, 17, 19, 23, 32, 38

| Story writing: | Most lessons. |
|---|---|
| Writing: | Lessons 1, 5, 6, 7, 10, 13, 15, 18, 21, 24, 27, 29, 31, 34, 37 |
| Word Formation: | Lessons 28, 30, 33 |

## INVENTORY OF SKILLS:      LESSONS 41 – 80

**Alphabetical order:**
Lessons 50, 58, 65, 68, 79

**Individual letter recognition:**
Lessons 41, 43, 45, 48, 51, 54, 57, 60, 63, 66, 69, 72

**Colors:**      Lessons 46, 59, 70, 71, 77

**Following Directions/Listening:**
Lessons 42, 53, 62, 73, 80

**Name:**      Lesson 62

**Numbers:**
  **Counting:**      Lesson 68

**Patterns:**      Lessons 53, 77

**Phonics**
  **Initial sounds:**

| Kk: | Lessons 41, 42, 50 |
|---|---|
| Cc: | Lessons 43, 44, 50, 61 |
| Ff: | Lessons 45, 46, 50 |
| Hh: | Lessons 48, 49, 50 |
| Gg: | Lessons 54, 55 |
| Jj: | Lessons 57, 58, 61 |
| Vv: | Lessons 60, 61 |
| Ww: | Lessons 63, 64, |
| Yy: | Lessons 69, 70 |
| Zz: | Lessons 72, 73 |
| Qu: | Lessons 75, 76 |
| Xx: | Lessons 78, 79 |

**Initial consonant review:**
Lessons 50, 55, 61, 71, 77, 80

**Vowels- short:**

| Oo: | Lessons 51, 52, 64 |
|---|---|
| Uu: | Lessons 66, 67, 80 |

**Vowel review:**      Lessons 64, 74, 80

**Position and Direction:**
    **Left to Right:**    Lessons 68, 74

    **Up/down; under/over; in front of/beside:**
        Lessons 53, 56, 73, 80

**Pronoun:**    Lessons 1 - 68

**Sentences:**    Lessons 68, 74

**Sequence:**
    **Stories:**    Lessons 42, 62

    **Alphabet:**    Lessons 47, 50, 56, 58, 65, 68, 79

**Shapes:**    Lessons 46, 53, 59, 70

**Story writing:**    Most lessons.

**Writing:**    Lessons 41, 43, 45, 48, 51, 54, 57, 58, 60, 63, 66, 69, 72, 75, 78

**Word Formation:**    Lessons 52, 66

## INVENTORY OF SKILLS    LESSONS 81 - 120

**Alphabetical order:**
    Lesson 81

**Colors (including word recognition):**
    Lessons 82, 86, 90, 95, 99, 103

**Following Directions/Listening:**
    Lessons 82, 89, 91, 98, 100

**Enrichment Activities:**
    Lessons 85 (#3), 88 (#3), 93 (#3), 97 (#3), 100 (#2), 102 (#3), 106 (#3), 109 (#3), 111 (#3), 113 (#3), 117 (#2), 119 (#3)

**Name, Age, Address:**
    Lesson 81

**Numbers:**
    **Numerals**    Lesson 100, 119

    **Number word recognition:**
    Lesson 107, 112, 118, 119

**Patterns:**
    Lesson 108 and in selected activities

Phonics
Consonant digraphs:

| | |
|---|---|
| Sh: | Lessons 105, 106 |
| Ch: | Lessons 110, 111 |
| Th (soft): | Lessons 115, 117 |
| Th (hard): | Lessons 116, 117 |

**Final consonant:**

| | |
|---|---|
| __b: | Lesson 106 |
| __ck: | Lesson 106 |
| __d: | Lesson 111 |
| __g: | Lesson 111 |
| __k: | Lesson 117 |
| __l: | Lesson 117 |

**Initial consonant review:**

Lessons 85, 88, 93, 97, 102

**Long vowels:**

| | |
|---|---|
| a: | Lessons 84, 85, 91, 119 |
| e: | Lessons 87, 88, 91, 113 |
| i: | Lessons 92, 93, 119 |
| o: | Lessons 96, 97, 113 |
| u: | Lessons 101, 102, 119 |

**Short vowel review:**

Lessons 83, 94, 100, 104, 108

**Silent e:** Lesson 83

**Poetry:** throughout, especially Lessons 81, 86, 90, 93

**Position and Direction concepts:**

Lessons 82, 98

**Rhymes:** Lessons 85, 88, 93, 97, 102

**Sentences:** Lessons 68, 74

**Sequence:**
  **Stories:** Lessons 91, 104, 113

  **Alphabet:** Lessons 83, 104, 113

**Shapes (including word recognition):**

Lessons 82, 98, 109, 114, 120

**Size words:** Lesson 100

| Story writing: | Most lessons, especially Lessons 85, 88, 93, 97, 102, 106, 111, 117 |
|---|---|
| Writing: | Lessons 86, 90, 95, 97, 103, 107, 109, 112, 114, 119, 120 |
| Word Formation: | in many activities. |

## INVENTORY OF SKILLS:    LESSONS 121- 160

**Colors:**         Lessons 139, 150, 155

**Following Directions/Listening:**
Lessons 124, 126, 136, 139, 150, 154, 155, 159

**Enrichment Activities:**
Lessons 122 (#3), 124 (#3), 127 (#3), 132 (#3), 134 (#4)

**Name, age, address:**
Lessons 149, 160

**Numbers (including word recognition):**
Lessons 123, 128, 132, 140

**Patterns:**         Lessons 151 and in selected activities

**Phonics**
**Consonant digraphs (initial):**
wh:         Lessons 121, 122
All:         Lessons  121, 122, 124, 127, 135, 152, 158

**Consonant digraphs (final):**
Lesson 144

**Final consonant (individual):**
___ m:         Lessons 122, 129
___ p:         Lessons 122, 129
___ n:         Lessons 127, 129
___ r:         Lessons 127, 129
___ s:         Lesson 132
___ t:         Lesson 132
___ v:         Lesson 134
___ w:         Lesson 134
___ x:         Lesson 134
___ z:         Lesson 134

**Final consonant review:**
Lessons 138, 146, 159, 160

**Initial consonant review:**
>Lessons 136, 142, 152, 155, 157,158

**Long vowels review:**
>Lessons 140, 148, 151, 156

**Short vowel review:**
>Lessons 133, 134, 138, 142, 146, 154

**Position and Direction concepts:**
>Lessons 124, 133, 137, 139, 141, 150, 159

**Predicting Outcomes:**
>Lesson 143

**Rhymes:**   throughout especially lesson 143

**Sentences:**   Lessons 131, 134

**Sequence:**
   **Stories:**   Lessons 136, 157

   **Alphabet:**   Lessons 126, 129, 144, 153, 157

   **Numerical:**   Lessons 126, 148, 156, 157

**Shapes (including word recognition):**
>Lessons 125, 130, 135, 147, 150, 154

**Story writing:**   Most lessons, especially 122, 147

**Writing:**   Lessons 123, 125, 128, 130, 133, 137, 141, 145, 147

**Word Formation:**   in many activities, especially: 131, 134, 138, 142, 148

**OBJECTIVES:**
1. To follow directions.
2. To recognize and write first name.
3. To identify family members by name.
4. To recognize and tell age.

**MATERIALS:** pencils, name cards, crayons, Bible. Optional: photographs, tactile letters.

**TEACHING PAGES 1, 2, and 3:**

1. Turn to page 1. Read what Sam and Jip are saying. Write the first name of the child on the first line. Have the child trace and say their name. Have the child copy on the next line. If children have difficulty, help them. Many 5 and 6 year olds are not yet ready to write. Encourage them to do the best they can and help them finish, if needed.

2. Introduce page 2 by talking about the names of family, friends, and pets. Have the children look at page 2 and talk about who they will place on the page. Be flexible. If some children are from a single-parent family, have no brothers or sisters, or no pets, they may put in grandparents, friends, or extended family. Have the children draw and color pictures for each box. If photographs are available, they may be used. Write the name of each person/animal pictured for the children.

3. Introduce page 3 by asking how old the children are. Talk about the pictures. Count the candles on Sam's and Jip's cakes. Read the page and help the children write their ages in the space provided.

**EXTENDED ACTIVITIES:**

1. Make name cards for the children (first names only). Have the children decorate the space around the names with favorite colors and pictures. Keep them where children can see them easily.

2. Make name cards for members of the family and decorate with pictures of things each member likes.

3. Make a collage or mobile of all the family members. Write names on the back.

4. Talk about the importance of names. What would it be like if no one had a name? What if everyone had the same name?

5. Talk about the importance of names in the Bible. Tell the children that in many books of the Bible God chooses names for people or changes the name if He has a special job for someone. Read Genesis 17: 5 & 15, where God changes Abram's and Sarai's names, and Genesis 35:10 (Jacob/Israel).

What is your name?

Teacher Check

My name is

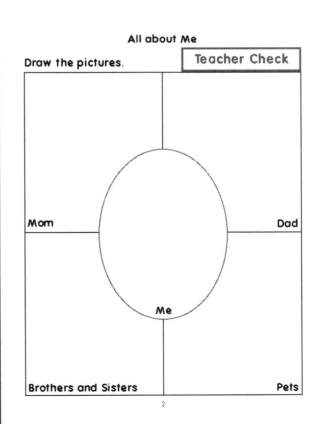

All about Me

Draw the pictures.

Teacher Check

Mom

Dad

Me

Brothers and Sisters

Pets

6. Talk about the name that is above all other names, Jesus (Philippians 2:9-11), how Jesus got His name (Mt. 1:21, Lk. 1:31), and about when Jesus told us to ask the Father for anything in His name (Jn. 14:14).

7. Start a chart of Bible names* that the children know. Add to it as they learn more.

8. If you have large tactile letters (letters made of felt, sandpaper, sponge, etc.), have the children make their names, close their eyes and feel the letters, trace and say the letters.

9. Have the children continue to practice their first names each day and with each lesson.

## SUGGESTED READING/ STORY IDEAS:

1. Find stories at the library about names or books of names.

2. Read the story of how John the Baptist got his name (Lk. 1:5-25; 57-64). Children can draw pictures or act out the story.

*Note: Biblical names and words will often be too difficult for the children to read. The lists, and later, the booklet are to familiarize the children with the Bible. Saying and seeing these names and words often will facilitate this and will, eventually, lead to the ability to read them.

## OBJECTIVES:
1. To follow directions.
2. To know and be able to say their address.

**MATERIALS:** pencils, crayons, pictures of different types of houses from different countries, pictures of animal/insect houses.

## TEACHING PAGES 4 and 5:
1. Talk about the picture on page 4. What kind of house do Sam and Jip have? What is an address? Why do people have addresses? Could people find your house without one? How would the mailman or a delivery man find your house?

2. Talk about where the children live: house, apartment, big city, small town, farm.

3. Read the page with the children. Help children write their addresses.

4. To prepare for page 5, have the children describe where they live. Have them draw a picture of where they live. Talk about the pictures. What is their favorite part of their house?

## EXTENDED ACTIVITIES:
1. Make cards with the children's addresses.
2. Talk about the differences in houses around the world: igloo, tent, huts, houseboats, castles, caves, and so on.
3. Talk about animal, bird, and insect houses.
4. Find pictures of houses in the Holy Land and talk about the kind of house where Jesus may have grown up.
5. Periodically, review the children's addresses with them orally until they know them.

## SUGGESTED READING/ STORY IDEAS:
1. Books about houses from the library.
2. Read "The Little House" by Virginia Burton. Ask if the children know of any houses in their area that might have a similar story.

We live at 22 Dog Bone Lane.

**Where do you live?**

Teacher Check

I live at 1302 Rice Rd Fulton MO 65251

4

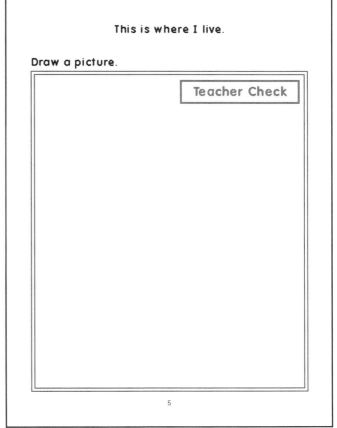

**This is where I live.**

**Draw a picture.**

Teacher Check

5

31

## OBJECTIVES:
1. To get excited about reading.
2. To find what words children already recognize.

**MATERIALS:** pencils, pictures of signs or frequently seen names.

## TEACHING PAGES 6 and 7:
1. On page 6, talk about the picture. What are they saying? Do the children agree with them? Have the children read the answer with you and trace it.

2. Most children have seen many street signs, fast food symbols and signs, and names of places they visit frequently. On page 7, explore with the children words they already recognize, and can "read".

3. Use the spaces at the bottom to write other words the children may know.

## EXTENDED ACTIVITIES:
1. Make a list, or use individual 3"x 5" cards, of words the children know. Add to the list as more words are learned.
2. Make a class list of words everyone knows.

## SUGGESTED READING/ STORY IDEAS:
1. Have each child create a story using the words already known. Help with connecting words or rebus (pictures) for sense. Write their stories out for them using the Story Book section at the back of their books.
2. Illustrate stories.
3. Find Bible stories that talk about where people lived (*Abraham, Moses*, etc.). Read and discuss what it would have been like to live in that period of time.

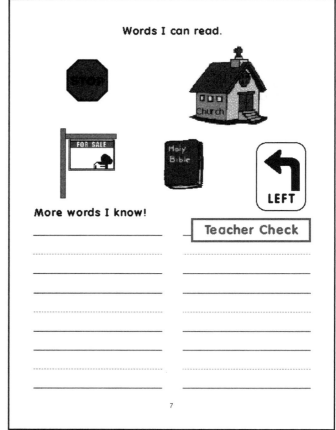

## OBJECTIVES:

1. To say the alphabet.
2. To recognize upper and lower-case letters.

**MATERIALS:** pencils, alphabet cards (or 3″ x 5″cards), books, and songs.

## TEACHING PAGES 8 and 9:

1. Everything has a name. Letters have names, too. Have the children point to each letter on page 8 as you say it in alphabetical order. Repeat the process and have the children say the letters with you. Tell the children that small letters are called lower-case letters.

2. Repeat the process for page 9. Tell the children that big letters are called capitals or upper-case letters. Use the alphabet song as you point to the letters.

## EXTENDED ACTIVITIES:

1. Make flash cards with both small and capital letters, perhaps the capital on one side of the card and the small letter on the other. Let the children who may know the alphabet help those who do not know it.

2. Make a large set of alphabet cards (both capital and small letters) out of some textured materials — cotton, felt, velour, sandpaper, and so on. Let the children feel the letter as well as see it. As the children learn more letters, games can be played by having the children select a letter with their eyes closed and try to guess what it is by feeling it. Three-dimensional letters, such as those that come with magnetic boards, are also good for this experience.

3. Sing the alphabet song frequently.

4. Alpha Omega Publications has a *Rev-Up for Learning: Reading, Writing & Arithemetic* DVD which will help the student learn the alphabet sequence and form all 26 letters.

5. Play a game to see if the children can think of a person's name for each letter of the alphabet. What letters do they see in their own names? Have them find and circle those letters. Check.

## SUGGESTED READING/ STORY IDEAS:

1. Find as many alphabet books and poems as possible and read often.

2. Prepare a notebook or binder as an alphabet book to be used for alphabet stories as new letters are introduced.

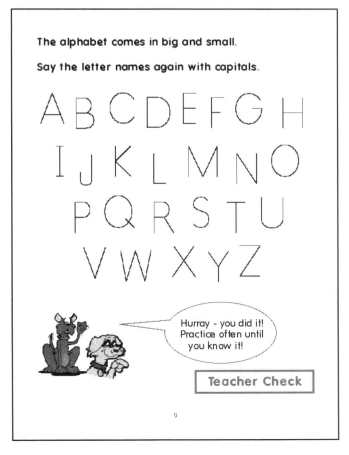

**OBJECTIVES:**
1. To form circles in preparation for writing.
2. To learn the correct way to write.
3. To learn to work from left to right.

**MATERIALS:** pencils, crayons, chart paper or tagboard.

**TEACHING PAGES 10 and 11:**
This lesson introduces the writing process. **A few cautions follow:**

1. Do not begin formal writing activities until the children have the proper coordination skills. They need proper eye-hand coordination and fine motor skills to hold the pencil correctly and to form letters and words. If the children have difficulties, do some simple exercises with them. Do not force them to do something they simply are not physically ready to do. The lines and spacing for writing in most books is limited. If the children need a larger space in which to write properly, use a chalk board, large paper, or other large surface where they can work more easily.

2. When they are ready to write, guide them in the proper way to hold the pencil. Remind them that writing is done from the left side of the page to the right side, and show them how this works. Always demonstrate correct letter formation so that they do not get into habits that will be more difficult to correct later.

3. Help the children to finish words, sentences, or activities which are difficult for them.

4. All the letters of the alphabet are made with circles, parts of circles, and straight lines. Circles should be made by starting at the top and going to the left. Many children make circles by starting at the bottom and will need help in making them correctly.

**Introduce Page 10:**
1. Ask the children what shape they see at the top of the page (some will call it a circle; some, an o). Tell them to put their fingers on top of the circle and trace around it to the left, following the arrow. Do the same with the other three circles.

2. Have the children put their fingers on the first circle on the lines and trace it. Have them pick up their pencils and trace the dotted circle, following the arrow. Then have them trace the dotted circle without the arrow. Finish the first line, making their own circles.

3. Take a break and have the children trace circles in the air, on their desks, on the floor, and so on.

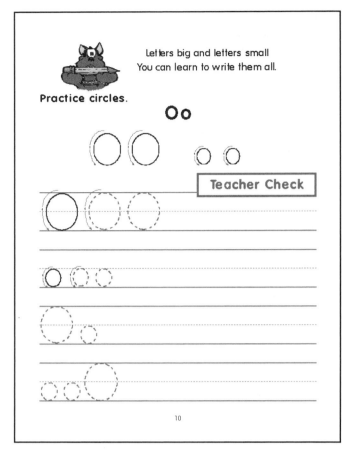

Letters big and letters small
You can learn to write them all.

**Practice circles.**

Oo

Teacher Check

10

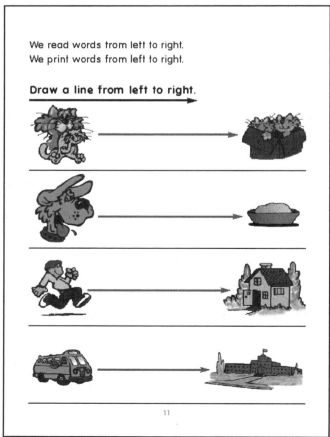

We read words from left to right.
We print words from left to right.

**Draw a line from left to right.**

11

4. Do the next two lines in the same way, reminding them to start at the top and to go to the left.

5. The final two lines introduce the children to simple patterns. Have the children trace the first two circles with their pencils, then ask them which should come next, a large circle or a small circle (large). Work together until you think they can finish the pattern by themselves. Do the final row in the same way. (two small circles, one large circle, two small, and so on).

6. If the children tire, break this lesson up or move to page 11 and then come back to complete this page.

**Introduce Page 11:**

1. To prepare the children for this page, play some left-right games. Ask them to raise their left hands, to touch their right eyes, to put their right elbows on their left knees, and so on. Go slowly at first; then, a little faster. This exercise not only helps them to practice left and right, but it also helps them to learn the parts of the body. Give extra help to any child who has difficulty distinguishing the left side from the right side, the left hand from the right, and so on.

2. Hold up a book with very large print. Tell the children that we always read from left to right. Read a sentence, drawing your hand from left to right under it as you read. Repeat this activity several times.

3. Remind the children that on page 10 they learned that we also write from left to right. Show them a wall calendar which has squares for each day of the week moving from left to right.

4. Have the children look at page 11. Tell them to put their fingers on the line and arrow under the direction. Read the direction. Have the children trace the arrow and tell which way it goes (left to right). Have them put their fingers on the first picture and ask one child to tell what he sees. Ask what is in the picture at the opposite side of the page. Then ask one to tell what he thinks will happen. (Mother cat will carry the kitten to the box.) Have them trace the dotted line from Mother cat to the box, first with a finger, then with a crayon. Do the same with the next line. Let the children finish the page independently. When all are finished, let them tell what is happening in each instance.

**EXTENDED ACTIVITIES:**

1. Do additional left-right activities with the children who have difficulty. Practice drawing lines from left to right, moving objects from left to right, walking from the left side of the room or yard to the right.

2. Make a chart for left and right. Print the words *Left* and *Right* at the top of a large sheet of construction paper or tagboard. Trace the child's right hand on the top right side of the chart and his left hand on the top left side of the chart. Divide the lower part of the chart in two columns. Have the children draw or find pictures of things that they do with each hand or that come in right and left pairs such as mittens, shoes, and skates.

3. Practice making circles by having the children write large and small circles in the air, and on the wall or floor with their fingers.

4. The writing practice section of the book has a page for additional circle practice. **DO NOT** do this page on the same day as this lesson. Use it over a period of days to review circles.

**SUGGESTED READING/ STORY IDEAS:**

1. Read story books and emphasize moving through the book and reading from left to right.

2. Create a felt book or make a felt board. Make a variety of felt people and objects to use to create stories. Use to create stories about left and right.

**OBJECTIVES:**
1. To write straight lines.
2. To form letters correctly.
3. To say the alphabet.
4. To recognize that everything has a name.

**MATERIALS:** pencils, 3" x 5" cards or self-stick note papers.

**TEACHING PAGES 12 and 13:**

1. On page 12, ask the children to look at the lines at the top of the page. Tell them to point first to the longer lines, then to the shorter lines. Ask them to look at the next set of lines. Tell them to put their fingers at the top of the line and to follow the arrow down. Repeat this activity with all the lines.

2. Follow the same procedure with the two rows that follow, tracing first with the finger, then with a pencil staying within the lines. Have the children complete the lines on their own.

3. On page 13, have the children look at the letters of the alphabet and say them together. Ask them to find all of the letters that have circles, or parts of circles, and all that have sticks.

4. Read what Sam has to say about names. Have the children begin to name things in the room. Have the children name the pictures on the page. Tell them that much of reading has to do with the names of things around them.

**EXTENDED ACTIVITIES:**

1. Continue talking about naming things: at home, at church, at school. Write any names of things that the children know on the board or a large sheet of paper. See how many of these names the children can "read".

2. Using 3" x 5" cards or self-stick note papers, write the names of some familiar objects and attach them to the objects so that the child will see them often and begin to associate the name with the object.

3. Additional practice for sticks and circles can be found on the second page of the writing practice section. Again, **DO NOT** do them all with the lesson or even on the same day, but use them in small sections as review.

**SUGGESTED READING/ STORY IDEAS:**

1. Read Genesis 2:19 to the children. Have them act out Adam's "naming" of every living creature. Discuss what names they might have given to specific animals if they were Adam.

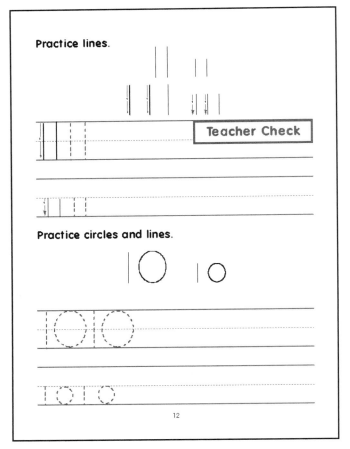

2. Have the children make a mural on large paper or butcher paper of Adam naming all the creatures. Write the names of each creature above or below when they have finished. Have the children retell the story.

## OBJECTIVES:

1. To recognize capital *A* and small *a*.
2. To write capital *A* and small *a*.
3. To recognize the sound of short *a*.

**MATERIALS:** pencils, chart paper or tagboard, magazines or catalogues.

## TEACHING PAGES 14 and 15:

1. Ask the children to put their fingers on the box on page 14. Ask if anyone can name the letter in it. If no one can, tell them that it is the letter *a*.

2. Tell them to look at the pictures. Say the name of each picture and have them repeat it after you. Ask them what sound the *a* makes at the beginning of each name. Tell them that this sound is called short *a*. Ask the children to give other words with the same sound.

3. Have the children put their fingers on the first *a* and follow the arrows to make first the circle and then the stick. Do the same with the other *a*'s in the row. Be sure that they start at the top of the circle.

4. Have the children trace the *a*'s at the beginning of each line, then finish the line independently. If children get tired, space this writing assignment so that they can benefit from it and not simply race through it.

5. Use the same procedure for the capital *A*, first tracing, then copying the letter. Walk around the room and make sure everyone is making the letters correctly. Give help if needed. Remind the children to keep the letters within the lines.

6. Begin working on the short *a* sound by stressing it in the pictures and words on page 14: *apple, ant, Adam,* and the last *a* in *Abraham*. Tell them that the *a* sound at the beginning of *Abraham* will be learned later.

7. Move to page 15 and have the children name the pictures on the page. Have them name them again stressing the short *a* sound. Let them trace the first *a* with their fingers, then with a pencil. Have them write *a* on the line under each picture saying the word as they do so.

8. Have the children think of words that begin with the short *a* sound (*am, at, and,* etc.).

9. Read the following list of words (or a similar list if you have one). Have the children either raise their hands or hold up a card with an *a* printed on it whenever they hear the short *a* sound. Examples: *ant, on, mat, egg, fan, bat, sun, can, sat*

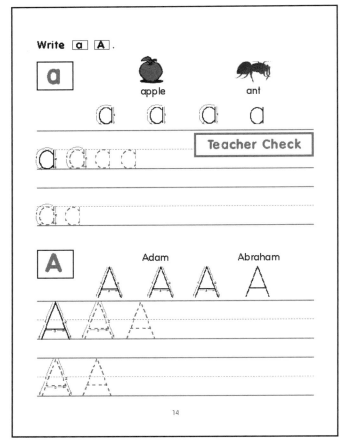

Write a A.

a    apple    ant

*a  a  a  a*

Teacher Check

A    Adam    Abraham

*A  A  A  A*

14

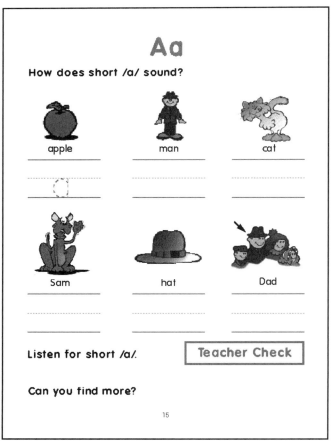

## Aa

**How does short /a/ sound?**

apple          man          cat

Sam          hat          Dad

**Listen for short /a/.**          Teacher Check

**Can you find more?**

15

**EXTENDED ACTIVITIES:**

1. Let the children who are able, write some short *a* words.

2. Play a rhyming game. Say a word such as *man* or *bat* and ask the children to say words that rhyme with the word given.

3. Make a short *Aa* chart using words and pictures from magazines.

4. Use the Alpha Omega Publications *Rev-Up for Learning: Reading, Writng, & Arithmetic* DVD as a supplement.

**SUGGESTED READING/ STORY IDEAS:**

1. Select easy books from the library which emphasize short a words, such as *The Cat in the Hat* or *Green Eggs and Ham*.

2. Find short *a* names and words from Bible stories the children may know: *Adam, animals, apple, Samuel, Daniel*.

Note: Many lessons in this volume present the word for a given picture. The purpose for this is so that the children begin to associate words with the objects they name. It is not necessary for the children to read the words at this time. Some children may be able to read them. Encourage these children to do so, but do not require *all* children to read them. Some will not be ready until they have learned all the sounds needed to read the word.

**OBJECTIVES:**

1. To recognize capital *A* and small *a*.
2. To write capital *A* and small *a*.
3. To recognize the sound of short *a*.
4. To find words and pictures with the short *a* sound.
5. To work from left to right.

**MATERIALS:** pencils, crayons, old magazines or catalogues, scissors, paste or glue, notebook or binder.

**TEACHING PAGES 16 and 17:**

1. Page 16 is a short *a* review and reinforcement page. It gives the children an opportunity to work with you to find pictures and words which have the short *a* sound. Talk about the short *a* work done in Lesson Six.

2. Have the children trace both the capital and small short *a* on the page.

3. Have the children look through magazines and catalogues to find pictures and words that have the short *a* sound. This page may be a collage of written words, drawings, cut and paste words and pictures. Help the children stress the short *a* sound when they find it. Help as needed with the writing, cutting, and pasting to complete the page.

4. To teach page 17, have the children put their fingers on the arrow. Have them follow the direction words from left to right as you read the direction.

5. Ask the children to look at the first two pictures and tell what is happening. Have them trace the line first with a finger and then with a crayon or pencil.

6. Tell them to look carefully at the next set of pictures to see what is happening and then to draw a line between them with a crayon or pencil. Discuss the page when everyone has finished. Ask the children to tell what is happening in each set. Encourage them to use complete sentences when answering.

**EXTENDED ACTIVITIES:**

1. Add to the short *Aa* chart if new words or pictures have been found.

2. Make a short *Aa* letter puppet. Puppets are a very good way to teach little children. Alphabet puppets are helpful for teaching both the names and sounds of the letters. Hand puppets, finger puppets, paper-bag puppets, or sock puppets are

My Aa page.

16

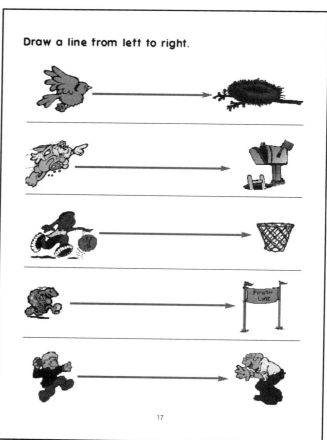

**Draw a line from left to right.**

17

all made easily. Name the puppet for the letter, i.e. *Andrew Apple, Benny Barn, Cathy Candy*, and so on. Many good books on puppets and alphabet learning are available at libraries or through school supply stores and catalogues.

3. As a home activity, have the children begin an alphabet scrapbook. Stress that the children are to do most of the work themselves, but ask the parents and family to help them find pictures. The children will do one page for each letter as they learn them in class. When all the letters have been completed, the children can bring their scrapbooks to school and share them with the class. In the home school share them with extended family and friends. The scrapbook should be kept for the entire year so that the children can review the letters and sounds they have learned and so that they can add new letter sounds and blends as they learn them. A looseleaf format would make the addition of pages easier and allow the addition of pages for more pictures and words for each sound as the children learn more. The children should begin their scrapbooks with the short *a* page. Instruct them to write *Aa* neatly at the top of the page. Tell them to ask their parents for old magazines that they might use to find pictures. Have them ask their parents to help them find pictures with the short *a* sound. Tell the children to cut the pictures out carefully (some may need help) and to paste them on the *Aa* page. Later the children can add words to their pages.

4. Do some left-right activities: lift your left foot, touch your right ear, put your right hand on your left foot, and so on. These activities can be done before you do the page, after you do the page, or at both times.

5. Have the children march around the room or out in the yard. Have them turn right or left on your command. March without music at first and have them say left, right as they march. Children who do not know which foot is left could have a piece of yarn tied around the left ankle.

6. The practice writing pages in the back of the children's book has a page for additional *Aa* practice. Use for review and practice a little each day.

**SUGGESTED READING/STORY IDEAS:**
1. Have the children review all the short *a* words and pictures they have found. Have the children make up short *a* stories. These stories can be dictated to the teacher or an aide and then

illustrated by the children. These stories may also be *rebus* stories, substituting pictures for words. A book of alphabet stories could be kept for each child.

2. Use the *Aa* puppet to tell the story.

## OBJECTIVES:

1. To identify the basic shapes of a *circle*, *triangle*, *square*, and *rectangle*.
2. To understand the words for basic shapes.
3. To recognize basic shapes within simple objects.
4. To work from left to right.
5. To recognize the colors *red*, *blue*, *green*, and *yellow*.

**MATERIALS:** pencils or crayons (especially *red*, *yellow*, *green*, and *blue*), objects with basic shapes or shapes cut from construction paper, or magazines.

## TEACHING PAGES 18 and 19:

1. The purpose of these pages is to introduce the children to the basic shapes. It is not necessary for the children to know or to be able to read the name of each shape. The names are presented simply so that the children may begin to associate the word with the shape. The reading of the name will be presented later.

2. Ask if anyone knows the names of the first shape on page 18. Have the children point to each shape, trace it with their fingers, and say the name after you. Ask the children to find objects in the room for each of the four shapes.

3. On page 19, ask if anyone knows the name of the first shape (square). Point out that a square has four sides that are exactly the same length. Have the children trace the square with their fingers. Ask them to find an object on page 19 that has a square shape. Have them tell what that object is (block). Have them trace the heavy square on the side of the block, then trace the line from the square to the block. Find other objects in the classroom or home with a square shape. Hold up a block or cube to show that all the sides are squares.

4. Follow the same procedure for the other shapes. Find an object to hold up for each one. Point out that triangles all have three sides but do not all look alike, and rectangles all have four sides —two longer sides and two shorter sides.

## EXTENDED ACTIVITIES:

1. The children may color the shapes on page 18. Color the square blue. Color the circle red. Color the rectangle orange. Color the triangle green.

2. Have the children find pictures in magazines that have the shapes. Outline the basic shape with a crayon. They could mount the pictures on tagboard making a separate chart for each shape.

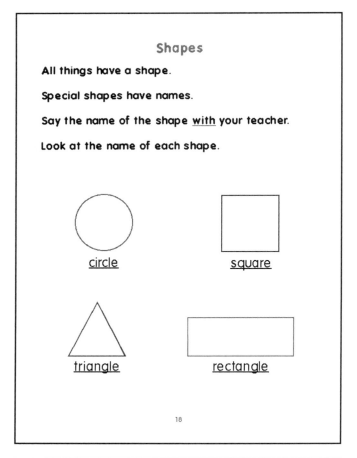

**Shapes**

All things have a shape.

Special shapes have names.

Say the name of the shape <u>with</u> your teacher.

Look at the name of each shape.

circle          square

triangle        rectangle

18

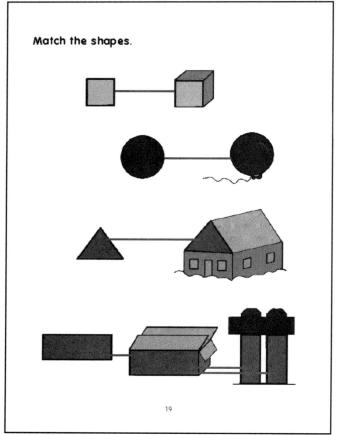

**Match the shapes.**

19

**SUGGESTED READING/ STORY IDEAS:**

1. Find shape books at the library and have available for children to look through and read.

2. Have the children choose one shape (either circle, square, rectangle, or triangle) and make up a story about what their world would be like if that shape were lost and nothing with that particular shape could be found or used. The story may be scripted on separate paper or in the Story Book section at the back of their books.

## OBJECTIVES:

1. To recognize capital *B* and small *b*.
2. To write capital *B* and small *b*.
3. To recognize the sound of *Bb*.

**MATERIALS:** pencils, Bible, tagboard, old magazines, scissors, paste or glue, alphabet or flash cards for *Bb*.

## TEACHING PAGES 20 and 21:

1. Have the children put their fingers on the letter in the box on page 20. Tell them that the letter has a name, *b*, and also a sound that they can hear at the beginning of the word *bat*. Repeat the sound and the word several times and have the children repeat it after you. Do the same with the words *boy* and *baby* on the top of the page and *Bible* and *Bethlehem* at the middle of the page. Have the children notice what happens to their lips when they say the *b* sound. Ask them to hold their hands in front of their mouths when they say the sound. Do they feel any air? (Alpha Omega's *Color Phonics*–illustrates the formation of sounds.)

2. Ask the children if they can think of more words that begin with the sound of *b*.

3. Have the children trace the *b* by following the arrows first for the line, then for the circle. Have them say the name of the letter to themselves as they trace it. Have them trace the letters on the lines and finish each line by themselves. Give help if necessary.

4. Follow the same procedure for the capital *B* on the bottom part of the page. Say the word *Bible*. Have the children repeat it emphasizing the *b* sound at the beginning and again in the middle of the word.   Have them do the same with *Bethlehem*. Complete the page as described in number three above. If children tire while writing, move on to page 21 and let them complete the writing after a break. Continue throughout the year with this procedure of spacing writing activities.

5. Have the children say the names of all the pictures on page 21 (*box, baby, bed, bow, ball, bell*). Ask where they hear the *b* sound (in the beginning except for *baby* which has both beginning and middle).

6. Read a list of words such as those which follow. Have the children raise their hands or hold up a card with *b* on it when they hear the *b* sound. Examples: *boy, cat, bat, bush, dog, burn, dig, big*.

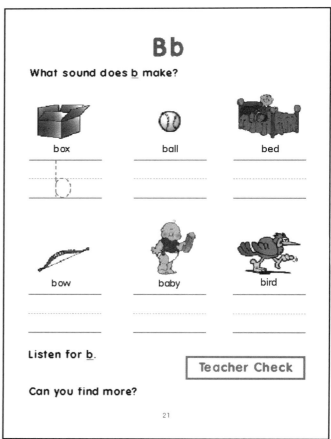

7. Ask the children to look around the classroom or home and find things which begin with the letter *b*.

## EXTENDED ACTIVITIES:

1. Hold up the Bible and ask how many know what it is. Write the word *Bible* on the board. Have the children find the word on page 20 and circle it. Point out that *Bible* has a *b* sound in the beginning and the middle.

2. Make a *Bb* chart.

3. Add to the Bible name chart begun in Lesson One. If you wish, begin a Bible booklet listing names, words, and pictures from the Bible for the letters of the alphabet.

## SUGGESTED READING/ STORY IDEAS:

1. Ask the children if they know a Bible story about a burning bush. Read Exodus 3:2 and tell the children the story of Moses and the burning bush. Have the children act out or draw pictures of the story.

2. Read Matthew 2:1 and 5, Ruth 1:19, or any other verses that tell about Bethlehem or someone who lived in Bethlehem. Use a simple globe or map to show the children where Bethlehem is located.

## OBJECTIVES:

1. To recognize capital *B* and small *b*.
2. To write capital *B* and small *b*.
3. To recognize the sound of *Bb*.
4. To identify basic shapes — *circle*, *triangle*, *square*, and *rectangle*.
5. To tell the difference in sizes and positions of objects.
6. To match shapes of different sizes and in different positions.
7. To recognize the colors *red*, *blue*, *green*, and *yellow*.

**MATERIALS:** pencils, crayons (especially red, blue, green, and yellow), magazines or newspapers, paste or glue, basic shapes of different sizes cut out of construction paper, materials to make puppet, alphabet scrapbook, kitchen sponges or thin foam, water based paint.

## TEACHING PAGES 22 and 23:

1. For page 22, review and reinforce the sound of the letter *b*, proceed as on page 16 (Lesson Eight), numbers 1, 2, and 3.

2. For page 23, use the basic shapes made from construction paper to review the name for each shape. Tell the children to look at the shape and to name it. Ask them to draw a line between the two shapes that are the same. The first one is done for them.

3. To check the children's understanding of numbers and their counting abilities, have the children count the number of squares on the entire page (4), the number of circles (4), the number of rectangles (4), and the number of triangles (4). If they have learned to write any numerals have them number each shape, 1, 2, 3, 4. Help as needed.

## EXTENDED ACTIVITIES:

1. Add to the *Bb* chart if new pictures and words have been found. Remember, when adding words to these charts, it is not essential that the children be able to read all of the words at this time. The words can be read to them. The recognition of the letter and listening to the sound of the letter as read by others are the important lessons for now.

2. Make a *Bb* puppet.

3. Add to the alphabet scrapbook at home.

4. Give each child a section of the newspaper (ads with larger letters are a good place to start). Have them circle all the *Bb*'s they find with a

My Bb page.

22

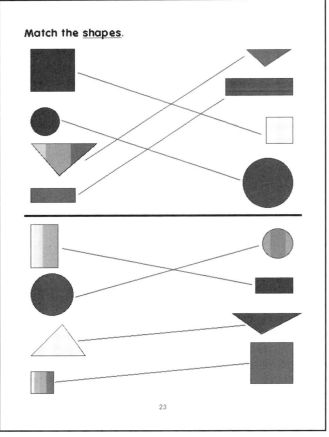

Match the **shapes**.

23

crayon or pencil. This helps them to identify the letter *Bb* even though it is in a different type of print.

5. Give the children each a sheet of construction paper with one of the shapes drawn on it and ask them to draw a picture using the shape.

6. Have the children make a shape booklet. Each child can contribute a page on which he has drawn a variety of things using all the shapes or one object that has all the shapes in it.

7. Cut basic shapes out of sponges or foam. Dip the shapes in a small amount of paint and print on plain paper. You may also brush the paint on the sponge in small amounts. Try different colors and overlapping shapes.

8. Additional practice for writing the letter *Bb* is found in the writing practice section at the back of the children's books.

**SUGGESTED READING/ STORY IDEAS:**

1. Write a story using as many *Bb* words as they can. Pictures may be used in place of words where appropriate. Write out the story for the children and let them add illustration. Add this story to the alphabet Story Book.

2. Have a child or several children use the *Bb* puppet to tell the story.

## OBJECTIVES:

1. To recognize the colors — *red, blue, green,* and *yellow.*

2. To recognize basic shapes — *circle, square, rectangle,* and *triangle.*

3. To match shapes and objects of the same color.

**MATERIALS:** red, blue, green, and yellow crayons, objects and basic shapes in the four colors, red, blue, green, and yellow construction paper.

## TEACHING PAGES 24 and 25:

1. Read page 24 to the children. Look at the names for each color. The purpose here, as with the shape names, is not to learn to read the words, but to begin associating the word with the color.

2. Have the children name things in the classroom or home for each color.

3. Have the children name the objects in the top box on page 25. Ask them to name the color of each object. Have them draw a line from the object in the left column to its match in the right column. At the bottom of the page, have the children find and circle the shape that matches.

## EXTENDED ACTIVITIES:

1. Have each child choose a color of construction paper. Ask the children to use that paper to make something that they like. They may draw a picture or cut out something. Have the children tell why they chose that color, what they made with their color, and what other things might come in that color.

2. Set up folders or small boxes (shoe boxes or oatmeal cartons) for each shape and color.
Have the children find small objects or pictures of things which can be put in the different boxes. For example, round objects or pictures of objects that are circular would be put in the *Circle* box, red objects or pictures of red objects would be put in the *Red* box.

## SUGGESTED READING/ STORY IDEAS:

1. Have the children create oral stories, for their construction paper project.

2. Periodically, spread out all the objects in one of the shape or color boxes and have the children write a story or poem trying to use all of the things represented there.

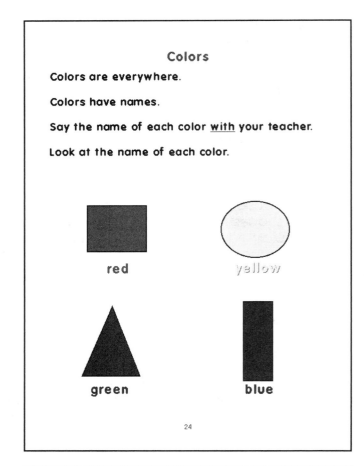

**Colors**

Colors are everywhere.

Colors have names.

Say the name of each color <u>with</u> your teacher.

Look at the name of each color.

red          yellow

green          blue

24

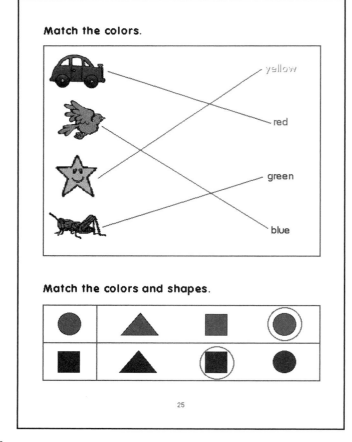

**Match the colors.**

yellow

red

green

blue

**Match the colors and shapes.**

25

## OBJECTIVES:

1. To recognize capital *T* and small *t*.
2. To write capital *T* and small *t*.
3. To recognize the sound of *Tt*.

**MATERIALS:** pencils, crayons, Bible, magazines or newspapers, paste or glue, chart paper or tagboard, flash cards for *Tt*.

## TEACHING PAGES 26 and 27:

1. To introduce *Tt* on pages 26 and 27, follow the procedures for pages 20 and 21 (Lesson Ten). Stress the words *tent, top, Thomas,* and *Timothy* on page 26.

2. Read a list of words such as those which follow. Have the children raise their hands or hold up a card with a *t* on it when they hear the *t* sound. Examples: *tiger, bag, Thomas, table, dog, time, tell, box, tight.*

3. Ask the children where they feel their tongues when they say the *t* sound (lightly touching the roof of the mouth). If they put their hands in front of their mouths, do they feel their breath?

4. Ask the children to find objects in the classroom, outdoors, or at home which begin with the sound *t*.

## EXTENDED ACTIVITIES:

1. Make a *Tt* chart.
2. Add to Bible booklet or chart.

## SUGGESTED READING/ STORY IDEAS:

1. Read Genesis 2:9 and 16; John 20:24 through 29; 2 Timothy 1:1 through 5; and any other references that contain the words *tent, tree, Thomas, Timothy,* or *Tobias.*

2. Have the more advanced students write and illustrate a story about : *Paul, the tentmaker; Timothy; Thomas; Jesus in the Temple; the Tower of Babel;* or any other Bible words or stories that could be included in the *Tt* section of the Bible booklet.

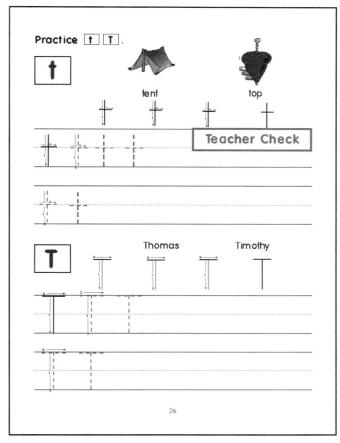

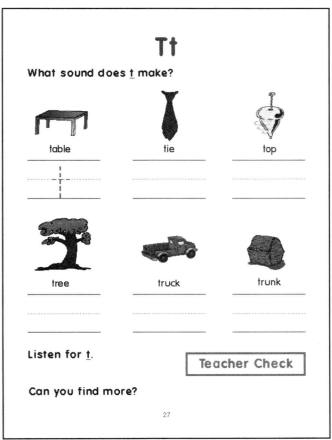

**OBJECTIVES:**
1. To recognize capital *T* and small *t*.
2. To write capital *T* and small *t*.
3. To recognize the sound of *Tt*.
4. To recognize basic shapes in common objects.
5. To recognize the colors *red*, *blue*, *green*, and *yellow*.
6. To follow directions.
7. To listen carefully.

**MATERIALS:** pencils, crayons, magazines and newspapers, paste or glue, materials to make puppet, alphabet scrapbook.

**TEACHING PAGES 28 and 29:**
1. On page 28 reinforce and review the sound *Tt*, follow the procedures for page 16, numbers 1, 2, and 3 (Lesson Eight).
2. On page 29, the children are required to listen to directions and follow them. (See the introduction of Teacher Notes, for activities to build listening skills.) Read the following directions slowly and clearly. Read each direction only once.
*Read:*
Put your finger on the truck.
Take your pencil. Pause.
Draw a circle around the green wheel. Pause.
Draw an X on the yellow wheel. Pause.
Draw a box around the truck. Pause.
Put your finger on the house.
Take your pencil. Pause.
Draw a circle around the triangle part of the house. Pause.
Draw a face in the square window.
Check.

**EXTENDED ACTIVITIES:**
1. Make *Tt* puppet.
2. Add to alphabet scrapbook at home.
3. Give the children a page from a newspaper or catalogue. Have them circle or cut out words that begin with *Tt*. Read the words for the children. Have them share the different words they found.
4. Add to the *Tt* chart, if new words or pictures have been found.
5. Additional practice for writing the letter *Tt* can be found in the writing practice section of the children's book.
6. Additional activities can be done to reinforce page 29. Have the children name each shape they recognize on the truck and the house. Ask them to point to the blue rectangles. Ask what color the triangle is, and so on.

My Tt Page.

28

Listen and find.      **Teacher Check**

29

**SUGGESTED READING/ STORY IDEAS:**

1. Write a story using as many *Tt* words as they can. Pictures may be used in place of words where appropriate. Write the story for the children and let them add illustration. Add to alphabet Story Book.

2. Have a child or several children use the *Tt* puppet to tell the story.

**OBJECTIVES:**
1. To recognize capital *M* and small *m*.
2. To write capital *M* and small *m*.
3. To recognize the sound of *Mm*.

**MATERIALS:** pencils, crayons, Bible, magazines or newspapers, paste or glue, chart paper or tagboard, alphabet or flash cards for *Mm*, 3" x 5" cards.

**TEACHING PAGES 30 and 31:**
1. To introduce *Mm* on pages 30 and 31, follow the procedures for pages 20 and 21 (Lesson Ten). Stress the words *man, mother, Mark,* and *Mary* found on page 30.
2. Read a list of words such as those which follow. Have the children raise their hands or hold up a card with an *m* on it when they hear the *m* sound. Examples: *man, nut, mouse, needle, Marie, box, mat.*
3. Have the children tell you how they make the *m* sound (lips together, sound inside). Does this sound remind them of something good to eat?
4. Have the children look around the classroom, outdoors, or at home for other things that begin with the *Mm* sound.

**EXTENDED ACTIVITIES:**
1. Make an *Mm* chart.
2. At this point in the readiness program, the children have learned sufficient sounds to be able to make new words. All children may not be ready for this activity, but some will. Make a kind of letter game for them: using 3" x 5" cards, cut the cards in half so that each card is 1 1/2" x 2 1/2". On each card, print one of the letters already learned (short *a, b, t, m*). Make several of each letter. Have the children spread the cards out and see if they can form any words. Examples: *at, am, bat, mat.* Have them use the words they make in a sentence. Help as needed. If the children are not ready and find this activity difficult, then wait several more weeks and try again.
3. Talk about names and words from the Bible that begin with the *Mm* sound: *Mary, Moses Mark, Matthew, Mother, man, manna.* Add these to Bible list or booklet.

**SUGGESTED READING/ STORY IDEAS:**
1. Read selected sections of the life of Moses (Exodus). If the children have a Bible, have them find the Gospel of Mark.

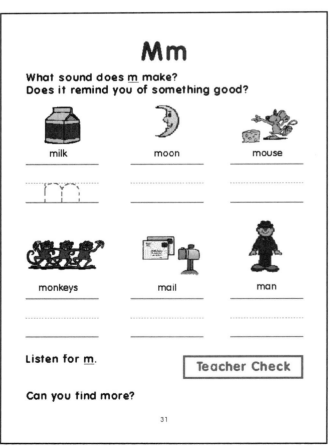

2. Read parts of Luke. Chapters 1 and 2 talk about Mary, Jesus' mother, and her story.

3. Have the more advanced students write a play on one of the *Mm* Bible figures. Have the class act it out.

**OBJECTIVES:**

1. To recognize capital *M* and small *m*.
2. To write capital *M* and small *m*.
3. To recognize the sound of *Mm*.
4. To distinguish different shapes.
5. To recognize shapes in more than one position.
6. To match shapes that are different sizes.

**MATERIALS:** pencils, crayons, magazines and newspapers, paste or glue, materials to make puppet, alphabet Scrap Book, construction paper, selection of basic shapes in different sizes.

**TEACHING PAGES 32 and 33:**

1. To reinforce and review the sound *Mm* on page 32, follow the procedures for page 16, numbers 1, 2, and 3 (Lesson Eight).

2. Tell the children to look at the shape in the box at the beginning of the row on the top of page 33. Ask them to look at the shapes in the long box. Have them circle all the shapes that are the same. Remind the children that some shapes may be a different size or in a different position than the first one. Read the directions for the children at the bottom of the page.

**EXTENDED ACTIVITIES:**

1. Make an *Mm* puppet.
2. Add to alphabet scrapbook at home.
3. Give the children a page from a newspaper or catalogue. Have them circle or cut out words that begin with *Mm*. Read the words for the children. Have them share the different words they have found.
4. Add to the Mm chart, if new words or pictures have been found.
5. Additional practice for writing the letter *Mm* can be found in the writing practice section of the children's book.
6. If children have learned to write numerals 1 through 4, have them number the shapes in each row of the long box at the top of the page and count as they write.
7. For an art project, give the children various sizes and colors of all the shapes or let them choose their own. Have them arrange the shapes on a sheet of construction paper to make designs, animals, objects, or people.
8. If some children have difficulty with shapes, have an aide, a volunteer, or an older student work with them. Provide pictures of objects with basic shapes, several construction paper or cardboard models of each shape in different

My Mm page.

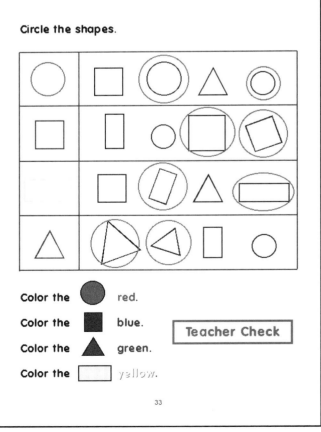

Circle the shapes.

Color the ● red.
Color the ■ blue.
Color the ▲ green.
Color the ▭ yellow.

Teacher Check

sizes. Have the children match shapes or pick out shapes from pictures, objects in the room, and so on.

**SUGGESTED READING/ STORY IDEAS:**

1. Write a story using as many *Mm* words as they can. Pictures may be used in place of words where appropriate. Write a story for the children and let them add illustration. Add to alphabet Story Book.

2. Have a child or several children use the *Mm* puppet to tell the story.

3. Have the children create a story for their art project in activity 7 above.

## OBJECTIVES:

1. To recognize the initial consonants: *t, b.*
2. To recognize short *a.*
3. To tell the difference in the size and position of objects.
4. To follow directions.
5. To distinguish degrees of size.

**MATERIALS:** pencils or crayons, *Tt, Bb,* and short *Aa* charts, pictures or objects which show *big* and *little,* basic shapes in various sizes.

## TEACHING PAGES 34 and 35:

1. Using the charts, review the initial *Tt, Bb,* and short *Aa* pictures which the children have found.

2. On page 34, have the children put their fingers on the letter in the first box (*t*), ask them what sound *t* makes. Then ask the children to name the pictures in each box. Which ones begin with the sound for *t*? Ask them to circle the pictures which begin with the *t* sound.

3. Repeat this process for the *b* and short *a* boxes.

4. To prepare for the activity on page 35, place two books on the table, one big and one little. Ask the children to tell which is the *big* object and which is the *little* one. Repeat this exercise using other objects and the shape patterns.

5. This activity is a listening activity. Tell the children that you will give them directions. Tell them that they must listen very carefully because you will say the direction only one time. Make it clear that you will not repeat the direction. Direct the children to put their fingers on the picture of the *cup* (do not repeat this direction). Ask them to look at the pictures and to trace an *X* on the *big circle* (do not repeat this direction). Make note of those who have not followed the directions. Ask them to put their fingers on the picture of the *fish* (do not repeat this direction). Have them take their pencils and put an *X* on the *small square* (do not repeat this direction). Follow the same procedure for the third and fourth boxes (*small triangle, big rectangle*).

## EXTENDED ACTIVITIES:

1. If children need extra drill on the initial consonants *Tt, Bb,* or short *Aa,* practice using the sound for a day. Make a set of cards for each sound (self adhesive note sheets work well). Help the children to find things which have the same sound as *Tt,* or *Bb,* or short *Aa,* whichever sound causes the problem. Let them take a letter card and attach it to the objects which begin with the

**Circle the pictures.**

34

**Put an X on the picture.**

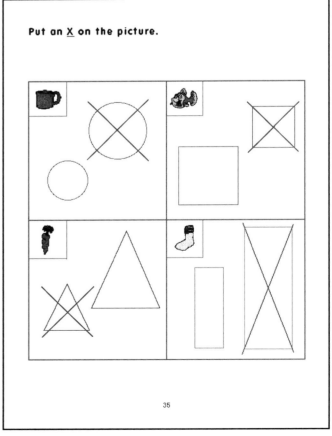

35

sound. Leave the letter cards in place for several days, even as new sounds are added. Example: The children would place a letter card *t* on a *table, towel, top,* and so on. This can be used for drill or for reinforcement when new sounds are added.

2. Make a large envelope for each sound. Collect pictures and words which begin with the *t* sound. Place the pictures and words in the envelope. The children can review them often, either independently or with an aide or older student.

3. Sharpen listening skills by playing a game like "Simon Says".

4. Have children practice the letters already learned in the writing practice section of the their book.

## SUGGESTED READING/ STORY IDEAS:

1. Find stories or poems about *big* and *little, large* and *small.*

2. Read the story of David and Goliath (1 Samuel 17). Have the children illustrate the story emphasizing how big Goliath was and how small David was. Have them act out the story if they are able.

## OBJECTIVES:

1. To recognize capital *R* and small *r*.
2. To write capital *R* and small *r*.
3. To recognize the sound of *Rr*.

**MATERIALS:** pencils, crayons, Bible, magazines or newspapers, paste or glue, chart paper or tagboard, alphabet or flash cards for *Rr*, 3" x 5" cards.

## TEACHING PAGES 36 and 37:

1. To introduce *Rr* on pages 36 and 37, follow the procedures for pages 20 and 21 (Lesson Ten). Stress the words *rose, rabbit, Ruth,* and *Ray* on page 36.

2. Read a list of words such as those which follow. Have the children raise their hands or hold up a card with an *r* on it when they hear the *r* sound. Examples: *run, man, rabbit, now, ride, ribbon, box, radio.*

3. How is the *r* sound made? Ask the children to tell you what happens with their teeth when they make the *r* sound.

## EXTENDED ACTIVITIES:

1. Make an *Rr* chart.

2. Have the children who are able, play the letter game introduced in extended Activity 2 for pages 30 - 31(Lesson Fifteen). Add *r* cards to those already made. Have the children spread the cards out and see if they can add more words to those found before. Examples: *rat, ram, art.* Have them use the words they make in a sentence. Add to the list of words and names they are able to form and sound out with the sounds already learned. Help as needed. Reminder: If the children are not ready and find this activity difficult, then wait several more weeks and try again.

3. Talk about names and words from the Bible that begin with the *Rr* sound: *Rebekah, Ruth, the letter to the Romans, Rachel, Red Sea, Resurrection,* and so on. Add these to Bible list or booklet.

## SUGGESTED READING/ STORY IDEAS:

1. Read or tell the children the story of Ruth in the Bible.

2. Read the story of the crossing of the Red Sea (Exodus 13:18; 14:20-31).

3. Have the children act out or illustrate either story.

## OBJECTIVES:

1. To recognize capital *R* and small *r*.
2. To write capital *R* and small *r*.
3. To recognize the sound of *Rr*.
4. To recognize basic shapes in objects around them.

**MATERIALS:** pencils, crayons, magazines and newspapers, paste or glue, materials to make puppet, alphabet scrapbook, objects that contain basic shapes.

## TEACHING PAGES 38 and 39:

1. To reinforce and review the sound *Rr* on page 38, follow the procedures for page 16, numbers 1, 2, and 3 (Lesson Eight).

2. Prepare the children for page 39 by holding up objects that contain basic shapes. Trace the shape with your finger (the side of a box for a square or rectangle, the round wheel on a toy, the triangle formed by the top of a closed milk carton, and so on).

3. Tell the children to look at the shape in the first box on page 39 and to find two objects that have the same shape. Read the direction and do the first box with them. Have the children finish the last three boxes on their own. Help as needed. Check.

## EXTENDED ACTIVITIES:

1. Make an *Rr* puppet.
2. Add to alphabet scrapbook at home.
3. Give the children a page from a newspaper or catalogue. Have them circle or cut out words that begin with *Rr*. Read the words for the children. Have them share the different words they found.
4. Add to the *Rr* chart, if new words or pictures have been found.
5. Additional practice for writing the letter *Rr* can be found in the writing practice section of the children's book.
6. For those children having difficulty seeing basic shapes in objects, set up a corner where they can work with an aide. Have available several objects (boxes, toys, balls, books, blocks, envelopes, and so on) so that the children can practice looking for basic shapes in the things around them.
7. Go to the boxes for the individual shapes (made in Lesson Twelve, Extended Activity 2, page 24 and 25) and have the children look at the objects and pictures they have collected. Have them trace with their fingers the shape they are working with on each object.

My Rr page.

38

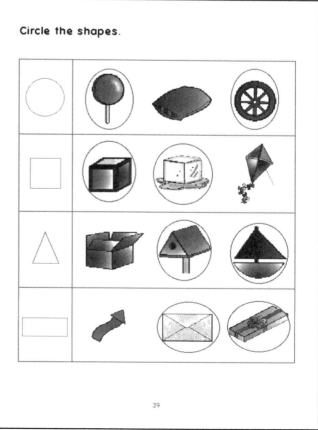

Circle the shapes.

39

**SUGGESTED READING/ STORY IDEAS:**

1. Write a story using as many *Rr* words as they can. Pictures may be used in place of words where appropriate. Write the story for the children and let them add illustration. Add to alphabet Story Book.

2. Have a child or several children use the *Rr* puppet to tell the story.

## OBJECTIVES:

1. To listen carefully.
2. To follow a direction given only once.
3. To match letters.
4. To write the letters *r, t ,m,* and *b.*
5. To recognize initial sounds *r, t, m,* and *b.*

**MATERIALS:** pencils or crayons, alphabet flash cards, charts made for *Rr, Tt, Mm,* and *Bb.*

## TEACHING PAGES 40 and 41:

1. The first activity on page 40 is another listening activity. Tell the children you will read a sentence, and they are to find the picture that matches the sentence and circle it. Tell them to listen very carefully because you will read the directions only once. Make sure that the directions are read slowly and clearly. Tell them to put their fingers on the *ball* and to listen carefully.
Read: *The black cat is eating.*
Circle the picture for the sentence. Tell them to put their fingers on the *apple* and to listen carefully.
Read: *The pig is running.*
Circle the picture for the sentence. Tell them to put their fingers on the *flower* and to listen carefully.
Read: *The boy is sitting.*
Circle the picture for the sentence. When they have finished, have them put their pencils away and take out a crayon. Then read the sentence again. If any children marked the wrong picture, tell them to circle the correct picture with the crayon.

2. To prepare for the second activity, review the alphabet song, or have the children recite the alphabet with you while looking at the letters on a chart.

3. Read the directions. Have the children look at the first letter then find and circle the letter like it in the long box. Let the children complete the activity independently.

4. Read the directions for page 41. Ask the children to put their fingers on the letter in the first box and trace it. Ask who can name the letter (*r*). Have the children copy the letter on the line next to it. Ask the children to name the pictures in the long box next to the letter. When they have finished ask them to circle the picture that begins with the letter *r.* Follow the same procedure for the remaining boxes. Note children who have problems with any of the letter sounds.

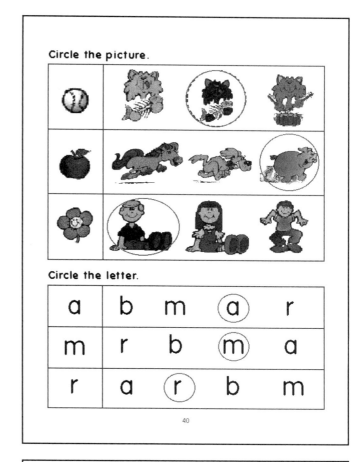

**EXTENDED ACTIVITIES:**

1. Reinforce listening by playing some direction games. Give the children three directions, such as these: *Stand up, Walk three steps, Touch your toes.* This can be done individually with a different set of directions for each or as a group. Say the directions only once.

2. Repeat the first activity on page 40 with different directions. Examples:

*ball*: Put an *X* on the cat that is playing a musical instrument.

*apple*: Put a box around the horse.

*flower*: Circle the picture that shows someone standing.

3. If children are having difficulty identifying letters of the alphabet, play games with the flash cards. Spread them on the table and ask the children to find individual letters. Making or purchasing alphabet *Lotto* or *Bingo* games are also good ways to reinforce letter recognition.

4. More advanced students may be able to give you a word or picture for each letter in the activity at the bottom of page 40.

5. If children are able to count and write numerals to 5, have them count and number all of the letters in each row of the same activity.

6. For children with difficulty identifying the initial sounds of *r, t, m,* and *b,* see page 34, Lesson Seventeen, Activity 1.

**SUGGESTED READING/ STORY IDEAS:**

1. Find and read books that encourage the children to listen and do.

2. Bring in some counting books for the children to read.

3. Read simple nursery rhymes which the children can act out.

## OBJECTIVES:

1. To recognize capital *E* and small *e*.
2. To write capital *E* and small *e*.
3. To recognize the short sound of *Ee*.

**MATERIALS:** pencils and crayons, Bible, tagboard or chart paper, magazines or newspapers, glue or paste, scissors.

## TEACHING PAGES 42 and 43:

1. For procedures for teaching page 42 and 43, see pages 14 and 15 (Lesson Seven). Stress the short sound of *e* in *egg*, *elephant*, and *Esther* on page 42.

2. Read a list of words such as the following. Have the children raise their hands or hold up a card with *e* on it when they hear the short *e* sound. Examples: *egg, bat, men, elephant, man, pet.*

## EXTENDED ACTIVITIES:

1. Make a short *Ee* chart.
2. Play a rhyming game with short *e* words. Say a word such as *hen* or *get* and *see* if the children can find other words that rhyme with them.
3. For more advanced children, continue the letter game begun in Lesson Fifteen, pages 30 and 31, Extended Activity 2. Help children to sound out new words with the sounds they have learned. Examples: *met, bet.* They can also review other words they have made: *mat, bat, rat.*
4. Talk about names and words in the Bible which have the short *e* sound: *Esther, Exodus, Ezra, Bethlehem* (all three *e*'s), and so on.

## SUGGESTED READING/ STORY IDEAS:

1. Read or tell the story of Esther.
2. Read stories or poems which emphasize short *e* sound.
3. Write a story or poem with the short *e* rhyming words found by the children.

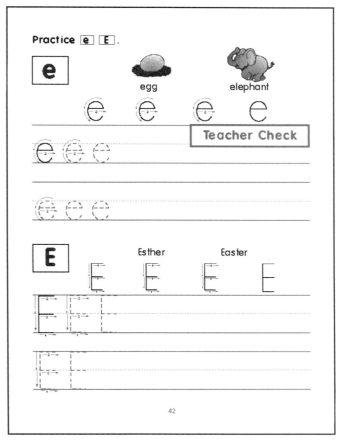

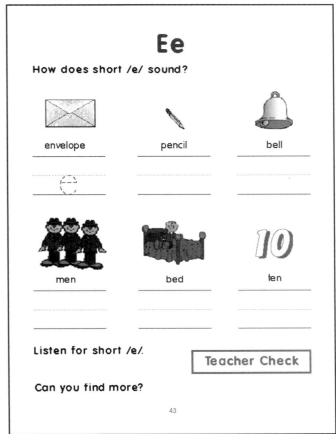

**OBJECTIVES:**
1. To recognize capital *E* and small *e*.
2. To write capital *E* and small *e*.
3. To recognize the short sound of *Ee*.
4. To review the alphabet.

**MATERIALS:** pencils, crayons, magazines and newspapers, paste or glue, materials to make puppet, alphabet scrapbook, alphabet flash cards or chart.

**TEACHING PAGES 44 and 45:**
1. To reinforce and review the sound of short *Ee* on page 44, follow the procedures for page 16, numbers 1, 2, and 3 (Lesson Eight).

2. Have all the children read the alphabet together on page 45. Then, with the help of an aide, have each child point to the letters and read the alphabet. Mark letters that cause problems for further drill.

3. Ask the children what letters of the alphabet have already been studied (*a, b, e, m, r, f*). Have them circle these letters. Ask them to find the letters in their names and put a box around them.

**EXTENDED ACTIVITIES:**
1. Make a short *Ee* puppet.
2. Add to alphabet scrapbook at home.
3. Give the children a page from a newspaper or catalogue. Have them circle or cut out words that have the sound of short *Ee*. Read the words for the children. Have them share the different words they found. Help as needed because most of the short *e* words will be within the words rather than initial sounds.
4. Add to the *Ee* chart, if new words or pictures have been found.
5. Additional practice for writing the letter *Ee* can be found in the writing practice section of the children's book.
6. Have an aide or older student work with children who have difficulty matching letters. Play recognition games with alphabet cards or blocks, or with alphabet *Lotto* or *Bingo* type games.

**SUGGESTED READING/ STORY IDEAS:**
1. Have the children review all the short *e* words and pictures they have found. Have the children make up a short *e* story. This story can be dictated to the teacher or an aide and then illustrated by the children. This story may also be a rebus stories, substituting pictures for words. Add to alphabet Story Book.
2. Use the *Ee* puppet to tell the story.

My Ee page.

44

**Read the alphabet to your teacher.**

**Circle the letters we have done.**

**Sing the alphabet song.**

45

## OBJECTIVES:

1. To review basic shapes: *circle*, *square*, *triangle*, and *rectangle*.

2. To review the colors: *red*, *blue*, *yellow*, and *green*.

3. To review initial sounds of *m*, *b*, *t*, and *r*.

**MATERIALS:** pencils and crayons (especially red, blue, yellow, and green), drawing paper, review charts for *m*, *b*, *t*, and *r*, objects with basic shapes.

## TEACHING PAGES 46 and 47:

1. Briefly review the basic shapes on page 46 by asking the children to identify the shape in each of the boxes at the beginning of each row. Have the children name each of the pictures in the first long row. Ask the children to find all of the triangles in the long box (*hat, ice cream cone*). Ask them to trace the circle on the hat and to draw a circle around the triangle portion of the cone. Repeat this procedure for the other rows on the page. If children have problems, review the shape which causes the problem.

2. To prepare for page 47, ask the children to name things in the room which begin with each of the letters *m*, *b*, *t*, and *r*. Take each letter individually. Have the children look at the picture and ask them to name as many items as they can. Ask them to take their *red* crayons and find all of the objects which begin with the *m* sound. Give time to complete this. Then go on to the other sounds and colors ( *blue*– bee, bird, *green*– tree, tent, *yellow*– roof, rabbit, rainbow, *red*– man, mailbox).

## EXTENDED ACTIVITIES:

1. Have the children name the pictures on page 46 and give the beginning sounds of as many as they are able.

2. Ask the children to group the pictures on page 46. Examples: Ask them to find furniture items (*mirror, lamp, table, rug, drawer*). Ask them to find food items (*banana, ice cream cone*). Ask them to find toys (*balloon, block*). Ask for the remaining items (*hat, suitcase, window*).

3. Have those who are able, number each of the groups with a different color (furniture items number 1 through 5 with a red crayon, and so on).

4. Review any sounds that were a problem on page 47 using charts, alphabet scrapbook, or letter cards.

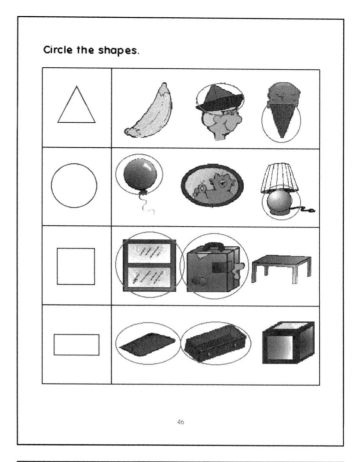

**Circle the shapes.**

46

**Color.**

47

5. Ask the children to draw animals using only circles and the shape of the mirror (oval). While the oval is not introduced here, the children can become aware of the shape.

6. Have the children complete or add to the picture on page 47.

## SUGGESTED READING/ STORY IDEAS:

1. Write or tell stories about the animals the children drew.

2. Find books at the library which show how to draw animals, objects, and people from basic shapes.

## OBJECTIVES:

1. To recognize capital *S* and small *s*.
2. To write capital *S* and small *s*.
3. To recognize the sound of *Ss*.

**MATERIALS:** pencils, crayons, Bible, magazines or newspapers, paste or glue, chart paper or tagboard, alphabet or flash cards for *Ss*, 3" x 5" cards.

## TEACHING PAGES 48 and 49:

1. To introduce *Ss* on pages 48 and 49, follow the procedures for pages 20 and 21 (Lesson Ten). Stress the words *soap, sun, Saviour,* and *Samson* on page 48.

2. Read a list of words such as those which follow. Have the children raise their hands or hold up a card with an *s* on it when they hear the *s* sound. Examples: *Sam, ham, sister, salt, rabbit, sight.*

3. The *s* sound is fun to make. Have the children tell you where their tongues are for this sound (not quite touching the roof of the mouth).

## EXTENDED ACTIVITIES:

1. Make an *Ss* chart.

2. Have the children, who are able, play the letter game introduced in Activity 2 for pages 30 - 31. Add *s* cards to those already made. Have the children spread the cards out and see if they can add more words to those found before. Examples: *sat, Sam, set, bats.* Have them use the words they make in a sentence. Add to the list of words and names they are able to form and sound out with the sounds already learned. Help as needed. Reminder : If the children are not ready and find this activity difficult, then wait several more weeks and try again.

3. Talk about names and words from the Bible that begin with the *Ss* sound: *Sarah, Samson, Samuel, Solomon, Sabbath, sacrifice, Son of God, Samaritan, salvation, Saul* and so on. Add these to Bible list or booklet.

## SUGGESTED READING/ STORY IDEAS:

1. Read or tell the children the story of Samuel in the Bible.

2. Read the story of the Samaritan Woman (John 4).

3. Have the children act out or illustrate either story.

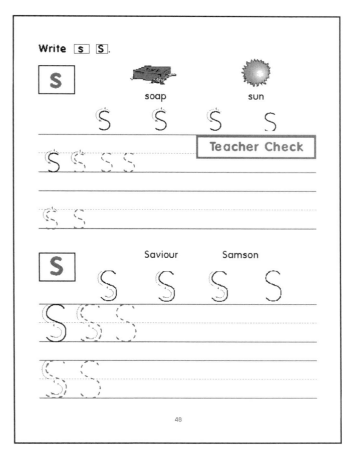

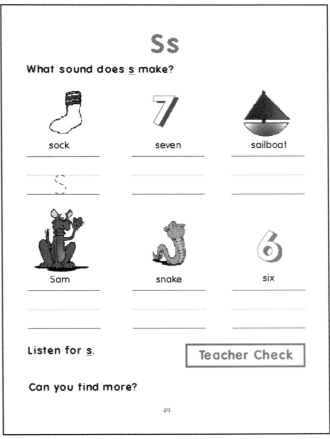

## OBJECTIVES:

1. To recognize capital *S* and small *s*.
2. To write capital *S* and small *s*.
3. To recognize the sound of *Ss*.
4. To review recognition of capital and small letters, *Aa, Bb, Ee, Mm, Rr, Ss,* and *Tt*.
5. To recognize individual letters at the beginning of words.

**MATERIALS:** pencils, crayons, magazines and newspapers, paste or glue, materials to make puppet, alphabet scrapbook.

## TEACHING PAGES 50 and 51:

1. To reinforce and review the sound *Ss* on page 50. Follow the procedures for page 16, numbers 1, 2, and 3 (Lesson Eight).

2. Have the children look at page 51 and read the letters in the first column of the first box (*a, t, m, r*). Ask them to find the capital letter which matches the (*a*) and point to it. Check. Have them draw a line between the small *a* and the capital *A*. Ask the children to do the same for each of the other letters. Repeat the procedure for the second box (*E, B, S*).

3. At the bottom of page 51, ask the children to read the letter at the beginning of each box. Ask them to find the one word in the long box which begins with the initial letter. Circle the word. Complete the page noting any difficulties the children have. If a child does have difficulty, isolate the rows and words so that they can be seen more clearly.

## EXTENDED ACTIVITIES:

1. Make an *Ss* puppet.
2. Add to alphabet scrapbook at home.
3. Give the children a page from a newspaper or catalogue. Have them circle or cut out words that begin with *Ss*. Read the words for the children. Have them share the different words they found. Ask them if they can use some of the words in sentences.
4. Add to the *Ss* chart, if new words or pictures have been found.
5. Additional practice for writing the letter *Ss* can be found in the writing practice section of the children's book.

## SUGGESTED READING/ STORY IDEAS:

1. Write a story using as many *Ss* words as they can. Pictures may be used in place of words where appropriate. Write the story for the children and let them add illustration. Add to alphabet Story Book.
2. Have a child or several children use the *Ss* puppet to tell the story.

My Ss page.

50

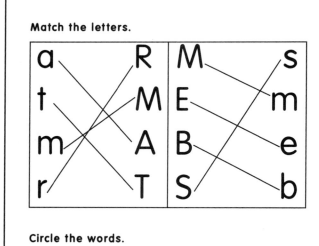

**Match the letters.**

**Circle the words.**

| a | an | so |
| b | at | bat |
| m | to | man |
| t | ran | to |

51

**OBJECTIVES:**

1. To read simple words and sentences.
2. To make simple words and sentences.
3. To read the word *I*.
4. To recognize the pronoun *I*.
5. To listen carefully.
6. To follow a direction given only once.
7. To write first name clearly and without help.

**MATERIALS:** pencils, crayons, name cards.

**TEACHING PAGES 52 and 53:**

1. On page 52 the children are introduced to reading and copying simple words and to reading simple sentences. Tell the children that this page is like the word game they have played with the individual letter cards. The words on this page are already "made" for them. Ask them to put their finger on the first word (*at*). Have them sound out the word. Help if needed. Ask the children to trace the word with their fingers. Then have the children trace with their pencils. Finally have them copy the word on the lines next to the word. Follow the same procedure for the remaining words.

2. To prepare for the sentence portion of this page, the words *I* and *a* will have to be presented because they use sounds which the children have not yet learned. Ask the children whom they are talking about when they say "*I*." Tell them that the word *I* is the same as the capital letter *I*. Have them write the letter *I* on their desks with their fingers. Then have them point to the word *I* as it appears on the page in the sentences. Ask if anyone can read the first sentence. Praise all efforts and attempts.

3. Tell the children that the word *a* is a helping word that we use very often in sentences when we are talking about one thing. The sound of the word *a* is different from the short *a* sound they have learned and also different from the name for the letter *Aa*. Say the word *a* and have the children repeat it. Have them point to it in the second sentence and say it again. Read the remaining sentences with the children pointing to the word *a* and repeating it.

4. If the children are able, make more words and sentences with the sounds they know.

5. Page 53 is an activity page to continue building listening skills and following directions. Read the page direction. Tell the children that they will be given a direction only once. Tell them that they will draw a circle around the picture that fits the sentence you will read. Have the children

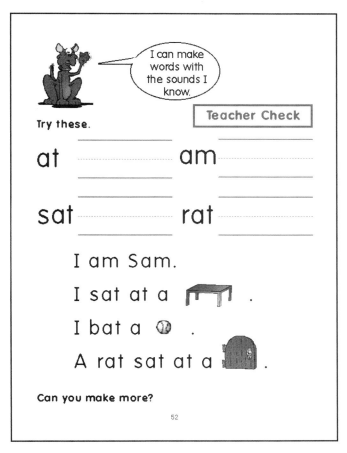

Try these.

at      am

sat      rat

I am Sam.

I sat at a 🪑 .

I bat a ⚾ .

A rat sat at a 🚪 .

**Can you make more?**

52

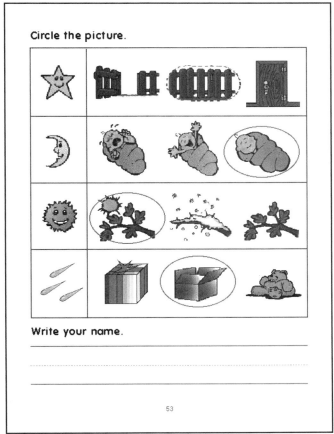

**Circle the picture.**

**Write your name.**

53

put their fingers on the *star*. Read this sentence only once. *The gate is shut.*

Have the children circle the proper picture. Do the same with the other three boxes. Fingers on *moon*. Read. *The baby is asleep.* Fingers on *sun*. Read. *It is summer.* Fingers on *raindrops*. Read. *The present is open.*

6. At the bottom of the page, ask the children to write their first names. They may use their name cards to copy if needed. Check spelling and letter formation.

**EXTENDED ACTIVITIES:**

1. If some children are still having difficulty with the listening activity, do the activity again using different direction sentences. Have them circle the pictures with a crayon. Examples: Put your finger on the *star*. Circle the *open gate*. Put your finger on the *moon*. Circle the *happy baby*. Put your finger on the *sun*. Circle the *winter picture*. Put your finger on the raindrops. Circle the *present that was in the box.*

2. If children still have difficulty forming words, have an aide or older student work with them. As before, if a child is simply not ready for reading, do not go beyond the level of endurance.

**SUGGESTED READING/ STORY IDEAS:**

1. Strengthen listening skills, by reading short stories to the children and asking specific recall questions.

2. Have the children make up a story for the *moon* and *raindrop* rows of page 53.

## OBJECTIVES:

1. To recognize capital *N* and small *n*.
2. To write capital *N* and small *n*.
3. To recognize the sound of *Nn*.

**MATERIALS:** pencils, crayons, Bible, magazines or newspapers, paste or glue, chart paper or tagboard, alphabet or flash cards for *Nn*, 3" x 5" cards.

## TEACHING PAGES 54 and 55:

1. To introduce *Nn* on pages 54 and 55, follow the procedures for pages 20 and 21 (Lesson Ten). Stress the words *nest, nut, Naomi,* and *Noah* on page 54.

2. Read a list of words such as those which follow. Have the children raise their hands or hold up a card with an *n* on it when they hear the *n* sound. Examples: *nice, mat, Nathan, big, neighbor, needle.*

3. Ask the children how they make the *n* sound. Where are their tongues? (top of mouth) How is the *n* sound different from the *m* sound?

## EXTENDED ACTIVITIES:

1. Make an *Nn* chart.

2. Have the children who are able, play the letter game introduced in Activity 2 for pages 30 – 31. Add *n* cards to those already made. Have the children spread the cards out and see if they can add more words to those found before: Examples: *net, Nan, ran, man.* Have them use the words they make in a sentence. Add to the list of words and names they are able to form and sound out with the sounds already learned. Help as needed. Reminder: If the children are not ready and find this activity difficult, then wait several more weeks and try again.

3. Talk about names and words from the Bible that begin with the *Nn* sound: *Nathan, Noah, Naomi, Nazareth, nation,* and so on. Add these to Bible list or booklet.

## SUGGESTED READING/ STORY IDEAS:

1. Read or tell the children the story of Noah in the Bible (Genesis chapters 6–8).

2. Have the children act out or illustrate some aspect of the story.

3. Ask the children if they remember the story of Ruth. Who was Naomi? Review the story.

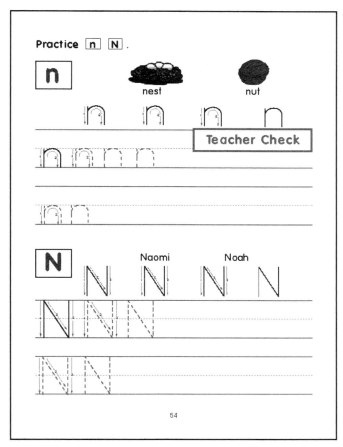

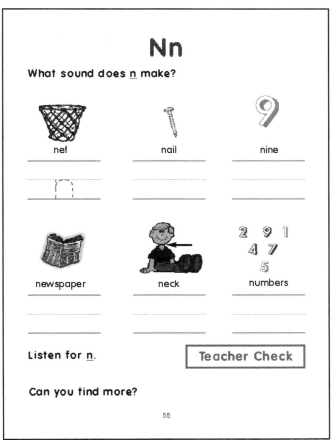

**OBJECTIVES:**
1. To recognize capital *N* and small *n*.
2. To write capital *N* and small *n*.
3. To recognize the sound of *Nn*.
4. To read new words.

**MATERIALS:** pencils, crayons, magazines and newspapers, paste or glue, materials to make puppet, alphabet scrapbook.

**TEACHING PAGES 56 and 57:**
1. To reinforce and review the sound *Nn* on page 56, follow the procedures for page 16, numbers 1, 2, and 3 (Lesson Eight).
2. Page 57 is an extension of the activity begun on page 52 (Lesson Twenty-six). Follow procedures from page 52 and the caution to use only with children who are ready for this activity. If children are not ready, come back to this activity several weeks or even months later. You will need to help sound out and spell *man, ten, net, tent*.

**EXTENDED ACTIVITIES:**
1. Make an *Nn* puppet.
2. Add to alphabet scrapbook at home.
3. Give the children a page from a newspaper or catalogue. Have them circle or cut out words that begin with *Nn*. Read the words for the children. Have them share the different words they have found.
4. Add to the *Nn* chart, if new words or pictures have been found.
5. Additional practice for writing the letter *Nn* can be found in the writing practice section of the children's book.

**SUGGESTED READING/ STORY IDEAS:**
1. Write a story using as many *Nn* words as they can. Pictures may be used in place of words where appropriate. Write the story for the children and let them add illustration. Add to alphabet Story Book.
2. Have a child or several children use the *Nn* puppet to tell the story.

My Nn page.

56

Make new words with the sound of /n/.

Teacher Check

an      ran

tan      fan

Ann      Ben

57

**OBJECTIVES:**
1. To recognize the capital *D* and small *d*.
2. To write capital *D* and small *d*.
3. To recognize the sound of *Dd*.

**MATERIALS:** pencils, crayons, Bible, magazines or newspapers, paste or glue, chart paper or tagboard, alphabet or flash cards for *Dd*, 3"x 5" cards.

**TEACHING PAGES 58 and 59:**
1. To introduce *Dd* on pages 58 and 59, follow the procedures for pages 20 and 21 (Lesson Ten). Stress the words *dog, duck, Daniel,* and *David* on page 58.

2. Read a list of words such as those which follow. Have the children raise their hands or hold up a card with a *d* on it when they hear the *d* sound. Examples: *doctor, boy, daddy, dark, ball, man, Douglas.*

3. How do the children make the *d* sound? Are their tongues in the same place as they put them for the letter *t*? What is the difference? Explain that some letters let air pass through and have a softer sound (*t, s, p*). Other letters need the children's voices to be heard (*b, d, n,* and so on).

**EXTENDED ACTIVITIES:**
1. Make a *Dd* chart.
2. Have the children who are able, play the letter game introduced in Activity 2 for pages 30–31. Add *d* cards to those already made. Have the children spread the cards out and see if they can add more words to those found before. Examples: *Dan, dad, mad, add.* Have them use the words they make in a sentence. Add to the list of words and names they are able to form and sound out with the sounds already learned. Help as needed. Reminder: If the children are not ready and find this activity difficult, then wait several more weeks and try again.

3. Talk about names and words from the Bible that begin with the *Dd* sound: *David, Daniel, Deborah, Damascus, deity, Dan,* and so on. Add these to Bible list or booklet.

**SUGGESTED READING/ STORY IDEAS:**
1. Ask the children what they know about the stories of David, Daniel, and Deborah in the Bible. Read or discuss at least one of these stories.

2. Have the children make a storybook of one of the stories. They may tell or read it to their families.

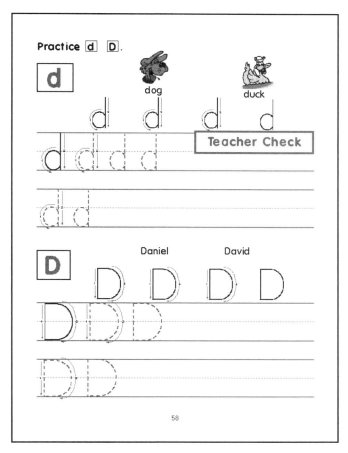

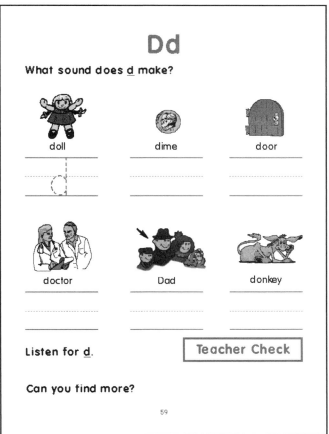

## OBJECTIVES:

1. To recognize the capital *D* and small *d*.
2. To write capital *D* and small *d*.
3. To recognize the sound of *Dd*.
4. To recognize and read simple words and sentences.

**MATERIALS:** pencils, crayons, magazines and newspapers, paste or glue, materials to make puppet, alphabet scrapbook.

## TEACHING PAGES 60 and 61:

1. To reinforce and review the sound *Dd* on page 60, follow the procedures for page 16, numbers 1, 2, and 3 (Lesson Eight).

2. Page 61 is an extension of the activity begun on page 52 (Lesson Twenty-six). Follow procedures from page 52 and the caution to use only with children who are ready for this activity. If children are not ready, come back to this activity several weeks or even months later. Help with spelling of *man* and *bat*.

## EXTENDED ACTIVITIES:

1. Make a *Dd* puppet.
2. Add to alphabet scrapbook at home.
3. Give the children a page from a newspaper or catalogue. Have them circle or cut out words that begin with *Dd*. Read the words for the children. Have them share the different words they have found.
4. Add to the *Dd* chart, if new words or pictures have been found.
5. Additional practice for writing the letter *Dd* can be found in the writing practice section of the children's book.

## SUGGESTED READING/ STORY IDEAS:

1. Write a story using as many *Dd* words as they can. Pictures may be used in place of words where appropriate. Write the story for the children and let them add illustration. Add to alphabet Story Book.
2. Have a child or several children use the *Dd* puppet to tell the story.

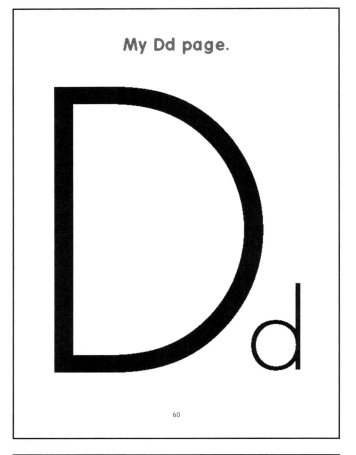

My Dd page.

60

Try these short /a/ words.

Teacher Check

Sam................... ran ...................

Dad................. rat .................

Ann and Dan ran.

**Can you find more?**

61

## OBJECTIVES:
1. To recognize capital *P* and small *p*.
2. To write capital *P* and small *p*.
3. To recognize the sound of *Pp*.

**MATERIALS:** pencils, crayons, Bible, magazines or newspapers, paste or glue, chart paper or tagboard, alphabet or flash cards for *Pp*, 3" x 5" cards.

## TEACHING PAGES 62 and 63:
1. To introduce *Pp* on pages 62 and 63, follow the procedures for pages 20 and 21 (Lesson Ten). Stress the words *pig, pail, Peter, Pam,* and *Paul* on page 62.

2. Read a list of words such as those which follow. Have the children raise their hands or hold up a card with a *p* on it when they hear the *p* sound. Examples: *paper, big, pizza, pipe, doll, Pamela, dog, penny.*

3. Have the children experiment with making the *p* sound and the *b* sound. Which one is louder (*b*)? Which is quieter (*p*)? Which lets more air through (*p*)?

## EXTENDED ACTIVITIES:
1. Make a *Pp* chart.

2. Have the children who are able, play the letter game introduced in Activity 2 for pages 30 – 31. Add *p* cards to those already made. Have the children spread the cards out and see if they can add more words to those found before: Examples: *pet, pan, Pam, Pat.* Have them use the words they make in a sentence. Add to the list of words and names they are able to form and sound out with the sounds already learned. Help as needed. Reminder: If the children are not ready and find this activity difficult, then wait several more weeks and try again.

3. Talk about names and words from the Bible that begin with the *Pp* sound: *Peter, Paul, Pilate, palm, Passover,* and so on. Add these to Bible list or booklet.

## SUGGESTED READING/ STORY IDEAS:
1. Ask the children what they know about the stories of Peter and Paul in the Bible. Read or discuss at least one of these stories.

2. Have the children act out the story of the conversion of Paul, the call of Peter, or any of the other stories from the gospels, Acts, or the letters of Peter and Paul.

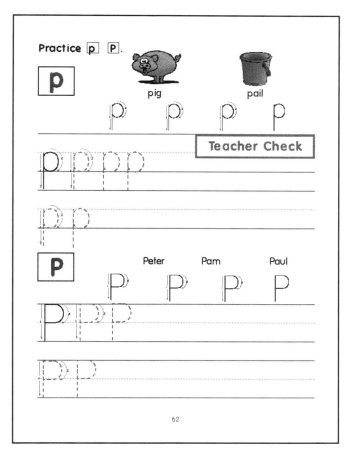

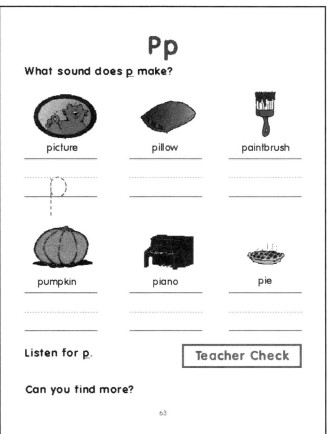

3. Ask the children if they know who Pilate was. Read one of the Gospel accounts of who Pilate was and what his role was in the Passion of Jesus (Matthew 27: 2-66; Luke 3:1; 23:1-25).

## OBJECTIVES:

1. To recognize capital *P* and small *p*.
2. To write capital *P* and small *p*.
3. To recognize the sound of *Pp*.
4. To review basic shapes.
5. To review colors *red, blue, green,* and *yellow*.
6. To follow directions.

**MATERIALS:** pencils, crayons, magazines and newspapers, paste or glue, materials to make puppet, alphabet scrapbook, basic shape cards, construction paper, pictures from calendars.

## TEACHING PAGES 64 and 65:

1. To reinforce and review the sound *Pp* on page 64, follow the procedures for page 16, numbers 1, 2, and 3 (Lesson Eight).

2. To teach page 65, read the direction. Explain that the children are to color all the circles on the page *red*, all of the squares *blue*, all of the rectangles *green*, and all of the triangles *yellow*. Have the children complete the page on their own. Accept all reasonable answers.

## EXTENDED ACTIVITIES:

1. Make a *Pp* puppet.
2. Add to alphabet scrapbook at home.
3. Give the children a page from a newspaper or catalogue. Have them circle or cut out words that begin with *Pp*. Read the words for the children. Have them share the different words they have found.
4. Add to the *Pp* chart, if new words or pictures have been found.
5. Additional practice for writing the letter *Pp* can be found in the writing practice section of the children's book.
6. Provide drill exercises for students who continue to have difficulty finding shapes.
7. Let the more advanced students make pattern pictures and puzzles. Using the construction paper or large calendar pictures, cut (or have the children cut) pictures into different shapes that can be fit back together as puzzles.

## SUGGESTED READING/ STORY IDEAS:

1. Write a story using as many *Pp* words as they can. Pictures may be used in place of words where appropriate. Write the story for the children and let them add illustration. Add to alphabet Story Book.
2. Have a child or several children use the *Pp* puppet to tell the story.

3. Find a book of nursery rhymes and tongue twisters. Read to the children anything which emphasizes the sounds already learned (*Peter Piper picked a peck of pickled peppers*, and so on).

**OBJECTIVES:**

1. To review initial sounds *d, n, p,* and *s*.

2. To read simple words and sentences with short *e* words.

**MATERIALS:** pencils and crayons, review charts or scrapbook pages for *d, n, p, s,* and short *e*.

**TEACHING PAGES 66 and 67:**

1. On page 66, have the children point to the first letter on the page (*d*). Ask them to trace the letter with their fingers and then to write the letter on the lines.

2. Ask them to name the pictures in the long box. Tell them to point to the one which begins with the *d* sound. When all have been checked, ask the children to circle the picture. Repeat this procedure for the remaining boxes.

3. Page 67 is an extension of the activity begun on page 52 (Lesson Twenty-six). This page deals primarily with short *e* words. Follow procedures from page 52 and the caution to use only with children who are ready for this activity. If children are not ready, come back to this activity several weeks or even months later. Help with spelling of *ten* and *net*. Note any confusion over these words.

**EXTENDED ACTIVITIES:**

1. Drill as needed with children who had difficulty with the beginning sounds reviewed here. Use games, charts, flash cards, or whatever materials are available to reinforce the sounds.

2. Ask the children who are able, to find more short *e* words which rhyme with those found on page 67.

**SUGGESTED READING/ STORY IDEAS:**

1. Go back and review the stories written by the children for *d, n, p, s,* and short *e*.

2. Ask the children to add to the stories or create a new story using all of the letters reviewed here.

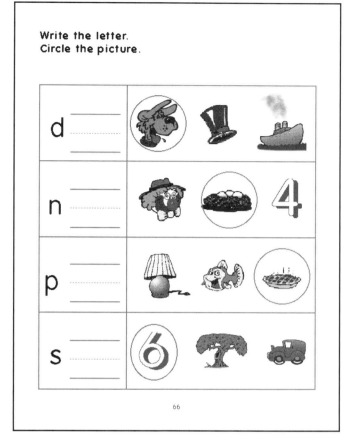

Write the letter.
Circle the picture.

d _____

n _____

p _____

s _____

66

Try these short /e/ words.

Teacher Check

men _____     pen _____

10 _____     🗑 _____

tent _____     red _____

Ben and Ted met ten men.

**Can you find more?**

67

## OBJECTIVES:
1. To recognize capital *I* and small *i*.
2. To write capital *I* and small *i*.
3. To recognize the sound of short *i*.

**MATERIALS:** pencils, crayons, Bible, magazines or newspapers, paste or glue, chart paper or tagboard, alphabet or flash cards for *Ii*, 3" x 5" cards.

## TEACHING PAGES 68 and 69:
1. For procedures for teaching page 68 and 69, see pages 14 and 15 (Lesson Seven).
Stress the short sound of *i* in *inch*, *igloo*, and *Israel*. Tell the children that the other Bible names they know, *Isaac* and *Isaiah*, have the sound of the pronoun *I* and will be studied later.
2. Read a list of words such as the following. Have the children raise their hands or hold up a card with *i* on it when they hear the short *i* sound. Examples: *it, egg, invitation, apple, sit, set, in, pin*.

## EXTENDED ACTIVITIES:
1. Make a short *Ii* chart.
2. Play a rhyming game with short *i* words. Say a word such as *pin* or *sit* and see if the children can find other words that rhyme with them.
3. For more advanced children, continue the letter game begun in Lesson Fifteen, pages 30 and 31, Activity 2. Help children to sound out new words with the sounds they have learned. Examples: *sit, bit*. They can also review other words they have made: *mat, bat, rat, met, ten, pen*.
4. Talk about names and words in the Bible which have the short *i* sound: *Israel, Ishmael*, and so on.

## SUGGESTED READING/ STORY IDEAS:
1. Read or tell the story of Jacob and how God changed his name to Israel (Genesis 35:10)
2. Read stories or poems which emphasize the short *i* sound.
3. Write a story or poem with the short *i* rhyming words found by the children.

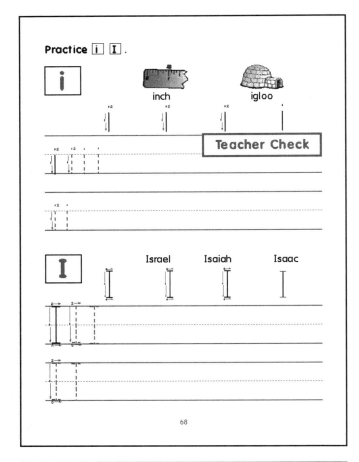

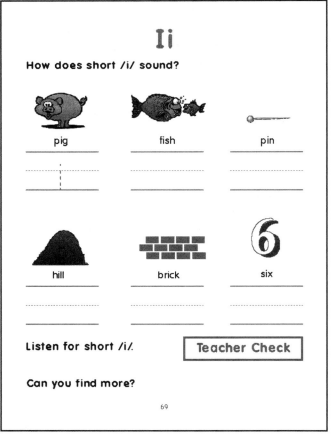

## OBJECTIVES:

1. To recognize capital *I* and small *i*.
2. To write capital *I* and small *i*.
3. To recognize the sound of short *i*.
4. To recognize and make new words with the short *i* sound.

**MATERIALS:** pencils, crayons, magazines and newspapers, paste or glue, materials to make puppet, alphabet scrapbook.

## TEACHING PAGES 70 and 71:

1. To reinforce and review the sound short *i* on page 70, follow the procedures for page 16, numbers 1, 2, and 3 (Lesson Eight).

2. Page 70 is an extension of the activity begun on page 52 (Lesson Twenty-six). Follow procedures from page 52 and the caution to use only with children who are ready for this activity. If children are not ready, do the activity with them and then come back to this activity several weeks or even months later. Have the children draw a line from the words *pin, mitt,* and *Jip* to the picture for each.

## EXTENDED ACTIVITIES:

1. Make a short *Ii* puppet.
2. Add to alphabet scrapbook at home.
3. Add to the *Ii* chart, if new words or pictures have been found.
4. Additional practice for writing the letter *Ii* can be found in the writing practice section of the children's book.

## SUGGESTED READING/ STORY IDEAS:

1. Write a story using as many short *Ii* words as they can. Pictures may be used in place of words where appropriate. Write the story for the children and let them add illustration. Add to the alphabet storybook.

2. Have a child or several children use the *Ii* puppet to tell the story.

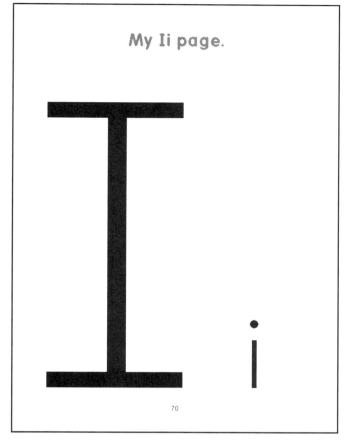

My Ii page.

70

Try these short /i/ words.

Teacher Check

Jip            tip

pin            dip

bin            sip

sit            mitt

71

## OBJECTIVES:

1. To listen carefully.
2. To follow directions given only once.
3. To put pictures in order.
4. To recognize and name the colors *brown*, *purple*, *pink*, and *orange*.

**MATERIALS:** pencils, brown, purple, pink, and orange crayons, tagboard and old books to make sequence cards, pictures or objects that are *brown*, *purple*, *pink*, and *orange*.

## TEACHING PAGES 72 and 73:

1. To prepare the children for page 72, ask them what they did before school today. What did they do first (get up, get dressed, eat breakfast)? Ask them what would happen if they had tried to eat breakfast before they got up. Talk about the order in which things are done. Tell them that the page they are about to do is about two children and something they do every week. Read the following sentences only once and have the children circle the appropriate picture. Have them put fingers on the picture in the box at the left to keep their place.

*Tie*: The children are going to church.
*Flower*: The children are sitting quietly in church.
*Leaf*: The children are leaving the church.

Check the exercise together. Talk about what is happening. Talk about going to church and let the children share experiences. Ask the children to listen, then read all three sentences again. Ask them to point to the circled picture that shows what happened first, then next, then last. Point out that a story is written this way.

2. To prepare for page 73, hold up a color card or object that is *brown*. Ask the children if they know what color the object is. Have them find other brown objects in the room. Repeat this process for *purple*, *pink*, and *orange*. Then look at the page and have the children point to each color and say its name with you. Once again, it is not important for the children to "read" the color name at this point, but to begin associating this word with the color. Reading color names will come later in the year.

## EXTENDED ACTIVITIES:

1. Find or draw three pictures that tell the beginning, middle, and end of an event. Mount them on cardboard and let the children put them in the proper order and tell the story. You can use old books or buy picture sequence cards from publishing companies or teacher supply stores.

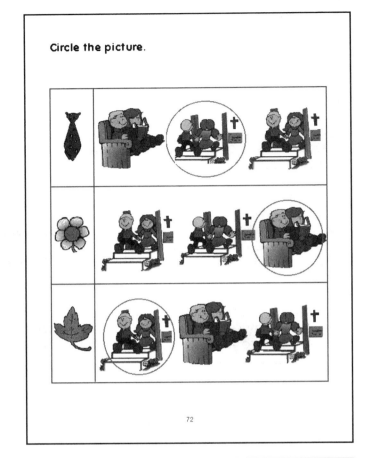

Circle the picture.

72

**More color names.**

brown          purple

pink          orange

**Say the names with your teacher.**

73

2. Make a box or an envelope for each of the new colors. Have children find objects and pictures for each and place in the box or envelope.

**SUGGESTED READING/ STORY IDEAS:**

1. Take a Bible story or fairy tale that the children know and tell it with the details OUT OF ORDER.  Ask the children to retell it using the correct order.

2. When the color boxes or envelopes have a number of things in them, ask the children to spread out the objects and pictures for one color and make up a story or a play using all of the items.

## OBJECTIVES:

1. To recognize capital *L* and small *l*.
2. To write capital *L* and small *l*.
3. To recognize the sound of *Ll*.

**MATERIALS:** pencils, crayons, Bible, magazines or newspapers, paste or glue, chart paper or tagboard, alphabet or flash cards for *Ll*, 3" x 5" cards.

## TEACHING PAGES 74 and 75:

1. To introduce *Ll* on pages 74 and 75, follow the procedures for pages 20 and 21 (Lesson Ten). Stress the words *lion, leaf, Luke,* and *Lord* on page 74.

2. Read a list of words such as those which follow. Have the children raise their hands or hold up a card with an *l* on it when they hear the *l* sound. Examples: *library, little, mine, Lois, bottom, Lisa*.

3. Have the children describe how the *l* sound is made. Does it need a voice? Does the tongue stay in one place or just touch the roof of the mouth for a second like the *t* and *d* sounds?

## EXTENDED ACTIVITIES:

1. Make an *Ll* chart.

2. Have the children who are able, play the letter game introduced in activity number 2 for pages 30 – 31. Add *l* cards to those already made. Have the children spread the cards out and see if they can add more words to those found before. Examples: *let, land, lit, ball, tall*. Have them use the words they make in a sentence. Add to the list of words and names they are able to form and sound out with the sounds already learned. Help as needed. Reminder : If the children are not ready and find this activity difficult, then wait several more weeks and try again.

3. Talk about names and words from the Bible that begin with the *Ll* sound: *Luke, Lord, lion, lamb, Leah, locusts,* and so on. Add these to Bible list or booklet.

## SUGGESTED READING/ STORY IDEAS:

1. Read 1 Samuel 17:34 and 35; Daniel chapter 6; the Gospel of Luke; and any other references that contain the words Lord, Luke, lion, or lamb.

2. Have the children illustrate and retell one of their favorite stories among those read.

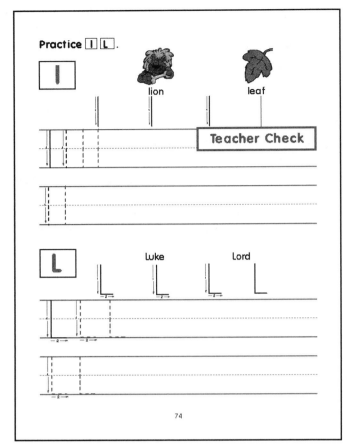

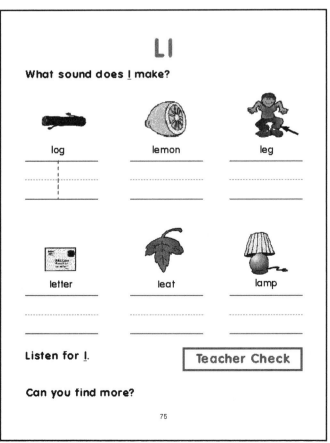

## OBJECTIVES:

1. To recognize capital *L* and small *l*.
2. To write capital *L* and small *l*.
3. To recognize the sound of *Ll*.
4. To identify colors: *red, blue, green, yellow, orange, brown, pink,* and *purple*.
5. To see shapes in different positions and sizes.

**MATERIALS:** pencils, crayons, magazines and newspapers, paste or glue, materials to make puppet, alphabet scrapbook, basic shape cards, color chart, drawing paper.

## TEACHING PAGES 76 and 77:

1. To reinforce and review the sound *Ll* on page 76, follow the procedures for page 16, numbers 1, 2, and 3 (Lesson Eight).

2. For page 77, use a color chart, individual pieces of colored paper with the color word written on it, or some similar color word combination to introduce the colors to the children. Some children may be able to recognize the color words, especially *red* and *blue*. Read the direction. Have the children look at the shape in the corner of the first box on the left and identify it (circle). Ask them to take their red crayon. Have them match the name on the crayon to the name under the circle. Tell the children to draw a red circle around the shape in the big box that matches the shape in the corner box. In the second box ask the children to identify the shape in the corner box (square). Ask them to take their blue crayon, match the name, and draw a blue circle around the matching shape. Continue this same procedure — identify shape, take crayon, match, circle shape — for the remainder of the page. Remind them that the shapes will be different sizes and in different positions than the shape in the small box.

## EXTENDED ACTIVITIES:

1. Make an *Ll* puppet.
2. Add to alphabet scrapbook at home.
3. Give the children a page from a newspaper or catalogue. Have them circle or cut out words that begin with *Ll*. Read the words for the children. Have them share the different words they have found.
4. Add to the *Ll* chart, if new words or pictures have been found.
5. Additional practice for writing the letter *Ll* can be found in the writing practice section of the children's book.

My Ll page.

76

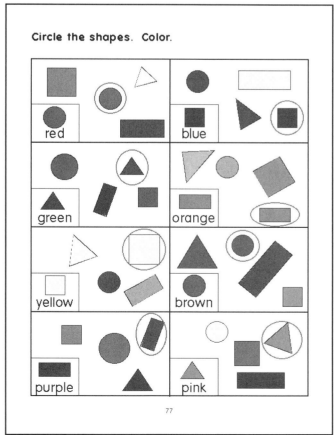

Circle the shapes. Color.

| red | blue |
| green | orange |
| yellow | brown |
| purple | pink |

77

6. Provide drill exercises for students who continue to have difficulty finding shapes.

7. Make a color chart for each child. Include both colored objects and the color words.

8. Give the children a sheet of white drawing paper and ask them to draw as many different triangles as they can. On the other side have them draw as many different rectangles as they can. Differences should be in sizes, positions, or size of the angles in the triangles.

## SUGGESTED READING/ STORY IDEAS:

1. Read books and poems that have color words and pictures in them.

2. Have the children pick one of the new colors and write a story or poem about it.

3. Write a story for the alphabet storybook using as many *l* words as possible. Write the story and have the children illustrate.

## OBJECTIVES:

1. To recognize and write first and last name.
2. To recognize and identify the alphabet.
3. To review the initial sounds *l, p, d, n, s,* and *r.*

**MATERIALS:** pencils, name cards with first and last names written on it, alphabet flash cards, charts or scrapbook pages for *l, p, d, n, s,* and *r.*

## TEACHING PAGES 78 and 79:

1. Read the first direction on page 78. Have the children point to each letter as they read it to you. Circle the letters they read without hesitation.

2. Give each child a name card with both first and last name written on it. Have the children practice their full names on the lines provided. Circle letters that the children still do not make correctly. Give the children extra help on these letters. Give them extra practice copying their name cards as needed.

3. For page 79, have the children break into groups. Give each group a letter (*l, p, d, n, s,* or *r*). Ask the children in the group to find in the room or to think of as many things as they can that begin with their letter. Have each group present what they have found. Ask the other groups if they can add any words to the group's collection. Allow each group time to share. Look at page 79. Read the directions. Have the children identify the pictures for each box. Let them do the page independently. Check. Reinforce any letters that are still weak.

## EXTENDED ACTIVITIES:

1. Divide a sheet of primary-lined paper in half from top to bottom. Put one letter the child needs to practice on each side at the top. Do the same on the other side with two different letters.

2. Have the children who know their letters help those who do not by working with them with flash cards or on the chalkboard.

## SUGGESTED READING/ STORY IDEAS:

1. Have the children make an alphabet story. The first child contributes an idea for *A,* the second for *B,* and so on until the entire alphabet is completed. Have the children work together to create a unifying theme or link to hold the story together.

2. Review the alphabet books, especially with children who continue to need help.

Read the alphabet to your teacher.

a b c d e f g h i
j k l m n o p q r
s t u v w x y z

Teacher Check

Write your name.

78

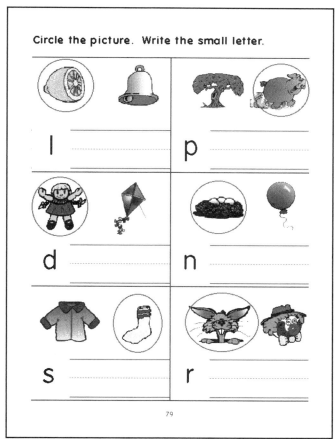

Circle the picture. Write the small letter.

l　　　　p

d　　　　n

s　　　　r

79

## OBJECTIVES:

1. To review recognition of capital and small letters, *Bb, Dd, Ll, Mm, Nn, Rr,* and *Tt.*
2. To review initial consonants *b, m,* and *t.*
3. To review short *a, e,* and *i.*

**MATERIALS:** pencils or crayons, alphabet chart or flash cards, charts, scrapbook pages, or stories for *b, m, t,* and short *a, e,* and *i.*

## TEACHING PAGES 80 and 81:

1. Have the children look at page 80 and read the letters in the first column of the first box (*R, T, M, B*). Ask them to find the small letter which matches the (*R*) and point to it. Check. Have them trace the line between the capital *R* and the small *r.* Ask the children to do the same for each of the other letters. Repeat the procedure for the letters in the second box (*n, d, l, p*).

2. At the bottom of page 80, ask the children to name the letter in the first box (*b*). Ask them to say the sound of *b.* Have them name the two pictures in the box and point to the one which begins with a *b.* Ask them to circle the picture. Complete the page in the same manner.

3. On page 81, the children will review the short sounds of *a, e,* and *i.* Remind the children that with short vowel sounds they are not just listening to the beginning sound of a word. Many times the short sounds are in the middle of the word. Review the short *a, e,* and *i* words and pictures that the children have gathered. Ask them to look at the top box on the page and point to the letter (*a*). Ask them what sound short *a* makes. Have them trace the *a* with their fingers. Ask them to name the three pictures in the box saying each one slowly so that the vowel sound is clearly heard. Have them point to the two pictures which have the short *a* sound (apple, ant). Ask them to circle the two pictures. Finally, have them write *a* on the lines, saying the short sound as they do so. Proceed in the same fashion with the remaining two boxes on the page.

## EXTENDED ACTIVITIES:

1. Use games, charts, or pictures to review and reinforce any sounds that children still find difficult.
2. Have an aide or older student work with children having difficulty with letter recognition.

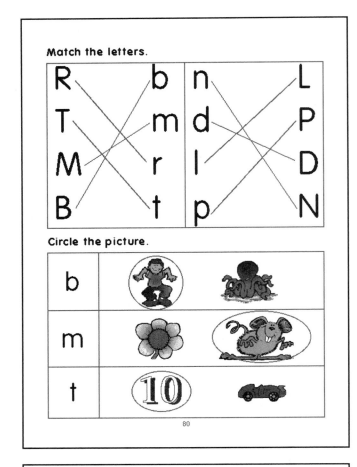

**Match the letters.**

**Circle the picture.**

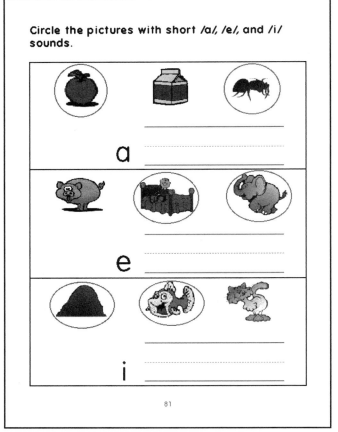

**Circle the pictures with short /a/, /e/, and /i/ sounds.**

**SUGGESTED READING/ STORY IDEAS:**

1. Reread books which emphasized short vowel sounds and have the children participate in the reading or telling of the story.

2. Review, add to, or write additional stories or poems for the sounds reviewed in this lesson.

## OBJECTIVES:
1. To recognize capital *K* and small *k*.
2. To write capital *K* and small *k*.
3. To recognize the sound of *Kk*.

**MATERIALS:** pencils, crayons, Bible, magazines or newspapers, paste or glue, chart paper or tagboard, alphabet or flash cards for *Kk*, 3" x 5" cards.

## TEACHING PAGES 82 and 83:
1. To introduce *Kk* on pages 82 and 83, follow the procedures for pages 20 and 21 (Lesson Ten). Stress the words *kitten*, *kite*, *Ken*, and *Kathleen* on page 82.

2. Read a list of words such as those which follow. Have the children raise their hands or hold up a card with a *k* on it when they hear the *k* sound. Examples: *kitchen, Bob, Katie, kind, doctor, kidding.*

3. The *k* sound is made in the throat. Have the children say the *k* sound and describe how it feels.

## EXTENDED ACTIVITIES:
1. Make a *Kk* chart.
2. Have the children who are able, play the letter game introduced in Activity 2 for pages 30 – 31. Add *k* cards to those already made. Have the children spread the cards out and see if they can add more words to those found before. Examples: *Ken, kit, Kim.* Have them use the words they make in a sentence. Add to the list of words and names they are able to form and sound out with the sounds already learned. Help as needed. Reminder: If the children are not ready and find this activity difficult, then wait several more weeks and try again.

3. Talk about names and words from the Bible that begin with the *Kk* sound: *King, kingdom,* and so on. Add these to Bible list or booklet.

## SUGGESTED READING/ STORY IDEAS:
1. Talk about Kings and the two Books of Kings in the Bible. How many Kings do they know (David, Solomon, and so on). Read a story about one of the Kings they know.

2. Read the Lord's Prayer and talk about what Jesus meant when He said "Thy kingdom come" (Luke 11:2; Matthew 6:10).

3. Read one of the many references to the kingdom of heaven in Jesus' teaching (Matthew chapter 13), or one of the references to the "keys to the kingdom" (Matthew 16:19).

4. Have the children retell one of the stories, illustrate a parable, or recite the Lord's Prayer.

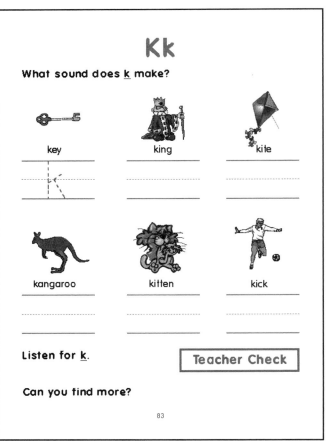

## OBJECTIVES:

1. To recognize capital *K* and small *k*.
2. To write capital *K* and small *k*.
3. To recognize the sound of *Kk*.
4. To listen carefully.
5. To follow directions given only once.
6. To put things in order.

**MATERIALS:** pencils, crayons, magazines and newspapers, paste or glue, materials to make puppet, alphabet scrapbook, sequence cards, drawing paper.

## TEACHING PAGES 84 and 85:

1. To reinforce and review the sound *Kk* on page 84, follow the procedures for page 16, numbers 1, 2, and 3 (Lesson Eight).

2. Have the children go to page 85. Read the following sentences only once. Have the children put their fingers on the small picture at the left to help keep their places. Ask the children to circle the picture that matches the sentence.
*Tomatoes*: Father is planting the garden.
*Beans*: The corn plants are just coming up.
*Peas*: John is pulling weeds out of the garden.
*Carrot*: John is eating corn from their garden. When the children have finished marking, talk about all the pictures in each box and be sure the children understand which is the correct picture if a mistake was made. Read the sentences over as a story and ask the children to write a number at the left of the boxes to show which happened first, second, third, and last (1, 2, 3, 4). Let several children retell the story.

## EXTENDED ACTIVITIES:

1. Make a *Kk* puppet.
2. Add to alphabet scrapbook at home.
3. Continue to use the newspaper activity if the children find it helpful.
4. Add to the *Kk* chart, if new words or pictures have been found.
5. Additional practice for writing the letter *Kk* can be found in the writing practice section of the children's book.
6. Talk about planting gardens and how the children can help. Let them share experiences. Let the children plant seeds in milk or egg cartons and watch them sprout.
7. Have the children divide a large sheet of drawing paper into three sections. Ask them to draw a sequence picture. Do several examples with them, such as:

My Kk page.

84

Circle the pictures.

85

caterpillar – cocoon – butterfly;
baby – child – adult;
sunrise – day – sunset;
summer – fall – winter.
Use sequences they are familiar with, such as those based on things that happen in their day (getting up, getting dressed, eating breakfast, and so on).

## SUGGESTED READING/ STORY IDEAS:

1. Have the children write stories for the sequence pictures and elaborate on them by using details, names, colors, and so on. Script the stories and display them with the pictures.

2. Continue to read simple stories to the children emphasizing the beginning, middle, and end of the story.

## OBJECTIVES:

1. To recognize capital *C* and small *c*.
2. To write capital *C* and small *c*.
3. To recognize the *k* sound of the letter *c*.

**MATERIALS:** pencils, crayons, Bible, magazines or newspapers, paste or glue, chart paper or tagboard, alphabet or flash cards for *Cc*, 3" x 5" cards.

## TEACHING PAGES 86 and 87:

1. To introduce *Cc* on pages 86 and 87, follow the procedures for pages 20 and 21 (Lesson Ten). Stress the words *carrot*, *cup*, *Christ*, *Christmas*, and *Carol* on page 86.

2. Read a list of words such as those which follow. Have the children raise their hands or hold up a card with a *c* on it when they hear the *k* sound of the letter *c*. Examples: *cat, Curt, Sam, curly, Christian, mother.*

## EXTENDED ACTIVITIES:

1. Make a *Cc* chart for words and pictures that begin with the *k* sound of the letter *c*.

2. Have the children who are able, play the letter game introduced in Activity 2 for pages 30 – 31. Add *c* cards to those already made. Have the children spread the cards out and see if they can add more words to those found before. Examples: *cat, can, cab.* Have them use the words they make in a sentence. Add to the list of words and names they are able to form and sound out with the sounds already learned. Help as needed. Reminder: If the children are not ready and find this activity difficult, then wait several more weeks and try again.

3. Talk about names and words from the Bible that begin with the *k* sound of the letter *c*: *Cain, camel, crucifixion, covenant, conversion,* and the *k* sound of *ch* as in *Christ, Christmas, Christian* and so on. Add these to Bible list or booklet.

## SUGGESTED READING/ STORY IDEAS:

1. Read the story of Cain and Abel (Genesis 4:1-16). Discuss with the children.

2. Read the Christmas story ( Luke chapter 2) and talk about the coming of Christ to save all of us from sin.

3. Have the children retell all or part of the Christmas story.

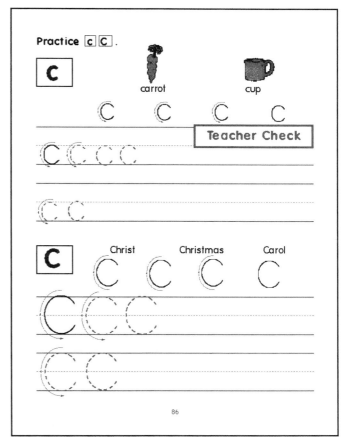

## OBJECTIVES:

1. To recognize capital *C* and small *c*.
2. To write capital *C* and small *c*.
3. To recognize the *k* sound of the letter *c*.
4. To recognize the *k* sound of the letters *ck*.

**MATERIALS:** pencils, crayons, magazines and newspapers, paste or glue, materials to make puppet, alphabet scrapbook.

## TEACHING PAGES 88 and 89:

1. To reinforce and review the *k* sound of *Cc* on page 88, follow the procedures for page 16, numbers 1, 2, and 3 (Lesson Eight).

2. On page 89, the children will have their first formal experience with sounds that come at the end of a word. Tell the children that in some words the *k* sound is spelled with two letters, *ck*. This pair of letters never comes at the beginning of a word, but very often it comes at the end of a word. Sometimes it comes in the middle of a word like *chicken*. Tell the children that this activity will look at words that end with *ck*. Have the children look at the first picture (*clock*). Ask them to say the word slowly. Where do they hear the *k* sound (beginning, end). Write the word *clock* on the board. Point out that the first *k* sound they hear is the letter *c* and that the final sound of *k* is made by the letters *ck*. Ask them to trace the *ck* on the lines under the picture of the clock. Repeat the process for the remaining pictures: say word, write on board, observe *ck* ending sound, write *ck* on the line. Have the children think of more words that end with a *k* sound. Sort out which ones end in *ck*.

## EXTENDED ACTIVITIES:

1. Make a puppet for the *k* sound of *c*.
2. Add to alphabet scrapbook at home.
3. Continue to use the newspaper activity if the children find it helpful.
4. Add to the *Cc* chart, if new words or pictures have been found.
5. Additional practice for writing the letters *Cc* and *ck* can be found in the writing practice section of the children's book.

## SUGGESTED READING/ STORY IDEAS:

1. Read stories about animals that have the *k* sound spelled with a *c*, or *ck*. Examples: *Ugly Duckling, Chicken Little*.
2. Create a story for the different *k* sounds. Add to the alphabet storybook.

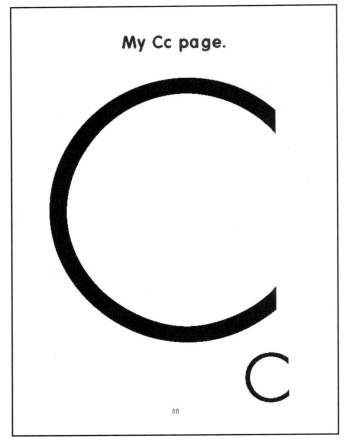

My Cc page.

88

ck

clock     sock     lock

tack     duck     truck

Can you find more?     **Teacher Check**

89

## OBJECTIVES:
1. To recognize capital *F* and small *f*.
2. To write capital *F* and small *f*.
3. To recognize the sound of *Ff*.

**MATERIALS:** pencils, crayons, Bible, magazines or newspapers, paste or glue, chart paper or tagboard, alphabet or flash cards for *Ff*, 3" x 5" cards.

## TEACHING PAGES 90 and 91:
1. To introduce *Ff* on pages 90 and 91, follow the procedures for pages 20 and 21 (Lesson Ten). Stress the words *fish, fan, Father,* and *Frank* on page 90.

2. Read a list of words such as those which follow. Have the children raise their hands or hold up a card with an *f* on it when they hear the *f* sound. Examples: *favor, find, popcorn, feather, mask, fun, new.*

3. Have the children put their hands in front of their mouths and make the *f* sound. What do they feel? Where are their teeth? (on their bottom lip)

## EXTENDED ACTIVITIES:
1. Make an *Ff* chart.

2. Have the children who are able, play the letter game introduced in Activity 2 for pages 30 – 31. Add *f* cards to those already made. Have the children spread the cards out and see if they can add more words to those found before. Examples: *fin, fan, fell.* Have them use the words they make in a sentence. Add to the list of words and names they are able to form and sound out with the sounds already learned. Help as needed. Reminder: If the children are not ready and find this activity difficult, then wait several more weeks and try again.

3. Talk about names and words from the Bible that begin with the *Ff* sound: *Father, fellowship, faith, fleece, feast, forgive* and so on. Add these to Bible list or booklet.

## SUGGESTED READING/ STORY IDEAS:
1. Return to the Lord's Prayer. Read to the children or pray together if they are able. To whom did Jesus teach us to pray? (Father) What is one of the things we ask in that prayer? (To forgive as we are forgiven) Talk about the Father's love for us and His forgiveness. If He can forgive us everything, how should we act toward those who hurt us?

2. Make a booklet of the Lord's Prayer for the children. Put one phrase on each page. Leave

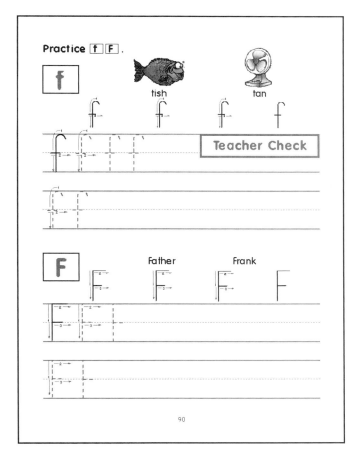

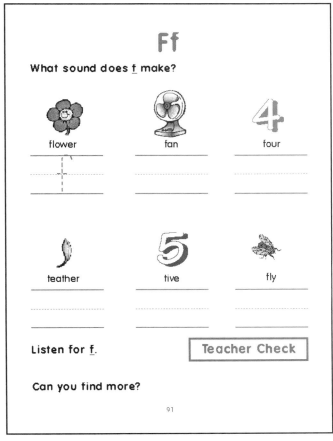

room for illustrations or designs the children want to add.  Keep this booklet in a special place to review often.  Review words already known (*Father, kingdom, forgive*).

## OBJECTIVES:

1. To recognize capital *F* and small *f*.
2. To write capital *F* and small *f*.
3. To recognize the sound of *Ff*.
4. To introduce the oval shape.
5. To review basic shapes.
6. To review colors.

**MATERIALS:** pencils, crayons, magazines and newspapers, paste or glue, materials to make puppet, alphabet scrapbook, basic shapes pictures and objects including the oval, color chart.

## TEACHING PAGES 92 and 93:

1. To reinforce and review the sound *Ff* on page 92, follow the procedures for page 16, numbers 1, 2, and 3 (Lesson Eight).

2. To prepare for page 93, hold up an *oval* object or a picture of an object for the children to see. Ask them to name the object. Ask if anyone knows the name of the shape. If no one knows, tell them that this object has an *oval* shape. Have the children find the *oval* on the top of the page and point to it. Tell them that the word for *oval* is printed next to the shape. Go to the picture. Ask the children to name each shape they see. Have them tell the color of each shape in the key. Instruct the children to color all of the rectangles *orange*, all of the circles *pink*, all of the triangles *purple*, all of the ovals *brown*, all of the squares *red*, and the birds *yellow*.

## EXTENDED ACTIVITIES:

1. Make an *Ff* puppet.
2. Add to alphabet scrapbook at home.
3. Continue to use the newspaper activity if the children find it helpful.
4. Add to the *Ff* chart, if new words or pictures have been found.
5. Additional practice for writing the letter *Ff* can be found in the writing practice section of the children's book.
6. Review colors and shapes that are a problem for some children.

## SUGGESTED READING/ STORY IDEAS:

1. Write a story using as many *Ff* words as they can. Pictures may be used in place of words where appropriate. Write the story for the children and let them add illustration. Add to alphabet storybook.
2. Have a child or several children use the *Ff* puppet to tell the story.

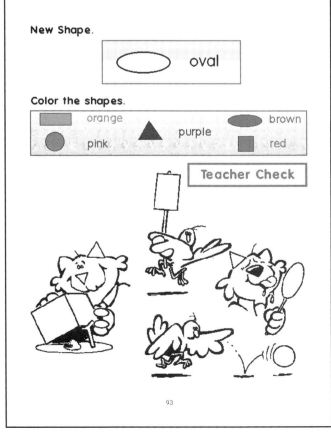

**OBJECTIVES:**

1. To review recognition of capital and small letters: *Aa, Bb, Cc, Dd, Ee.*
2. To put letters of the alphabet in order.

**MATERIALS:** pencils, alphabet chart or flash cards.

**TEACHING PAGES 94 and 95:**

1. Have the children look at page 94 and read the letters in the first column of the first box (*a, b, d, e, c*). Ask them to find the letter which matches and point to it. Check. Have them trace the line between the two small *a*'s. Ask the children to do the same for each of the other letters. Repeat the procedure for the letters in the second box and match to the capitals.

2. At the bottom of page 94, ask the children to read the letter at the beginning of each box.
Ask them to find the letter in the long box which matches it. Circle the letter. Complete the page noting any difficulties the children have. If a child does have difficulty, work with individual flash cards of the letters and with writing letters on large paper.

3. Prepare for page 95, by asking the children to recite as much of the alphabet as they are able. Drill the first six letters of the alphabet (*a, b, c, d, e, f*). Tell the children that the alphabet has an order, just as stories do. Ask them to point to the box at the top of the page. Have them point to and say the letters in the box. Tell them that the other boxes on the page each have one letter missing. Ask them to look at the first box and read the letters that are there (*a, c, d*). Ask if anyone can tell what letter is missing (*b*). (They may look at the box at the top of the page for help). If no one can tell you, go back to the top box and have the children say the letters again, match the *a*'s in the two boxes, match the *b* to the line for the missing letter, match the *c*'s and *d*'s. Ask the children to write the letter *b* on the line. Finish the remaining boxes in the same way taking as much time as needed. If some children do not understand, do the page together and then wait several weeks and repeat the exercise.

**EXTENDED ACTIVITIES:**

1. Practice alphabet sequencing by giving the children a set of alphabet flash cards and asking them to match them to a large alphabet chart.

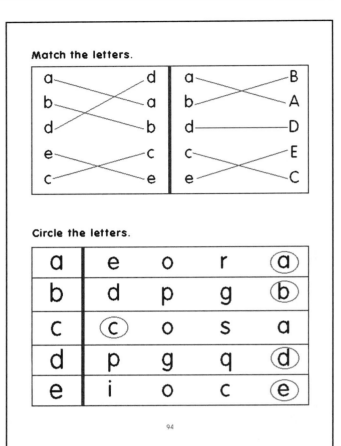

**Match the letters.**

**Circle the letters.**

94

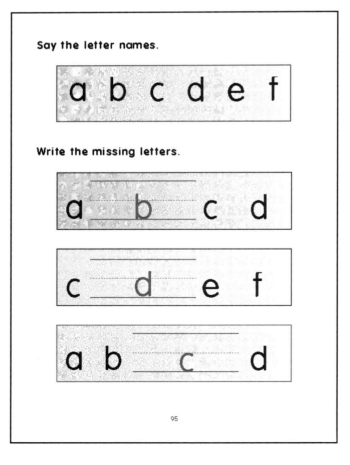

**Say the letter names.**

a b c d e f

**Write the missing letters.**

a b c d

c d e f

a b c d

95

2. Watch for children who consistently confuse *b* and *d*. These children may need extra help.

3. For those who are able, give each child an alphabet card. Ask the children to arrange themselves in alphabetical order.

4. Play alphabet *Bingo* or *Lotto* to reinforce letter recognition.

**SUGGESTED READING/ STORY IDEAS:**

1. Find new alphabet books from the library to explore. Talk about the order of the alphabet.

## OBJECTIVES:

1. To recognize capital *H* and small *h*.
2. To write capital *H* and small *h*.
3. To recognize the sound of *Hh*.

**MATERIALS:** pencils, crayons, Bible, magazines or newspapers, paste or glue, chart paper or tagboard, alphabet or flash cards for *Hh*, 3" x 5" cards.

## TEACHING PAGES 96 and 97:

1. To introduce *Hh* on pages 96 and 97, follow the procedures for pages 20 and 21 (Lesson Ten). Stress the words *hen, hat, Helen, Henry* on page 96.

2. Read a list of words such as those which follow. Have the children raise their hands or hold up a card with an *h* on it when they hear the *h* sound. Examples: *happy, find, Heather, baby, heart, have, home, man*.

3. Have the children hold their hands in front of their mouths when they say the *h* sound. What do they feel? Where does the sound come from? Is it a quiet sound?

## EXTENDED ACTIVITIES:

1. Make an *Hh* chart.

2. Have the children who are able, play the letter game introduced in Activity 2 for pages 30 – 31. Add *h* cards to those already made. Have the children spread the cards out and see if they can add more words to those found before. Examples: *had, hand, hat*. Have them use the words they make in a sentence. Add to the list of words and names they are able to form and sound out with the sounds already learned. Help as needed. Reminder: If the children are not ready and find this activity difficult, then wait several more weeks and try again.

3. Talk about names and words from the Bible that begin with the *Hh* sound: *hallowed, Ham, handmaid, Hannah, heaven, hope,* and so on. Add these to Bible list or booklet.

## SUGGESTED READING/ STORY IDEAS:

1. Read the story of the appearance of the angel to Mary (Luke 1:38); some translations have *handmaid* others do not. Discuss what it means to serve the Lord.

2. Read other passages that tell of *Ham*, Noah's son; of *Hannah*, Samuel's mother; of *heaven*.

3. Return to the Lord's Prayer booklet. Find *hallowed* and *heaven*.

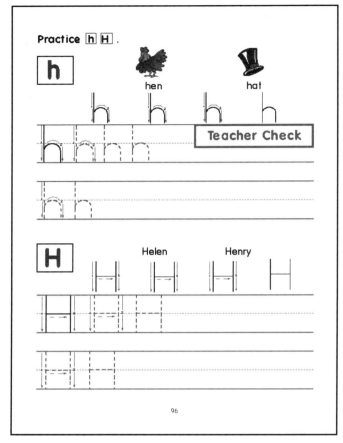

Practice h H.

h — hen — hat

Teacher Check

H — Helen — Henry

96

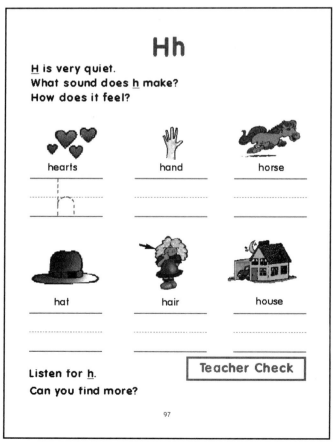

# Hh

<u>H</u> is very quiet.
What sound does <u>h</u> make?
How does it feel?

hearts          hand          horse

hat          hair          house

Listen for <u>h</u>.
Can you find more?

Teacher Check

97

## OBJECTIVES:

1. To recognize capital *H* and small *h*.
2. To write capital *H* and small *h*.
3. To recognize the sound of *Hh*.
4. To distinguish size: *big/little, large/small*

**MATERIALS:** pencils, crayons, magazines and newspapers, paste or glue, materials to make puppet, alphabet scrapbook, objects or pictures of objects that illustrate *big/little, large/small*.

## TEACHING PAGES 98 and 99:

1. To reinforce and review the sound *Hh* on page 98, follow the procedures for page 16, numbers 1, 2, and 3 (Lesson Eight).

2. To prepare for page 99, write the word *BIG* on one side of the board or a large sheet of paper and *LITTLE* on the other side of the board. Ask the children to tell you all the things they consider *big*. List them using pictures to represent the things whenever possible. Do the same for those things they consider *little*. Repeat the process for the words *large* and *small*. Ask the children to look at the page and to find the words for *big, little, large,* and *small*. This is a matching rather than a reading activity.

3. Tell the children that you will read a sentence for them only once. Ask them to circle the picture that matches the sentence. Have them put their fingers on the small boxes to keep their place. Say: Put your fingers on the *sock*. Listen to the sentence: John wanted a *small* tree for his yard. Circle the *small* tree. Put your fingers on the *bike*. Listen to the sentence: Janet lived in a very *large* house. Circle the *large* house. Put your fingers on the *ice cream cone*. Listen to the sentence: The baby chick is *little*. Circle the *little* baby. Put your fingers on the *kite*. Listen to the sentence: The *big* dog took care of the small dog. Circle the *big* dog. Check to see if all children have completed the page correctly.

## EXTENDED ACTIVITIES:

1. Make an *Hh* puppet.
2. Add to alphabet scrapbook at home.
3. Continue to use the newspaper activity if the children find it helpful.
4. Add to the *Hh* chart, if new words or pictures have been found.
5. Additional practice for writing the letter *Hh* can be found in the writing practice section of the children's book.
6. Take the children for a walk to the park and ask them to find examples of things which are *big*

My Hh page.

98

Size.

Circle the picture.

99

or *little*, *large* or *small*.  Continue to work with students who are having difficulties with size relationships.

**SUGGESTED READING/ STORY IDEAS:**

1.  Write a story using as many *Hh* words as they can.  Pictures may be used in place of words where appropriate. Write the story for the children and let them add illustration. Add to alphabet storybook.

2.  Have a child or several children use the *Hh* puppet to tell the story.

3.  Find library books which talk about size or stories which have reference to size, such as *The Three Bears, Jack and the Beanstalk, The Three Billy Goats Gruff,* and so on.

## OBJECTIVES:

1. To say the alphabet.
2. To recognize the letters of the alphabet.
3. To follow the order of the alphabet.
4. To follow directions.
5. To review the initial consonants: *c, f, p, k, d, h.*

**MATERIALS:** pencils and crayons, alphabet chart or flash cards, charts to review initial consonants: *c, f, p, k, d,* and *h.*

## TEACHING PAGES 100 and 101:

1. Prepare for page 100 by having the children sing the alphabet song. Then ask them to point to *A* on the picture. Ask them to read the alphabet through pointing to each letter as it is said. Watch to see if all follow. Have the children take their pencils and move from dot to dot as they say the alphabet once again. Check to see if anyone has difficulty. Give help as needed and note problem letters. When they have finished, they may color the picture.

2. Review the initial consonants *c, f, p, k, d,* and *h.* Have the children divide into six groups (three if the class is small). Give each group one or two letters. Ask them to find as many things as they can that begin with their letter(s). Give time for each group to share what they have found.

3. Ask the children to look at page 101. Have someone read the letter in the first box. Tell them to look at the pictures in the box and circle the one that begins with the *k* sound of the letter *c* (*cat*). Ask them to write the letter *c* on the line. Follow the same procedure for the remaining boxes. If some children are able, let them work independently. Check the page and give help as needed.

## EXTENDED ACTIVITIES:

1. Find or make other dot-to-dot alphabet pages for additional practice, especially for children having difficulty. Make sure that both the letters and the dots are large enough for the children to see clearly.

2. Review and reinforce any initial consonants that are causing problems.

## SUGGESTED READING/ STORY IDEAS:

1. Review, add to, or create new stories or poems for the consonants used in this lesson.

2. Subscribe to, or obtain from the library, children's magazines such as *Ladybug,* which provide stories and poems for children of kindergarten age.

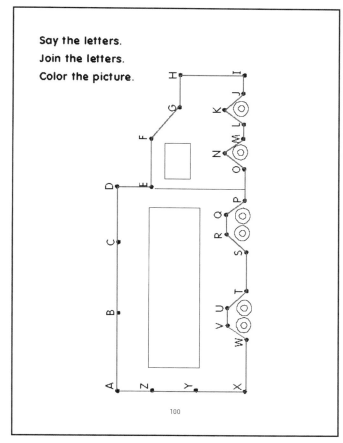

Say the letters.
Join the letters.
Color the picture.

100

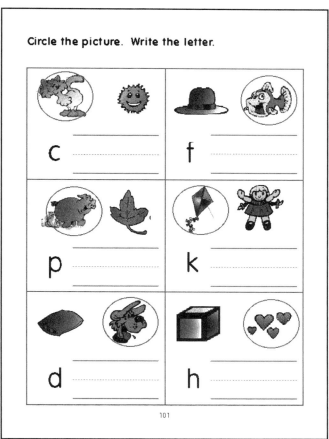

Circle the picture. Write the letter.

c          f

p          k

d          h

101

## OBJECTIVES:
1. To recognize capital *O* and small *o*.
2. To write capital *O* and small *o*.
3. To recognize the sound of short *Oo*.

**MATERIALS:** pencils and crayons, Bible, tagboard or chart paper, magazines or newspapers, glue or paste, scissors, flash cards for short *o*, 3"x 5" cards.

## TEACHING PAGES 102 and 103:
1. For procedures for teaching page 102 and 103, see pages 14 and 15 (Lesson Seven).
Stress the short sound of *o* in *ox, octopus, October, Oscar* on page 102.
2. Read a list of words such as the following. Have the children raise their hands or hold up a card with *o* on it when they hear the short *o* sound. Examples: *on, opposite, inch, Oliver, ant, egg, of, odd.*

## EXTENDED ACTIVITIES:
1. Make a short *Oo* chart.
2. Play a rhyming game with short *o* words. Say a word such as *hot* or *mop* and see if the children can find other words that rhyme with them.
3. For more advanced children, continue the letter game begun in Lesson Fifteen, pages 30 and 31, Activity 2. Help children to sound out new words with the sounds they have learned. Examples: *pot, not, on.* They can also review other words they have made; *mat, bat, rat, let, met, sit, pit.*

## SUGGESTED READING/ STORY IDEAS:
1. Write a story or poem with the short *o* rhyming words found by the children.
2. Find stories or poems which have short *o* rhymes.

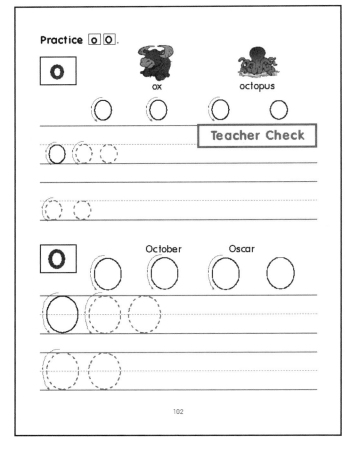

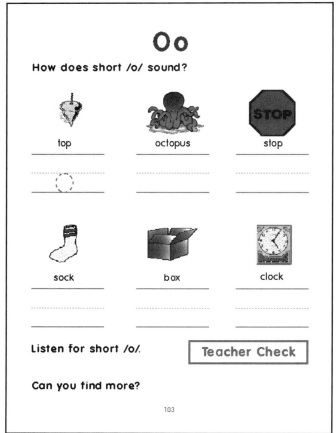

**OBJECTIVES:**
1. To recognize capital *O* and small *o*.
2. To write capital *O* and small *o*.
3. To recognize the sound of short *Oo*.
4. To make and read new words.

**MATERIALS:** pencils, crayons, magazines and newspapers, paste or glue, materials to make puppet, alphabet scrapbook.

**TEACHING PAGES 104 and 105:**
1. To reinforce and review the sound short *o* on page 104, follow the procedures for page 16, numbers 1, 2, and 3 (Lesson Eight).
2. Page 105 is an extension of the activity begun on page 52 (Lesson Twenty-six). Follow procedures from page 52 and the caution to use only with children who are ready for this activity. If children are not ready, do the activity with them and then come back to this activity several weeks or even months later. Have the children draw a line from the words *clock*, *top*, and *block* to the pictures.

**EXTENDED ACTIVITIES:**
1. Make a short *Oo* puppet.
2. Add to alphabet scrapbook at home.
3. Add to the *Oo* chart, if new words or pictures have been found.
4. Additional practice for writing the letter *Oo* can be found in the writing practice section of the children's books.

**SUGGESTED READING/ STORY IDEAS:**
1. Very few short *o* words are found for the Bible section. The most important is *God*. Ask the children to write or tell a story about who God is to them, to their families, and so on. Compile the stories in a class book or add them to the children's Bible booklet.
2. Have the children write a class poem beginning each line with "God is . . .".

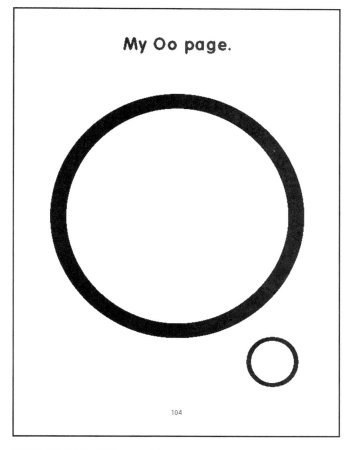

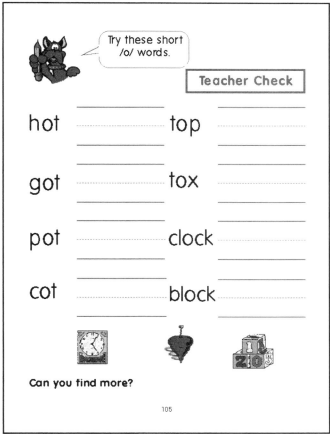

**OBJECTIVES:**
1. To recognize patterns.
2. To complete patterns.
3. To recognize color patterns.
4. To complete color patterns.
5. To recognize the position of one thing in relation to another.
6. To listen carefully.
7. To follow a direction given only once.

**MATERIALS:** crayons, flannel board and shapes, colored blocks, bears, or other manipulatives, color chart, drawing paper.

**TEACHING PAGES 106 and 107:**
1. Preparation for this session may take more than one class period. Spread over two days or as many as needed. Begin preparing for page 106 by putting shapes on the chalkboard or flannel board in the following patterns:
Square, circle, square, circle
Triangle, circle, triangle, circle
Square, rectangle, square
Ask the children to look carefully to see if they can tell which shapes should come next in each pattern. When they realize that a square continues the first pattern, add a square to the pattern. Continue the first pattern for at least two additional sets (square, circle, square, circle). Work with the second and third pattern in the same manner.

2. When children have mastered these simple patterns, put the following more complicated patterns on the board:
Square, circle, triangle
Circle, rectangle, circle, square
Square, triangle, circle
Follow the same procedures used with the simple patterns. These patterning activities can also be done with colored blocks or bears alternating colors instead of shapes (red, blue, red, blue; red, green, green, red, and so on).

3. When the children are ready, read the directions to page 106. Tell them that first they will complete the pattern in pencil for each row. Work only with the shapes, not the colors. Do not be concerned about the color words at this point. Do the first box together. Have the children trace the solid circle and square first. Then have them trace the broken circle. Ask them what shape should come next (*square*). Tell them to draw that shape. Ask them what shape should come next (*circle*). Have them draw the shape and so on until the row

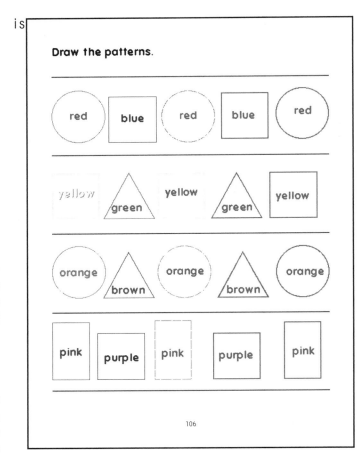

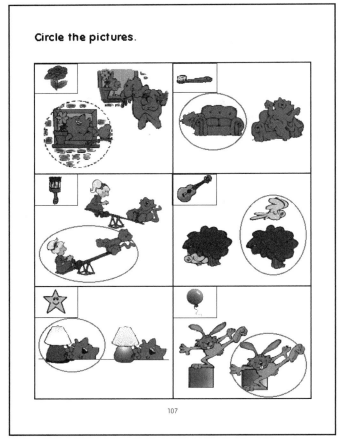

complete. Have the children finish the page by themselves. Walk around to see if anyone is having trouble.

4. After a break, or on another day, look at the page again. This time tell the children that they are looking for a color pattern. Have a color chart ready to help with words. Ask the children what color word they see in the first circle (*red*). Ask what color word they see in the first square (*blue*). Ask them what color the next circle should be (*red*). Ask them what color the next square should be (*blue*). Complete the first two rows with the children. Help them begin the last two rows to make sure they know what colors they need. Let them complete the last two rows on their own.

5. On page 107 read the direction. Ask the children to read them after you. Read the following sentences only once. Have the children circle the appropriate picture. Have them put their fingers on the small picture in the box to keep their places more easily.

| | |
|---|---|
| *Rose*: | The cat is looking *out* of the window. |
| *Toothbrush*: | The cat is *behind* the sofa. |
| *Paintbrush* | Mary is going *down*. |
| *Violin*: | The bird is *over* the bush. |
| *Star*: | The lamp is turned *off*. |
| *Balloon*: | The rabbit is *in front* of the box. |

Check each of the boxes together. Ask the children what is happening in the other picture in the box. Be sure they understand the difference between the two.

**EXTENDED ACTIVITIES:**

1. Have the children begin some patterns on drawing paper. Let them exchange papers and complete each others' patterns.

2. Divide a sheet of drawing paper into six sections.

Read the following sentences one by one and have the children draw in one of the boxes a picture representing each sentence.

A box is *under* the table.
A dog is *under* the bed.
The ball is going *over* the house.
The car is *in front* of the garage.
Tom is standing *beside* Mary.
The egg is *in* the nest.

**SUGGESTED READING/ STORY IDEAS:**

1. Find or create stories or rhymes that encourage the children to follow a pattern (*The House that Jack Built, Let's Go on a Lion Hunt, The Farmer in the Dell*). Have the children change them and add some variations of their own.

2. Have the children make up a story using as many position words as they can: *over, under, up, down, in front of, beside*.

**OBJECTIVES:**
1. To recognize capital *G* and small *g*.
2. To write capital *G* and small *g*.
3. To recognize the sound of *Gg*.

**MATERIALS:** pencils, crayons, Bible, magazines or newspapers, paste or glue, chart paper or tagboard, alphabet or flash cards for *Gg*, 3" x 5" cards.

**TEACHING PAGES 108 and 109:**
1. To introduce *Gg* on pages 108 and 109, follow the procedures for pages 20 and 21 (Lesson Ten). Stress the words *goat, girl, God,* and *Gabriel* on page 108. The sound introduced in this lesson is the hard sound of *g*. The soft *g* (*gentle*), is not introduced at this time.
2. Read a list of words such as those which follow. Have the children raise their hands or hold up a card with a *g* on it when they hear the *g* sound. Examples: *guess, boy, gift, gather, doll, mix, Galilee, car.*
3. Have the children say the *g* sound. Where does the sound come from? Is it a quiet sound?

**EXTENDED ACTIVITIES:**
1. Make a *Gg* chart.
2. Have the children who are able, play the letter game introduced in Activity 2 for pages 30 – 31. Add *g* cards to those already made. Have the children spread the cards out and see if they can add more words to those found before. Examples: *get, God, gift.* Have them use the words they make in a sentence. Add to the list of words and names they are able to form and sound out with the sounds already learned. Help as needed. Reminder: If the children are not ready and find this activity difficult, then wait several more weeks and try again.
3. Talk about names and words from the Bible that begin with the *Gg* sound: *God, Gabriel, Galilee, gate, Goliath, Gospel, glorify, grace, godliness,* and so on. Add these to Bible list or booklet.

**SUGGESTED READING/ STORY IDEAS:**
1. Review the story of David and Goliath. Have the children tell it.
2. Find Galilee on a map. Read any passages that speak of Galilee.
3. Read what the angel Gabriel did (Daniel 8: 16; 9:21; Luke 1: 19, 26).
4. Look at the four Gospels and read a short story from each.

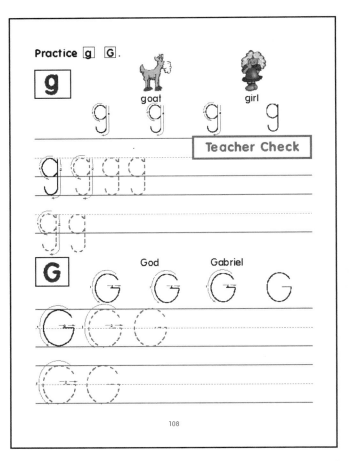

## OBJECTIVES:

1. To recognize capital *G* and small *g*.
2. To write capital *G* and small *g*.
3. To recognize the sound of *Gg*.
4. To review initial consonants: *p, s, f, r, l, g, b, t, n, d, g.*

**MATERIALS:** pencils, crayons, magazines and newspapers, paste or glue, materials to make puppet, alphabet scrapbook, charts for initial letter review.

## TEACHING PAGES 110 and 111:

1. To reinforce and review the sound *Gg* on page 110, follow the procedures for page 16, numbers 1, 2, and 3 (Lesson Eight).

2. To prepare the children for page 111, draw three boxes on the chalkboard, draw pictures and print letters similar to those on the page. (*cat — c* and *t; man — r* and *m; ball — b* and *g*). Point to the first picture on the board and ask the children to name it (*cat*). Ask them to say the beginning sound. Ask them to look at the two letters in the box and to tell which letter sound they hear at the beginning of the picture. Do the same with the other two boxes.

3. On page 111, read the directions. Do the first row of boxes on the page with the children. After naming all the pictures in the boxes, let them finish the exercise by themselves. When everyone has finished, have the children take turns naming the picture, giving the beginning sound, and naming the letter circled.

## EXTENDED ACTIVITIES:

1. Make a *Gg* puppet.
2. Add to alphabet scrapbook at home.
3. Continue to use the newspaper activity if the children find it helpful.
4. Add to the *Gg* chart, if new words or pictures have been found.
5. Additional practice for writing the letter *Gg* can be found in the writing practice section of the children's book.
6. Review initial sounds as needed.

## SUGGESTED READING/ STORY IDEAS:

1. Write a story using as many *Gg* words as they can. Pictures may be used in place of words where appropriate. Write the story for the children and let them add illustration. Add to alphabet Story Book.

2. Have a child or several children use the *Gg* puppet to tell the story.

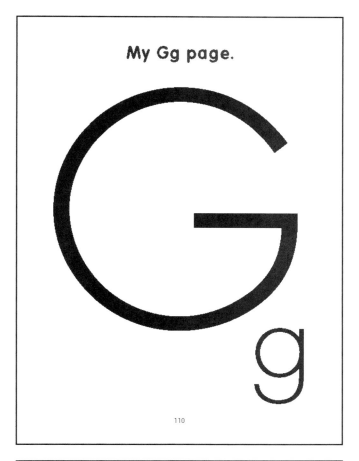

## OBJECTIVES:

1. To understand position words.
2. To recognize the positions of objects.
3. To complete part of the alphabet in the correct order.

**MATERIALS:** pencils, crayons, alphabet charts.

## TEACHING PAGES 112 AND 113:

1. To prepare the children for page 112, place one object on the table, one under the table, one behind the table, one in front of the table, and one beside the table. Name the object and ask a child to tell you where it is. Hold an object over the table and ask a child to tell where it is. Hold an object under the table and ask a child to tell where it is. Do this activity several times.
*Read*: Circle the glass *on* the table; Circle the cat *in* the box; Circle the bird flying *over* the roof; Circle the boy *under* his bed.

2. To prepare for the activity on page 113, put sequence letters on the chalkboard with several missing. See the following examples:

    a, ____, c, d;  f, ____, h, ____, ____, k;
    ____, m, ____, o, ____, and so on.

Have the children tell you which letters are missing. Be sure that the children have an alphabet posted or their alphabet chart for reference. Read all the letters together after the list has been completed.

3. Have the children look at page 113. Ask them to point to the letter box at the top of the page and say the letters first with you and then on their own. Complete the page following the procedures used for page 95 (Lesson Forty-seven, number 3).

## EXTENDED ACTIVITIES:

1. Say the alphabet aloud frequently, stopping every few letters so the children can add the next letter.

2. Do several drills on the board as in number 2 above.

3. Lay out series of letters with flash cards leaving a space for one or more letters. Have a selection of letters for the children's choice. Ask them to choose the missing letters and place them in the right position.

4. Play games which emphasize different positions and directions. Ask the children, for example, to put their pencils *in* their desks, *under* their books, and so on.

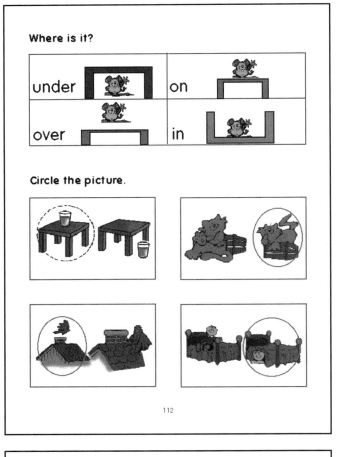

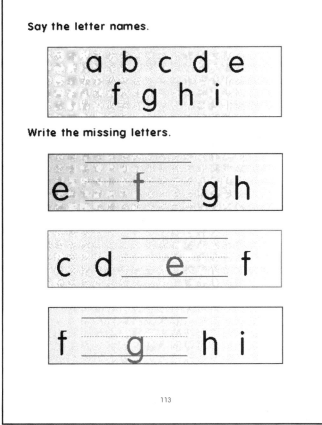

**SUGGESTED READING/ STORY IDEAS:**

1. Read books such as *Inside, Outside, Upside Down*, by Stan Berenstain to reinforce position words.

2. Play games or sing songs such as "Go in and out the window".

**OBJECTIVES:**
1. To recognize capital *J* and small *j*.
2. To write capital *J* and small *j*.
3. To recognize the sound of *Jj*.

**MATERIALS:** pencils, crayons, Bible, magazines or newspapers, paste or glue, chart paper or tagboard, alphabet or flash cards for *Jj*, 3" x 5" cards.

**TEACHING PAGES 114 AND 115:**

1. To introduce *Jj* on pages 114 and 115, follow the procedures for pages 20 and 21 (Lesson Ten). Stress the words *jar, jacket, Jesus,* and *Joseph* on page 114.

2. Read a list of words such as those which follow. Have the children raise their hands or hold up a card with a *j* on it when they hear the *j* sound. Examples: *joke, gift, Jane, jump, bottle, James,* and *just.*

3. Have the children say the *j* sound. Where are their teeth? Where does the sound come from? Is it a quiet sound? Can they feel any air passing through their lips?

**EXTENDED ACTIVITIES:**

1. Make a *Jj* chart.

2. Have the children who are able, play the letter game introduced in Activity 2 for pages 30 - 31. Add *j* cards to those already made. Have the children spread the cards out and see if they can add more words to those found before. Examples: *jet, jam, Jill.* Have them use the words they make in a sentence. Add to the list of words and names they are able to form and sound out with the sounds already learned. Help as needed. Some children may still find this difficult. If the children are not ready, wait several more weeks and try again.

3. Talk about names and words from the Bible that begin with the *Jj* sound: *Jesus, James, John, Jerusalem, Joseph, justice, Jacob, Jordan, Jew, Job,* and so on. Add these to Bible list or booklet.

**SUGGESTED READING/ STORY IDEAS:**

1. Read any of the many gospel stories about Jesus and talk to the children about how He loved little children and how important He is in their lives. Have them choose a favorite story to illustrate. Keep the drawings where the children can see them and be reminded of Jesus' love for them.

2. Read or tell parts of the story of Joseph (Genesis chapters 37–48). Have them act out one or more of these parts.

## OBJECTIVES:

1. To recognize capital *J* and small *j*.
2. To write capital *J* and small *j*.
3. To recognize the sound of *Jj*.
4. To put letters of the alphabet in order.

**MATERIALS:** pencils, crayons, magazines and newspapers, paste or glue, materials to make puppet, alphabet scrapbook, alphabet charts and flash cards.

## TEACHING PAGES 116 AND 117:

1. To reinforce and review the sound Jj on page 116, follow the procedures for page 16, numbers 1, 2, and 3 (Lesson Eight).

2. For page 117, follow the preparation and teaching procedures for page 95 (Lesson Forty-seven, number 3) and page 113 (Lesson Fifty-six, number 2).

## EXTENDED ACTIVITIES:

1. Make a *Jj* puppet.
2. Add to alphabet scrapbook at home.
3. Continue to use the newspaper activity if the children find it helpful.
4. Add to the *Jj* chart, if new words or pictures have been found.
5. Additional practice for writing the letter *Jj* can be found in the writing practice section of the children's book.
6. Review alphabet sequence.

## SUGGESTED READING/ STORY IDEAS:

1. Write a story using as many Jj words as they can. Pictures may be used in place of words where appropriate. Write a story for the children and let them add illustration. Add to alphabet storybook.

2. Have a child or several children use the *Jj* puppet to tell the story.

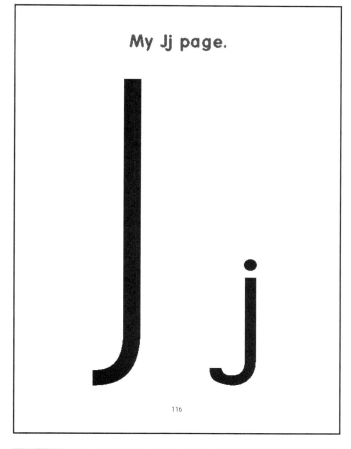

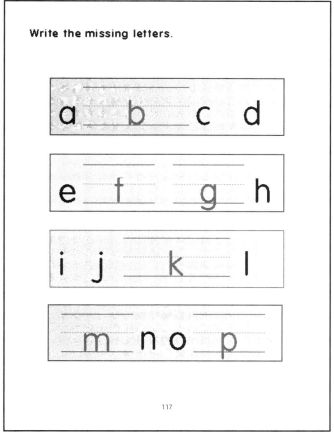

**OBJECTIVES:**

1. To review colors: red, blue, green, yellow, brown, orange, pink, and purple.

2. To recognize black and white.

3. To review basic shapes in different sizes and positions: circle, square, triangle, rectangle, and oval.

4. To review recognition of basic shapes in objects.

**MATERIALS:** pencils and crayons, objects and cards to review both shapes and colors, materials from the shape and color boxes or envelopes.

**TEACHING PAGES 118 AND 119:**

1. Prepare for page 118, by reviewing all the colors the children have learned. This can be done by having children list or find items for each color. It can also be done by dividing the children into groups and assigning one or two colors for each group to find. When they have done this, ask them to find or name some things that are *black*. Follow this activity by asking them to find or names things that are *white*.

2. Have the children look at the words *black* and *white* on the top of page 118. Ask them if they see these words anywhere else on the page. Have them show you where they find them. Tell the children to lay out crayons for *red, orange, blue, yellow, pink, white, green, black, brown,* and *purple*. Have them find the *red* crayon and match the name on the crayon to the first word in the box. Ask them to find the *red* square and point to it. Then have them trace the line from the word *red* to the *red* square with their *red* crayons. Follow this procedure for the remaining colors.

3. On page 119, read the directions to the children. Ask the children to put their fingers on the *circle* in the first column. Have them find the *circle* in the second column and point to it. Ask them to draw a line from the first *circle* to the second *circle*. Repeat this procedure with the *square*. Have the children note the two squares are not the same size. Ask the children to complete the two boxes at the top of the page. Remind them that they are matching the shape. The size and positions may be different, but they are to find the shapes that match. Read the direction at the bottom of the page and ask the children to circle all of the pictures in the row that contain the shape in the first box. Let children work independently. Walk around and check as they work.

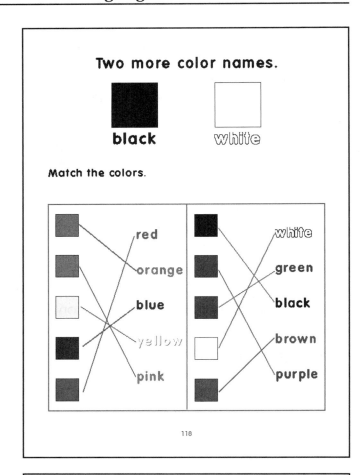

**Two more color names.**

**black**    white

**Match the colors.**

red
orange
blue
yellow
pink

white
green
black
brown
purple

118

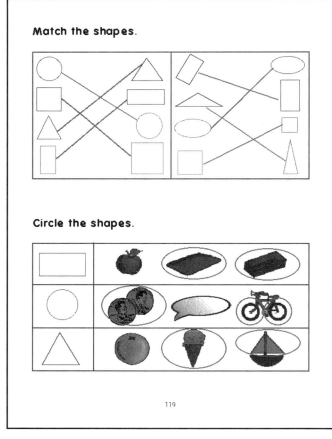

**Match the shapes.**

**Circle the shapes.**

119

**EXTENDED ACTIVITIES:**

1.  Review any colors or shapes that continue to be a problem for individual children.

2.  Play color or shape Bingo or Lotto games as a review for all children.

**SUGGESTED READING/ STORY IDEAS:**

1.  Ask the children to name several things which contain the shape of a circle. Put this list on the board. On a sheet of chart paper, write the title: *Round as a . . . .*  Have the children work on a poem which uses as many of the round or circular objects on the list as possible.
Examples:
Round as the sun in the deep blue sky,
Round as a balloon flying high,
Round as a circle on a paper of red,
Round as the pillow on Mother's bed,
Round as the world all blue and green, and so on.
Rhyming is not necessary, but will make it easier to remember.
Writing poems about other shapes or colors may be done as well.

2.  When the poem is finished, have the children illustrate it.

**OBJECTIVES:**
1. To recognize capital *V* and small *v*.
2. To write capital *V* and small *v*.
3. To recognize the sound of *Vv*.

**MATERIALS:** pencils, crayons, Bible, magazines or newspapers, paste or glue, chart paper or tagboard, alphabet or flash cards for *Vv*, 3" x 5" cards.

**TEACHING PAGES 120 AND 121:**
1. To introduce *Vv* on pages 120 and 121, follow the procedures for pages 20 and 21 (Lesson Ten). Stress the words *vase*, *vest*, *Vivian*, and *Vera* on page 120.
2. Read a list of words such as those which follow. Have the children raise their hands or hold up a card with a *v* on it when they hear the *v* sound. Examples: *vacation, fish, valley, gate, very, Veronica.*
3. Have the children say the *v* sound. Where are their teeth? Where does the sound come from? Is it a quiet sound? Can they feel any air passing through their lips? Ask them to make the sound of *f* and compare.

**EXTENDED ACTIVITIES:**
1. Make a *Vv* chart.
2. Have the children who are able, play the letter game introduced in Activity 2 for pages 30 - 31. Add *v* cards to those already made. Have the children spread the cards out and see if they can add more words to those found before. Examples: *vet, van.* Have them use the words they make in a sentence. Add to the list of words and names they are able to form and sound out with the sounds already learned. Help as needed. Some children may still find this difficult. If the children are not ready, wait several more weeks and try again.
3. Talk about names and words from the Bible that begin with the *Vv* sound: *vineyard, victory, vow,* and so on. Add these to Bible list or booklet.

**SUGGESTED READING/ STORY IDEAS:**
1. Read Matthew 20: 1 through 16 to the children (the parable of the laborers in the vineyard).
2. Talk about what a vow is. Read Genesis, 28: 20 - 21 which contains Jacob's vow to God. Emphasize that a *vow* is a very serious promise. Talk about *vows* that the children may know about, such as wedding vows.

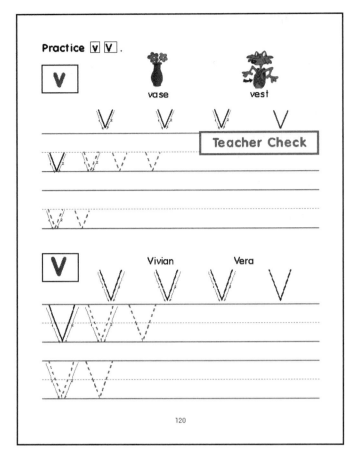

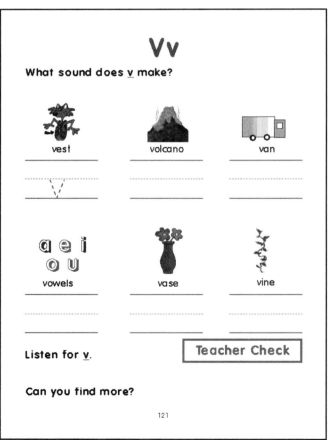

## OBJECTIVES:

1. To recognize capital *V* and small *v*.
2. To write capital *V* and small *v*.
3. To recognize the sound of *Vv*.
4. To review initial consonants: *c, f, p, j, m, l, t, p, s, b, d,* and *r*.

**MATERIALS:** pencils, crayons, magazines and newspapers, paste or glue, materials to make puppet, alphabet scrapbook, alphabet charts and flash cards, 3" x 5" cards.

## TEACHING PAGES 122 AND 123:

1. To reinforce and review the sound *Vv* on page 122, follow the procedures for page 16, numbers 1, 2, and 3 (Lesson Eight).

2. To prepare for page 123, say the words *jump, bake, pink,* and *tub* slowly and clearly. Ask the children to identify the beginning sound for each. Repeat the words one by one. Review the procedure used for page 111 (Lesson Fifty-five, number 2). Read the directions. Do the first row of boxes on the page with the children. Let them finish the exercise by themselves AFTER naming *all* of the pictures in the boxes. When everyone has finished, have the children take turns naming the picture, giving the beginning sound, and naming the letter circled.

## EXTENDED ACTIVITIES:

1. Make a *Vv* puppet.
2. Add to alphabet scrapbook at home.
3. Add to the *Vv* chart, if new words or pictures have been found.
4. Additional practice for writing the letter *Vv* can be found in the writing practice section of the children's book.
5. Make up a list of words beginning with *p, t, d,* and *b*. Have the children put their *p, t, d,* and *b* flash cards on their desks. Ask the children to hold up the proper card as a word is read. This activity immediately checks whether the children are hearing the sounds. Read all words slowly and clearly. Children who often confuse the sounds of *p, t, d,* and *b* may need to have their hearing checked.
6. Cut small pictures of things that begin with consonant sounds out of catalogues or old magazines. Paste them on 3" x 5" cards. Put the beginning letter on the back of the card. Have the children match the picture cards with an alphabet card. They can check themselves or have another child or the teacher do it.

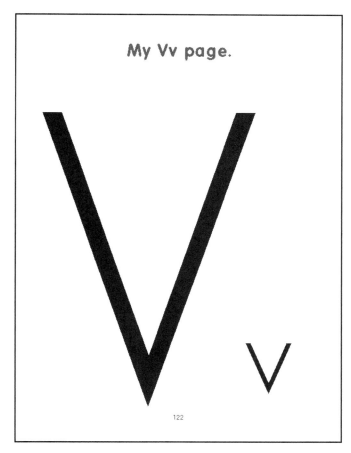

My Vv page.

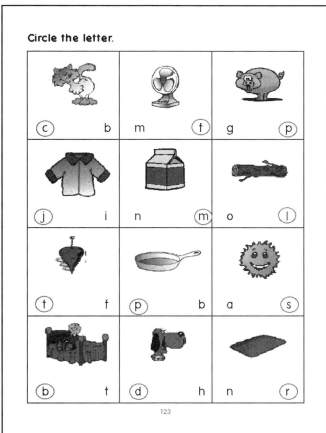

Circle the letter.

7. More advanced students can begin also listening for the ending sounds of words. Have them try the *ending* sounds for the pictures on page 123.

**SUGGESTED READING/ STORY IDEAS:**

1. Write a story using as many *Vv* words as they can. Pictures may be used in place of words where appropriate. Write the story for the children and let them add illustration. Add to alphabet Story Book.

2. Have a child or several children use the *Vv* puppet to tell the story.

## OBJECTIVES:

1. To listen carefully.
2. To follow directions given only once.
3. To review writing of names.
4. To review letter recognition.
5. To put things in order.

**MATERIALS:** pencils, crayons, alphabet chart or flash cards, sequence cards.

## TEACHING PAGES 124 AND 125:

1. Read the direction on page 124. Tell the children that you will read a sentence only once. They should listen carefully and circle the correct picture. Ask them to put their fingers on the picture while you read the sentence.
Read:
*Top:* The cat is wrapping a box.
*Kite:* The cat gives the box to the bird.
*Block:* The bird opens the box and finds a truck.
*Car:* The bird thanks the cat.
When they have circled the pictures, tell them to recall the story, to look at the pictures, and then to write a *1* in the box that shows what happened first, a *2* in the box next to what happened second, a *3* in the box next to what happened third, and a *4* in the box next to what happened last.

2. Tell the children that page 125 is a page they can do by themselves after you read the directions. They have done each type of activity before and should be able to do this on their own. Read the first direction slowly. Have the children write their names (first and last if they are able, if not, only the first). They may use their name cards if needed. Note letter formation. Read the second direction. Ask the children to do this activity on their own. Walk around and help anyone having difficulty. Read the third direction. Ask the children to circle the word that begins with the letter at the beginning of the row. Let them work independently. Again, walk around and help anyone having difficulty. Check together and note any letters which still give problems.

## EXTENDED ACTIVITIES:

1. For children who had difficulty with page 124, review earlier sequence Lessons (36 and 42) and any sequence cards that are available. When the review is complete, have the children take a crayon and do the page again. Read:
*Top:* The cat opens the box.
*Kite:* The cat takes a collar out of the box.
*Block:* The cat picks up the wrapping paper.
*Car:* The cat thanks the bird for the gift.

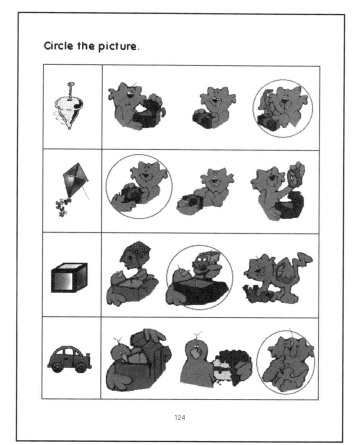

Circle the picture.

124

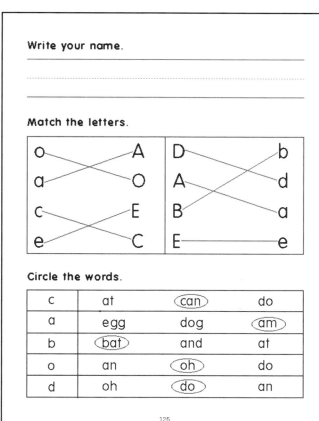

Write your name.

Match the letters.

Circle the words.

| c | at | can | do |
|---|-----|-----|-----|
| a | egg | dog | am |
| b | bat | and | at |
| o | an | oh | do |
| d | oh | do | an |

125

2. Have the children give a word for each letter in the matching boxes on page 125.

3. Have the more advanced children read any of the words in the last exercise that they are able to read. Have the children make up sentences for the words.

4. Ask the children if they can find any short *a, e,* or *o* words.

**SUGGESTED READING/ STORY IDEAS:**

1. Have the children make up a story about the cat and the bird using either of the sequences given for the page.

2. Continue to read to the children daily, pointing out the order of stories as you do so.

## OBJECTIVES:

1. To recognize capital *W* and small *w*.
2. To write capital *W* and small *w*.
3. To recognize the sound of *Ww*.

**MATERIALS:** pencils, crayons, Bible, magazines or newspapers, paste or glue, chart paper or tagboard, alphabet or flash cards for *Ww*, 3" x 5" cards.

## TEACHING PAGES 126 AND 127:

1. To introduce *Ww* on pages 126 and 127, follow the procedures for pages 20 and 21 (Lesson Ten). Stress the words *well, world, William,* and *Wally* on page 126.

2. Read a list of words such as those which follow. Have the children raise their hands or hold up a card with a *w* on it when they hear the *w* sound. Examples: *wallet, wonder, many, will, valley, water.*

3. Have the children say the *w* sound. How do they use their lips? Where does the sound come from?

## EXTENDED ACTIVITIES:

1. Make a *Ww* chart.

2. Have the children who are able, play the letter game introduced in Activity 2 for pages 30 - 31. Add *w* cards to those already made. Have the children spread the cards out and see if they can add more words to those found before. Examples: *wet, win, well.* Have them use the words they make in a sentence. Add to the list of words and names they are able to form and sound out with the sounds already learned. Help as needed. Some children may still find this difficult. If the children are not ready, wait several more weeks and try again.

3. Talk about names and words from the Bible that begin with the *Ww* sound: *walls, wells, work, world, worship, wisdom,* and so on. Add these to Bible list or booklet.

## SUGGESTED READING/ STORY IDEAS:

1. Review the story of the Samaritan woman at the well ( John 4:1–14). See how much the children remember. Stress the *w* words: *water, well, woman, worship.*

2. Read or tell the story of Joshua chapter 6. Have children retell or act out the story.

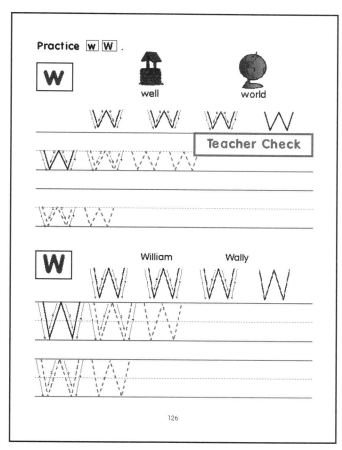

**OBJECTIVES:**
1. To recognize capital *W* and small *w*.
2. To write capital *W* and small *w*.
3. To recognize the sound of *Ww*.
4. To review the short vowel sounds of *a, e, i,* and *o*.

**MATERIALS:** pencils, crayons, magazines and newspapers, paste or glue, materials to make puppet, alphabet scrapbook, alphabet charts and flash cards, short vowel charts and stories.

**TEACHING PAGES 128 AND 129:**
1. To reinforce and review the sound *Ww* on page 128, follow the procedures for page 16, numbers 1, 2, and 3 (Lesson Eight).
2. Prepare for page 129 by reviewing pictures for each of the short vowels. Put a flash card for each of the letters on a table or desk in separate rows: *a, e, i, o*. Ask the children to place the pictures below the correct vowel. Ask the children to look at the page and find the *a* in the first box. Ask them to say the short *a* sound. Have them name each of the pictures in each row pronouncing the vowel sound very carefully. Tell them to circle the pictures in the row that have the short *a* sound. Follow the same procedure for the remaining sounds.

**EXTENDED ACTIVITIES:**
1. Make a *Ww* puppet.
2. Add to alphabet scrapbook at home.
3. Add to the *Ww* chart, if new words or pictures have been found.
4. Additional practice for writing the letter *Ww* can be found in the writing practice section of the children's book.
5. Ask the children if they can find rhyming words for each of the pictures circled.
6. Work with children who have difficulty with any of these sounds. Use pictures, charts, magazines, catalogues, games, or anything that will help to reinforce the sounds.

**SUGGESTED READING/ STORY IDEAS:**
1. Write a story using as many *Ww* words as they can. Pictures may be used in place of words where appropriate. Write the story for the children and let them add illustration. Add to alphabet Story Book.
2. Have a child or several children use the *Ww* puppet to tell the story.
3. Review any short vowel stories written by the children or storybooks with short vowel sounds that the children like.

My Ww page.

128

Circle the short vowel pictures.

| a | | | |
| e | | | |
| i | | | |
| o | | | |

129

**OBJECTIVES:**
1. To say the alphabet.
2. To recognize the letters of the alphabet.
3. To follow the order of the alphabet.

**MATERIALS:** pencils, crayons, alphabet chart or flash cards.

**TEACHING PAGES 130 AND 131:**
1. Prepare for page 130 by having the children sing the alphabet song. Then ask them to point to *a* on the picture. Ask them to read the alphabet pointing to each letter as it is said. Watch to see if all follow. Have the children take their pencils and move from dot to dot as they say the alphabet once again. Check to see if anyone has difficulty. Give help as needed and note problem letters. When they have finished, they may color the picture.

2. Have the children look at the first row on the top of page 131. Ask what letter they see at the beginning of the first row, small *i* . Tell them to look at all of the words in the long box. Have them point to the word *in* which is already circled for them. Ask what letter they see at the beginning of the word *in*. Have the children look at the other three words in the box (*lie, kit, if*). Ask the children to find another word that begins with a small *i*. Ask if anyone can read the word (*if*). Have all the children circle the word *it*. Move to the second box and repeat this procedure. If children have trouble sorting out the words in a single row, allow them to use a sheet of paper or a card to place under the row they are doing so that they are not distracted by the words in the following rows. Complete this activity with the children, or, if they are able, allow the children to complete it independently. Watch for any letters that still cause difficulty.

3. The matching activity at the bottom of the page is a type which has been done many times before. Most children should be able to do this independently. Help as needed for those who have problems.

**EXTENDED ACTIVITIES:**
1. Have the children who are able read the words in the boxes on page 131.
2. If you have not done so, make a set of alphabet cards for each child including both small and capital letters on separate cards. Make a larger set for your use. Hold up your card with a capital and have the children hold up the small letter, or you hold up the small letter and let the

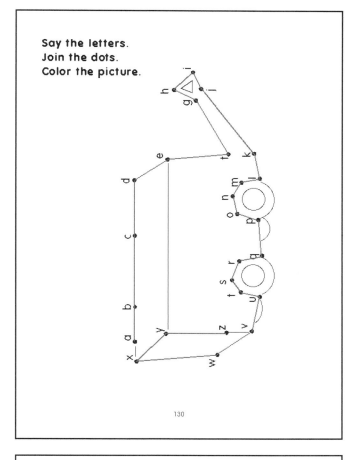

Say the letters.
Join the dots.
Color the picture.

130

**Circle the words.**

| i | in | lie | kit | it |
|---|-----|------|------|------|
| l | he | look | is | land |
| t | at | the | two | how |
| n | no | me | not | can |
| L | He | Lee | It | Larry |
| T | Look | At | To | Tom |
| I | Is | Low | In | Time |
| N | My | No | Nancy | He |

**Match the letters.**

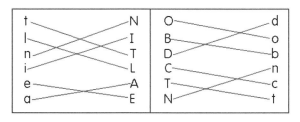

131

123

children hold up the capital. An aide or another child can also do this drill with children.

3. Use the words in the boxes in sentences.

**SUGGESTED READING/ STORY IDEAS:**

1. Using the alphabet puppets that have been made to this point, have the children put together a play about alphabet animals. The children will present this play in alphabetical order using the letters already learned.

2. Have a story time in which you read the alphabet stories written by the children for the letters learned.

## OBJECTIVES:

1. To recognize capital *U* and small *u*.
2. To write capital *U* and small *u*.
3. To recognize the short sound of *Uu*.

**MATERIALS:** pencils and crayons, Bible, tagboard or chart paper, magazines or newspapers, glue or paste, scissors, flash cards for short *Uu*, 3"x 5" cards.

## TEACHING PAGES 132 AND 133:

1. For procedures for teaching page 132 and 133, see pages 14 and 15 (Lesson Seven). Stress the short sound of *u* in *umbrella*, and *up* on page 132. Tell the children that the words *Uriah* and *United* have a different sound of *u* that they will learn later.

2. Read a list of words such as the following. Have the children raise their hands or hold up a card with *u* on it when they hear the short *u* sound. Examples: *under, on, apple, up, us, ant, understanding.*

## EXTENDED ACTIVITIES:

1. Make a short *Uu* chart.
2. Play a rhyming game with short *u* words. Say a word such as *nut* or *bug* and see if the children can find other words that rhyme with them.
3. For more advanced children, continue the letter game begun in Lesson Fifteen, pages 30 and 31, Activity 2. Help children to sound out new words with the sounds they have learned. Examples: *rug, up, hug.* They can also review other words they have made: *mat, bat, hot, met, sit, pit.*

## SUGGESTED READING/ STORY IDEAS:

1. Write a story or poem with the short *u* rhyming words found by the children.
2. Find stories or poems which have short *u* rhymes.

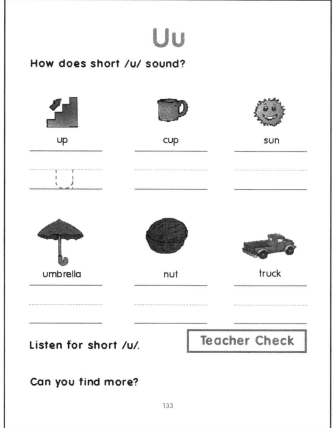

**OBJECTIVES:**
1. To recognize capital *U* and small *u*.
2. To write capital *U* and small *u*.
3. To recognize the short sound of *Uu*.
4. To make new words using the short sound of *Uu*.

**MATERIALS:** pencils, crayons, magazines and newspapers, paste or glue, materials to make puppet, alphabet scrapbook.

**TEACHING PAGES 134 AND 135:**
1. To reinforce and review the sound short *u* on page 134, follow the procedures for page 16, numbers 1, 2, and 3 (Lesson Eight).
2. Page 135 is an extension of the activity begun on page 52 (Lesson Twenty-six) Follow procedures from page 52 and the caution to use only with children who are ready for this activity. If children are not ready, do the activity with them and then come back to this activity several weeks later. Help with the spelling of *rug, sun, cup,* and *duck.*

**EXTENDED ACTIVITIES:**
1. Make a short *Uu* puppet.
2. Add to alphabet scrapbook at home.
3. Add to the *Uu* chart, if new words or pictures have been found.
4. Additional practice for writing the letter *Uu* can be found in the writing practice section of the children's books.

**SUGGESTED READING/ STORY IDEAS:**
1. Look for words for the Bible list. Many short *u* words contain the prefix *un-* (*unfaithful, unworthy, unjust, unholy, ungodly, unfruitful*). Explain to the children that *un-* usually means *not* (*not faithful, not holy, not godly, not fruitful*). The more positive words such as *upright, uphold, understanding* should also be discussed. When you have finished, ask the children if they can think of Bible figures who were *upright* and *understanding*. Can they think of those who were *unfaithful, unjust,* and so on? Review the stories of those figures the children name.
2. Go back in the Bible stories the children have already written or read and look for any of these characteristics.

My Uu page.

134

Try these short /u/ words.

Teacher Check

tub      bug

mud      mug

Can you find more?

135

**OBJECTIVES:**
1. To read from left to right.
2. To read and write the word *I*.
3. To recognize the pronoun *I*.
4. To recognize the order of the alphabet.
5. To put letters in alphabetical order.

**MATERIALS:** pencils, crayons, alphabet charts or flash cards.

**TEACHING PAGES 136 AND 137:**

1. Have the children look at the pictures on page 136 to see what is happening. Have them draw a line from left to right between the first two pictures. Ask a child to tell what is happening in the next box. Point to the sentence in the box and ask what it is. Tell the children that it is called a sentence. Ask them to follow along as you read it. Ask if the sentence tells what is happening in the pictures. Let one or two children read the sentence. Do the last box the same way. Ask what kind of letter is at the beginning of a sentence (capital letter). Tell them that the mark used at the end of the sentence is called a period. Ask them to draw a line from left to right in the last two boxes.

2. Ask the children whom they are talking about when they say "I". Remind them that the word *I* is the same as the capital letter *I*. Have them trace the letter *I* on their desks. Then have them point to the first set of lines. Tell them that the word *I* is to be written there to finish the sentence. Read the sentence. Have them write the *I* and then read the sentence with you. Finish the page in the same way.

3. Prepare for page 137, by asking the children to recite as much of the alphabet as they are able. Write the letters *l, m, n, o, p, q, r, s, t, u, v, w, x* on the board and ask the children to say the names as you point to the letters. Next write the following on the board:

m, n, ____, p, q Ask the children what letter is missing. They can look to the letters written on the board or to their alphabet charts for help. Continue this type of drill with three or four more sets. Ask them to point to the box at the top of page 137. Have them point to and say the letters in the box. Tell them that the other boxes on the page each have one letter missing. Ask them to look at the first box and read the letters that are there (*r, t, u*). Ask if anyone can tell what letter is missing (*s*). (They may look at the box at the top of the page for help). If no one can tell you, go back to the top box and have the children say the

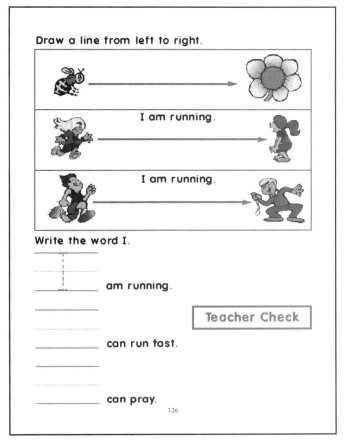

Draw a line from left to right.

I am running.

I am running.

Write the word I.

____ am running.

[ Teacher Check ]

____ can run fast.

____ can pray.

136

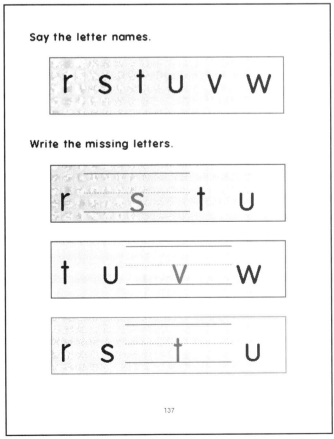

Say the letter names.

r  s  t  u  v  w

Write the missing letters.

r  ____  s  ____  t  ____  u

t  ____  u  ____  v  ____  w

r  ____  s  ____  t  ____  u

137

letters again, match the *r*'s in the two boxes, match the *s* to the line for the missing letter, match the *t*'s and *u*'s. Ask the children to write the letter *s* on the line. Finish the remaining boxes in the same way taking as much time as needed. If some children do not understand, do the page together and then wait several weeks and repeat the exercise.

**EXTENDED ACTIVITIES:**

1. If the children are able to count and write the numerals from 1 through 7, ask them to count the number of times they see the word *I* on page 136 (7). Have them write *1, 2, 3, 4, 5, 6, 7* next to the word *I* from the top to the bottom of the page. Ask them to count the number of words in the first direction (*7*). Ask them to write the numerals above the words. Example:

1,    2,    3,    4,    5,    6,    7.
*Draw   a   line   from   left   to   right.*

2. Continue to play alphabet sequence games with all the children and to give special attention to the children having difficulty. Distribute alphabet cards, in sequence, to the class. If the class is small, line the cards up on a table out of order and let the children take them off in order and place them along the chalkboard.

**SUGGESTED READING/ STORY IDEAS:**

1. Read the story of *Snow White and the Seven Dwarfs*, or another story with the number 7 (*The Little Tailor*, for example). Have the children illustrate the story in sections and then put those sections in order to form a book.

2. Use the alphabet puppets to act out the story.

## OBJECTIVES:

1. To recognize the capital *Y* and small *y*.
2. To write capital *Y* and small *y*.
3. To recognize the sound of *Yy*.

**MATERIALS:** pencils, crayons, Bible, magazines or newspapers, paste or glue, chart paper or tagboard, alphabet or flash cards for *Yy*, 3" x 5" cards.

## TEACHING PAGES 138 AND 139:

1. To introduce *Yy* on pages 138 and 139, follow the procedures for pages 20 and 21 (Lesson Ten). Stress the words *yarn*, *yellow*, *Yul*, and *Yuma* on page 138.

2. Read a list of words such as those which follow. Have the children raise their hands or hold up a card with a *y* on it when they hear the *y* sound. Examples: *you*, *yes*, *window*, *yesterday*, *baby*, *yarn*.

3. Have the children say the *y* sound. What are they doing with their teeth? Where does the sound come from?

## EXTENDED ACTIVITIES:

1. Make a *Yy* chart.

2. Have the children who are able, play the letter game introduced in Activity 2 for pages 30 - 31. Add *y* cards to those already made. Have the children spread the cards out and see if they can add more words to those found before. Examples: *yet*, *yam*, *yell*. Have them use the words they make in a sentence. Add to the list of words and names they are able to form and sound out with the sounds already learned. Help as needed. Some children may still find this difficult. If the children are not ready, wait several more weeks and try again.

3. Talk about names and words from the Bible that begin with the *Yy* sound: *yoke*, *yearn*, *years*, *youth*, and so on. Add these to Bible list or booklet.

## SUGGESTED READING/ STORY IDEAS:

1. Read Matthew 11:29-30 to the children. Ask if anyone knows what a *yoke* is in the sense used here. Show the children a picture of a *yoke* or draw a simple sketch on the board. Explain that the *yoke* made things easier for the animals even though it looked heavy and clumsy. Talk about the meaning of the word *yoke* as it applies to our lives. Ask the children what in their lives would be the *yoke* of Jesus.

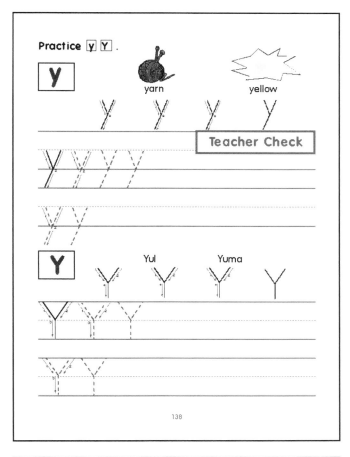

2. Review with the children stories from the Bible which involve young people *(David, Samuel, Joseph, Jesus,* and so on). How did they serve God? How can the children serve God even now?

## OBJECTIVES:

1. To recognize the capital *Y* and small *y*.
2. To write capital *Y* and small *y*.
3. To recognize the sound of *Yy*.
4. To review basic shapes.
5. To review basic colors.

**MATERIALS:** pencils, crayons, magazines and newspapers, paste or glue, materials to make puppet, alphabet scrapbook, basic shape and color cards, charts and pictures, shape pieces in a variety of colors and sizes, drawing paper.

## TEACHING PAGES 140 AND 141:

1. To reinforce and review the sound *Yy* on page 140, follow the procedures for page 16, numbers 1, 2, and 3 (Lesson Eight).

2. Read the direction on page 141 and ask the children to point to the *blue square* at the top of the page. Ask them to look at the picture and find the square. What is the square in this picture. Let them tell you what they find. Check. Tell them to color the square blue. Continue this procedure for the remaining shapes and colors. A background for the picture may be colored as the children choose.

## EXTENDED ACTIVITIES:

1. Make a *Yy* puppet.
2. Add to alphabet scrapbook at home.
3. Add to the *Yy* chart, if new words or pictures have been found.
4. Additional practice for writing the letter *Yy* can be found in the writing practice section of the children's book.
5. Review any colors or shapes that are causing problems for individual children.

## SUGGESTED READING/ STORY IDEAS:

1. Write a story using as many *Yy* words as they can. Pictures may be used in place of words where appropriate. Write the story for the children and let them add illustration. Add to alphabet storybook.

2. Have a child or several children use the *Yy* puppet to tell the story.

3. Give the children sets of shapes and ask them to create a character for a story from the shapes. It can be an animal, a person, or an imaginary creature. Ask them to tell the story. Script for the child and mount story and picture on large drawing paper.

My Yy page.

140

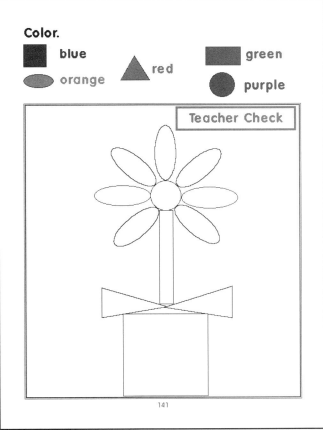

Color.

blue   red   green   orange   purple

Teacher Check

141

## OBJECTIVES:

1. To review colors: *red, black, yellow, orange, pink, green, brown, white, blue,* and *purple.*

2. To reinforce color word recognition in preparation for reading them.

3. To review initial consonants: *m, t, v, w, f, k, n, h,* and *g.*

**MATERIALS:** pencils and crayons, color chart with words and pictures, alphabet charts to review initial consonants: *m, t, v, w, f, k, n, h,* and *g.*

## TEACHING PAGES 142 AND 143:

1. On page 142, the children will check recognition of all the colors learned. The words are printed in the appropriate color so that actually reading the words is not yet necessary. To prepare for this page, if needed, have each child be a different color. That child is responsible for finding as many items in the room in his/her color as possible. Have a "Color Review" with each child in turn standing in front of the class and presenting all the things found in his/her color. Read the direction. Let the children do it independently. Check. Help those who are still having problems. If children have great difficulty distinguishing certain colors (blue, green, for example), they may need to have their eyes checked.

2. On page 143, read the direction. Ask a child to name the picture in the first box. Ask all the children to say the word *milk*. Ask what sound they hear at the beginning of the word. Have them trace the letter on the lines. Do the same with the rest of the boxes, having the children write the beginning letter on the lines.

## EXTENDED ACTIVITIES:

1. Have the children use the charts or picture cards to review initial consonants.

2. Give each child a sheet of drawing paper. Show them how to fold it into eight boxes. Draw a sample sheet on the board. On the sample write a consonant at the bottom of each box.

Have the children copy the letters onto their papers. Instruct them to draw a picture for each beginning sound.

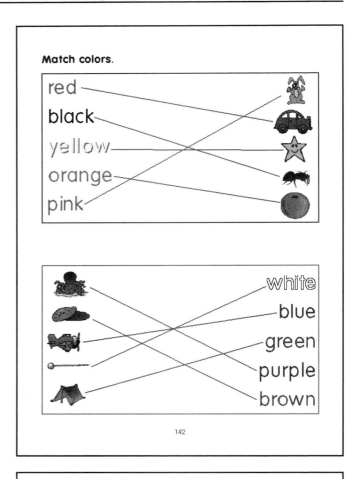

**SUGGESTED READING/ STORY IDEAS:**

1. Review the stories written for each beginning sound here. Add to or create new stories.

2. Write a poem trying to use all of the color words.

**OBJECTIVES:**
1. To recognize capital *Z* and small *z*.
2. To write capital *Z* and small *z*.
3. To recognize the sound of *Zz*.

**MATERIALS:** pencils, crayons, Bible, magazines or newspapers, paste or glue, chart paper or tagboard, alphabet or flash cards for *Zz*, 3" x 5"cards.

**TEACHING PAGES 144 AND 145:**
1. To introduce *Zz* on pages 144 and 145, follow the procedures for pages 20 and 21 (Lesson Ten). Stress the words *zero, zebra, Zion,* and *Zebedee* on page 144.
2. Read a list of words such as those which follow. Have the children raise their hands or hold up a card with a *z* on it when they hear the *z* sound. Examples: *zipper, zoo, sister, Zacharias, father, zero.*
3. Have the children say the *z* sound. What are they doing with their teeth? Where are their tongues? How is it different from the sound they learned for *s*?

**EXTENDED ACTIVITIES:**
1. Make a *Zz* chart.
2. Have the children who are able, play the letter game introduced in Activity 2 for pages 30 - 31. Add *z* cards to those already made. Have the children spread the cards out and see if they can add more words to those found before. Examples: *zip, zig-zag, buzz.* Have them use the words they make in a sentence. Add to the list of words and names they are able to form and sound out with the sounds already learned. Help as needed. Some children may still find this difficult. If the children are not ready, wait several more weeks and try again.
3. Talk about names and words from the Bible that begin with the *Zz* sound: *Zaccheus, Zacharias, Zion, Zebedee,* and so on. Add these to Bible list or booklet.

**SUGGESTED READING/ STORY IDEAS:**
1. Review the story of Elizabeth and Zacharias used in Lesson One (page 1).
2. Read the story of Zaccheus (Luke 19:1-10). Talk about what it would be like to have Jesus call you from a crowd and tell you that He was coming to your house. How would the children feel? What would they do? What preparations would they make? Ask the children to draw a picture of what they would do if Jesus came to their homes.
3. Act out either story using puppets.

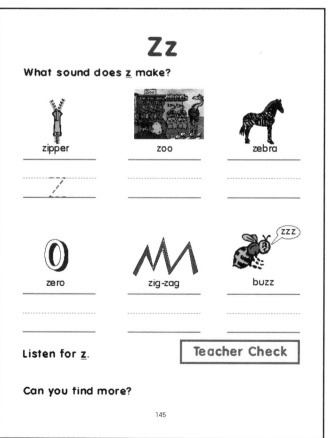

## OBJECTIVES:

1. To recognize capital *Z* and small *z*.
2. To write capital *Z* and small *z*.
3. To recognize the sound of *Zz*.
4. To listen carefully.
5. To follow directions given only once.
6. To recognize different size, position, and direction words.

**MATERIALS:** pencils, crayons, magazines and newspapers, paste or glue, materials to make puppet, alphabet scrapbook, objects or pictures that can be used to reinforce different positions, sizes, and directions.

## TEACHING PAGES 146 AND 147:

1. To reinforce and review the sound *Zz* on page 146, follow the procedures for page 16, numbers 1, 2, and 3 (Lesson Eight).

2. Tell the children that page 147 is another listening activity like those they have done before. Tell them that they must listen carefully because you will read the sentence only once.

Have them put their fingers on the small pictures for better reference. Have them circle the correct picture after you read each sentence.

Read:

*Grapes*: The hat is *on* the cat's head.

*Apple*: These stairs go *up*.

*Orange*: This glass is *small*.

*Carrots*: Jack jumps *out* of his box.

*Cake*: The ball is *beside* the table.

*Cookies*: The doll is *in* the box.

Check. If anyone misses an answer ask them to tell you what is going on in each picture in the box to determine whether or not the problem is a listening problem or a comprehension problem. If the child understands the pictures and describes them correctly, then the error may be one of inattention to the directions. Use other objects or movements to reinforce the concepts missed.

## EXTENDED ACTIVITIES:

1. Make a *Zz* puppet.
2. Add to alphabet scrapbook at home.
3. Add to the *Zz* chart, if new words or pictures have been found.
4. Additional practice for writing the letter *Zz* can be found in the writing practice section of the children's book.
5. Do additional activities with the children to reinforce the position, direction, and size concepts. Play "Simon Says" or similar games emphasizing *on*, *off*, *next to*, *up*, *down*, *over*, *under*, and so on.

My Zz page.

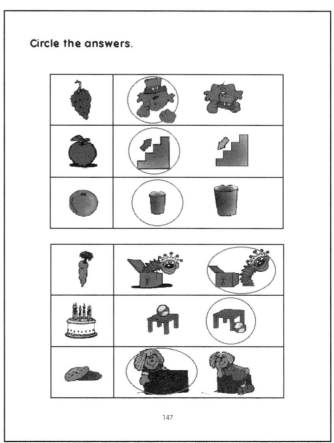

Circle the answers.

6.  If some children are still having great difficulty with the listening activity, repeat the activity using the following sentences:

Read:

*grapes:* The cat took *off* his hat.

*apple*: These stairs go *down*.

*orange*: This glass is *big*.

*carrots*: The box is *closed*.

*cake*: The ball is *on* the table.

*cookies*: The doll is *on top* of the box.

## SUGGESTED READING/ STORY IDEAS:

1. Write a story using as many *Zz* words as they can. Pictures may be used in place of words where appropriate. Write the story for the children and let them add illustration. Add to alphabet Story Book.

2. Have a child or several children use the *Zz* puppet to tell the story.

## OBJECTIVES:

1. To work from left to right.
2. To recognize that sentences read from left to right.
3. To recognize that a sentence begins with a capital letter and ends with a period.
4. To review all short vowel sounds.

**MATERIALS:** pencils and crayons, charts, picture card, and stories used for short vowel sounds.

## TEACHING PAGES 148 AND 149:

1. On page 148, have the children look at the pictures to see what is happening then draw a line from left to right between the two pictures. Ask them to do the first three sets and talk about them. Encourage the children to use complete sentences when telling what is happening in the pictures. Ask the children what is happening in the third box. Point out the sentence written in the box. Tell them that the sentence tells them in words what the pictures show. Read the sentence. Have the children repeat the sentence while moving their fingers from left to right under the sentence. Remind the children that a sentence begins with a capital letter and ends with a period. Point out the periods and have the children find them. Finish the page in the same manner.

2. To prepare for page 149, review the short vowel sound with the children having them repeat the sound after you and then make the sound on their own. Divide the children into five groups. Give each group a different short vowel sound. Give them about ten minutes to find all the words or pictures they can for their sound. Let them use the charts, objects in the room, and any stories written using the sound. Have each group report what they have found to the class. Put words on the board under the vowel sound.

3. Have the children look at the box on the top of page 149. Have them say first the name and then the vowel sound as they point to each letter. Read the direction. Have them name each picture emphasizing the vowel sound. Ask them to tell you what vowel sound they hear in the word *apple*. Have them circle the *a*. Continue this procedure for the remainder of the page.

## EXTENDED ACTIVITIES:

1. Have the children who are able, work at writing simple sentences like those on page 148. Help with spelling as needed.

Draw a line from left to right.

I can run.

A dog can run.

We can run.

148

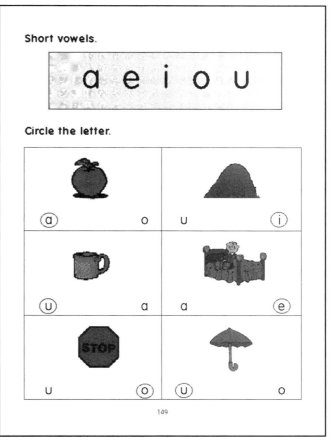

Short vowels.

a e i o u

Circle the letter.

149

2. Using charts and picture cards, review any vowel sounds which cause difficulty.

## SUGGESTED READING/ STORY IDEAS:

1. Have the children expand the simple sentences on page 148 into paragraphs or stories. They could take, for example, "A dog can run." Add to it: "The dog's name is Spot. Spot likes to run and play. He runs to John." They could write a story about the family in the first box, giving each person a name, talking about them going to church, telling how they got to church (did they walk, ride in a car), and so on.

2. The children could also tell stories about what happens after the pictures:
What did the family do in church?
Did the ball go in the basket?
What did the girl do after she reached the tree?
Why was she running?
What will the boy and the dog do next?
What will the children do when they are together?

**OBJECTIVES:**
1. To recognize capital *Q* and small *q*.
2. To write capital *Q* and small *q*.
3. To recognize the sound of *Qu*.

**MATERIALS:** pencils, crayons, Bible, magazines or newspapers, paste or glue, chart paper or tagboard, alphabet or flash cards for *Qq*, *Qu*, 3" x 5" cards.

**TEACHING PAGES 150 AND 151:**
1. To introduce *Qq*, *qu* on pages 150 and 151, follow the procedures for pages 20 and 21 (Lesson Ten). Stress the words *quail*, *quilt*, *Quentin*, and *Queen* on page 150.
2. Read a list of words such as those which follow. Have the children raise their hands or hold up a card with a *qu* on it when they hear the *qu* sound. Examples: *quack*, *quick*, *sister*, *quiet*, *money*, *quilt*.
3. Have the children say the *qu* sound. What are they doing with their lips? Do they move forward? What two letters does this sound remind them of (*kw*)?

**EXTENDED ACTIVITIES:**
1. Make a *qu* chart.
2. Have the children who are able, play the letter game introduced in Activity 2 for pages 30 - 31. Add *qu* cards to those already made. Have the children spread the cards out and see if they can add more words to those found before: Examples: *quick*, *quilt*. Have them use the words they make in a sentence. Add to the list of words and names they are able to form and sound out with the sounds already learned. Help as needed. Some children may still find this difficult. If the children are not ready, wait several more weeks and try again.
3. Talk about names and words from the Bible that begin with the *qu* sound: *question*, *quiet*, and so on. Add these to Bible list or booklet.

**SUGGESTED READING/ STORY IDEAS:**
1. The context of words with *qu* in the Bible may be difficult for the children to understand. Tell them that in the Gospels many people asked Jesus questions. Ask them to create with you a story or poem about the questions they would ask Jesus if He were in front of them.
2. Talk about the importance of *quiet* for hearing God's word and following God's Spirit. Give the children some quiet time to say a prayer in their hearts and to listen for a moment.

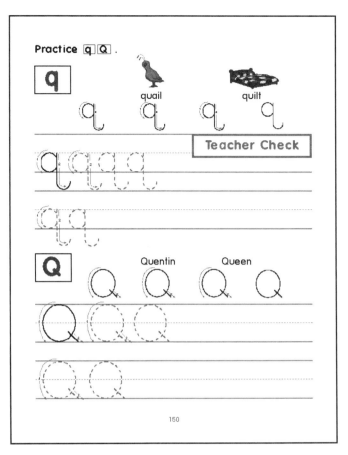

## OBJECTIVES:
1. To recognize capital *Q* and small *q*.
2. To write capital *Q* and small *q*.
3. To recognize the sound of *Qu*.
4. To recognize and match capital and small letters.

**MATERIALS:** pencils, crayons, magazines and newspapers, paste or glue, materials to make puppet, alphabet scrapbook, alphabet charts and flash cards.

## TEACHING PAGES 152 AND 153:
1. To reinforce and review the sound *Qu* on page 152, follow the procedures for page 16, numbers 1, 2, and 3 (Lesson Eight).

2. Read the direction at the top of page 153. The children should be able to do this activity on their own. If preparation is needed, put a similar activity on the board and have individual children come forward to draw a line from the capital to the small letter.

3. Read the direction at the bottom of page 153. Have the children look at the letter in the small box on the left and then find two words in the long box on the right that begin with that letter. Do the first box with the children. Let them complete the exercise independently. If needed, allow children to use a card or sheet of paper to place under each row as they work.

## EXTENDED ACTIVITIES:
1. Make a *Qu* puppet.
2. Add to alphabet scrapbook at home.
3. Add to the *Qu* chart, if new words or pictures have been found.
4. Additional practice for writing the letter *Qq*, *qu* can be found in the writing practice section.
5. Give each child a section of a newspaper. Put the words *the* and *The* on the board and have them find and circle as many as they can in five minutes. This can also be done with other simple words: *but*, *But*, *do*, *Do*, and so on.
6. Have the children who are able, read some of the words in the long boxes.
7. Have the children make up sentences for some of the words.

## SUGGESTED READING/ STORY IDEAS:
1. Write a story using as many *Qu* words as they can. Pictures may be used in place of words where appropriate. Write the story for the children and let them add illustration. Add to alphabet storybook.

2. Have a child or several children use the *Qu* puppet to tell the story.

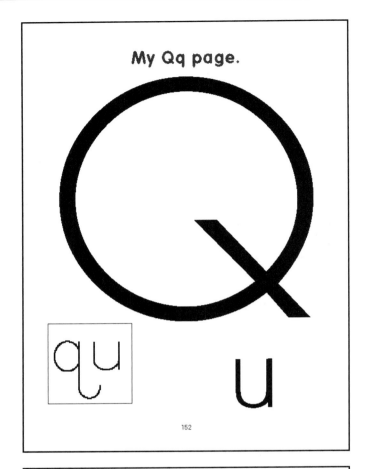

**My Qq page.**

152

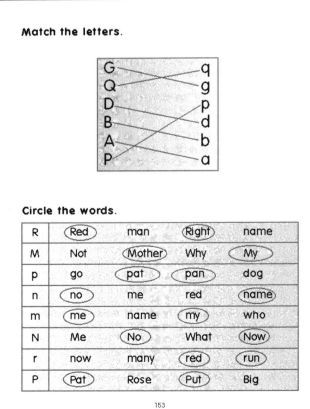

**Match the letters.**

**Circle the words.**

| R | Red | man | Right | name |
|---|---|---|---|---|
| M | Not | Mother | Why | My |
| p | go | pat | pan | dog |
| n | no | me | red | name |
| m | me | name | my | who |
| N | Me | No | What | Now |
| r | now | many | red | run |
| P | Pat | Rose | Put | Big |

153

## OBJECTIVES:

1. To review the initial consonants: *c, g, h, n, j, l, b, k.*
2. To build patterns.
3. To review colors.
4. To associate color words with the color.

**MATERIALS:** pencils, crayons (especially *blue, yellow, black, red, purple, orange, green, white*), shape cards or blocks, pattern cards, initial sound charts for *c, g, h, n, j, l, b, k,* strips of white paper (2" x 12"), strips of colored paper ( 1" x 6"), glue or paste.

## TEACHING PAGES 154 AND 155:

1. Read the directions for page 154. Ask the children to name the pictures on the page. Have them emphasize the beginning sound for each picture. Do the first box with them. If children are able, let them complete the page independently. If some children need help, take them aside in a group and do each box together.

2. For page 155, follow the procedures for page 106 (Lesson Fifty-three, numbers 1-4).

## EXTENDED ACTIVITIES:

1. Review any initial sounds that are still a problem for the children.

2. Continue the pattern activity by giving the children sets of shape blocks or cut shapes. Have them make their own color/shape patterns.

3. Purchase or make sets of pattern cards that the children can use to match patterns.

4. Give the children strips of paper about two inches wide and let them make up patterns of their own, color them, and mount them as a border for a bulletin board.

5. Give the children colored strips of paper about six inches long and an inch wide. Let them make paper chain color patterns and hang them around the room.

## SUGGESTED READING/ STORY IDEAS:

1. Read any poem that has a refrain. Talk about the "pattern" of the poem.

2. Read poems that rhyme. Show the children how the rhyme forms a "pattern".

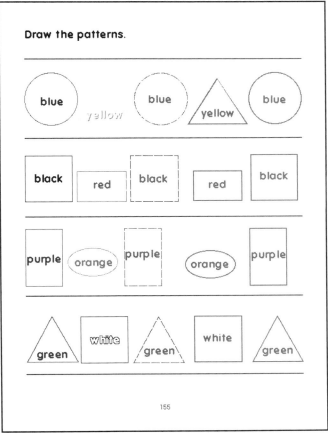

## OBJECTIVES:

1. To recognize capital *X* and small *x*.
2. To write capital *X* and small *x*.
3. To recognize the two sounds of *Xx*.

**MATERIALS:** pencils, crayons, Bible, magazines or newspapers, paste or glue, chart paper or tagboard, alphabet or flash cards for *Xx*, 3" x 5" cards.

## TEACHING PAGES 156 AND 157:

1. To introduce *Xx* on pages 156 and 157, follow the procedures for pages 20 and 21 (Lesson Ten). Stress the words *xylophone, Xavier, Xerxes* on page 156.

2. Read a list of words such as those which follow. Have the children raise their hands or hold up a card with an *x* on it when they hear the *x* sound. Examples: *xylophone, supper, fork, Xavier.*

3. Explain to the children that *Xx* has two sounds, one that sounds like a *z* and the other that sounds like a *k* and an *s* put together.

## EXTENDED ACTIVITIES:

1. Make an *Xx* chart.

2. Have the children who are able, play the letter game introduced in Activity 2 for pages 30 - 31. Add *x* cards to those already made. Have the children spread the cards out and see if they can add more words to those found before. Examples: *wax, fox, box*. Have them use the words they make in a sentence. Add to the list of words and names they are able to form and sound out with the sounds already learned. Help as needed. Some children may still find this difficult. If the children are not ready, wait several more weeks and try again.

## SUGGESTED READING/ STORY IDEAS:

1. Ask the children if they remember why Mary and Joseph had to travel to Bethlehem before Jesus was born. Reread Luke 2: 1-5, (some translations use taxed, others used census). Explain to the children that a census is a count of the people taken so that the government knows what tax to charge.

2. Talk about the men in the New Testament who were tax collectors (or tax-gatherers), Zaccheus (Luke 19:2) and Matthew (Matthew 9:9, 10:3). Explain to the children that being a tax collector was not a job that religious people respected. Both of these men decided to choose Jesus and follow Him. Have the children draw a picture of Matthew leaving his tax collection to follow Jesus.

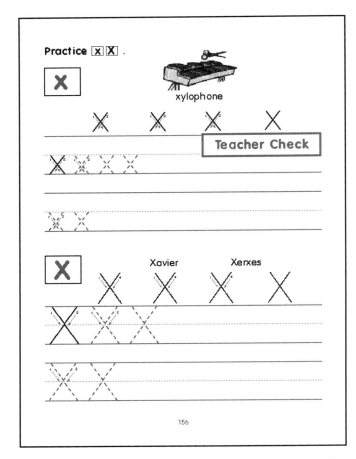

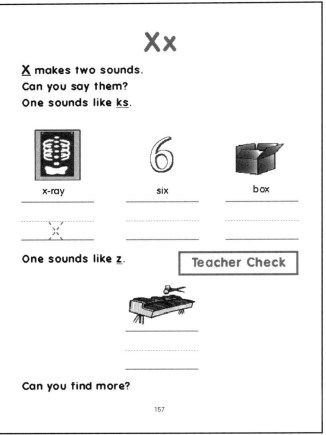

## OBJECTIVES:
1. To recognize capital X and small x.
2. To write capital X and small x.
3. To recognize the two sounds of Xx.
4. To say the alphabet.
5. To put the alphabet in order.

**MATERIALS:** pencils, crayons, magazines and newspapers, paste or glue, materials to make puppet, alphabet scrapbook, alphabet charts and flash cards.

## TEACHING PAGES 158 AND 159:
1. To reinforce and review the sound Xx on page 158, follow the procedures for page 16, numbers 1, 2, and 3 (Lesson Eight).

2. To prepare for page 159, have the children look at their alphabet charts and say the alphabet, pointing to each letter as they say it. Write the small letters of the alphabet on the board omitting several letters, for example:

a, ___, c, d, ___, f,
g, h, ___, j, k, ___,
m, n, o, ___, q, r, s,
___, u, v, w, ___, y, z.

Have individual children tell which letters are missing and come forward to write in the missing letter. Read the directions on page 159. Explain to the children that they must write in the missing letters. They may use their alphabet charts, if needed. Check. Correct letter formation as needed.

## EXTENDED ACTIVITIES:
1. Make an Xx puppet.
2. Add to alphabet scrapbook at home.
3. Add to the Xx chart, if new words or pictures have been found.
4. Additional practice for writing the letter Xx can be found in the writing practice section of the children's book.
5. Review alphabet sequence using flash cards.

## SUGGESTED READING/ STORY IDEAS:
1. Write a story for the letter Xx. Words may be used that end in x or that have x in the middle. Ask the children to tell which sound of Xx they hear in each word.
2. Read a book such as *Fox in Sox*, which has some words with Xx sounds.

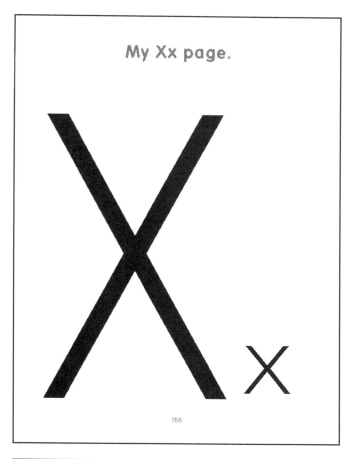

My Xx page.

158

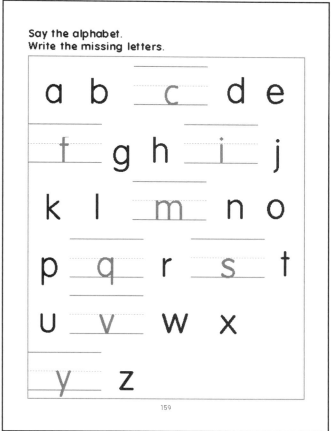

Say the alphabet.
Write the missing letters.

a b c d e
f g h i j
k l m n o
p q r s t
u v w x
y z

159

**OBJECTIVES:**

1. To review short *u*, and *a* sounds.
2. To review initial consonants: k, f, b, h, d, and t.
3. To review size, position, and direction words.
4. To listen carefully.
5. To follow a direction given only once.

**MATERIALS:** pencils, crayons, initial and short vowel charts, objects and pictures to reinforce size, position, and direction words.

**TEACHING PAGES 160 AND 161:**

1. Review all initial consonant sounds and short vowel sounds in preparation for page 160. This can be done by holding up picture cards or by slowly reading a list of words which includes a word for each sound. Have the children say the name of the sound or hold up the letter card which shows the letter for the sound. Read the directions for page 160. Have the children name each picture and circle the letter that they hear at the beginning of the word. Let children work independently, if they are able.

2. Ask the children to look at the picture on page 161. Ask them to have their red, blue, green, yellow, orange brown, pink, and purple crayons ready. Have them tell what they see in the picture. Tell them that you will read a sentence once and they are to follow your direction.

*Read:*

Take your blue crayon. Pause.
Circle the bird *under* the tree.
Take your green crayon. Pause.
Circle the cat *inside* the box.
Take your red crayon. Pause.
Draw a square *around* the thing up high in the sky.
Take your purple crayon. Pause.
Circle the cat *outside* the box.
Take your brown crayon. Pause.
Circle the bird *over* the tree.
Take your pink crayon. Pause.
Draw a flower *under* the *biggest* tree.
Take your orange crayon. Pause.
Draw a balloon *in* the girl's hand.
Take your yellow crayon. Pause.
Draw a kite *over* the small tree.

Check the activity with the children. Note the problem concepts.

**EXTENDED ACTIVITIES:**

1. Review initial consonants and short vowel sounds as needed.

2. Review color, position, size, and directions as needed.

3. Have children finish the pictures.

**SUGGESTED READING/ STORY IDEAS:**

1. Write a story for the pictures on page 161.

2. Write a poem using the words up, down, under over, inside, outside, big, and little.

## OBJECTIVES:

1. To review first and last name.
2. To recognize age.
3. To review address.
4. To say the alphabet.
5. To recognize both capital and small letters.

**MATERIALS:** pencil, crayons, alphabet chart or flash cards, name and address cards.

## TEACHING PAGES 1, 2, AND 3:

1. The first three pages of Volume Two review name, age, address, alphabet, and individual letter recognition. At this stage of the year, most children should not have problems with any of the pages. Please remember, however, that children at this age develop very differently. If some children are not ready to do this independently, assist them.

2. Page 1 reviews the child's name, age, and address. If children are able, let them do the page independently once directions have been given. They may use their name and address cards if needed. Circle any letters or numerals that need practice. Check formation of letters and numerals carefully.

3. Page 2 reviews the entire alphabet, both capital and small letters. Have the children say or sing the alphabet. Ask the children to point to individual letters. See activity 1 below.

4. Page 3 has the children, once again, practicing their names. Tell them that many times on school papers they will put their names on every page.

For the second activity, if necessary, put some simple letter matching activities on the board for the children to practice. Have the children do the matching independently if they are able.

Read the direction at the bottom of the page. Ask the children to put their fingers on the first letter and name it. Ask them if this letter is capital or small (small). Have them trace the letter on the lines. Is this letter capital or small (capital)? Tell the children that they are to write the *capital* letter for each *small* letter they see. The children may use page 2 or an alphabet chart for reference. Check letter formation.

## EXTENDED ACTIVITIES:

1. Use page 2 as a game board. Ask the children to do some of the following, giving the

My name is

My age is

I live at

**Say the alphabet for your teacher.**

direction only once: Examples: Circle the letters in their names with a red crayon. Put a blue box around the vowels. Circle the beginning sound of *sun* with a yellow crayon. (Several beginning sounds can be used, each with a different color.) Check individual letters by asking the children, for example, to circle the letter *Dd*. Many variations can be used.

2. The writing practice section of this volume has practice pages for names, for the entire alphabet in small letters, and for the entire alphabet in capital letters. Use these practice pages a little each day.

## SUGGESTED READING/ STORY IDEAS:

1. Ask the children to select a story from their alphabet Story Book. Reread the story to the children and ask some of them to act it out using the alphabet puppets.

2. Write an "Alphabet Poem" together as a class. Create two lines for each letter using rhymes for the second lines of every two letters.

Example:

"A" is for apple
So shiny and *bright.*
"B" is for bat
That flies in the *night.*
"C" is for cradle
Where baby *rocks.*
"D" is for my dog
When he chews my *socks.*
Continue through the alphabet.

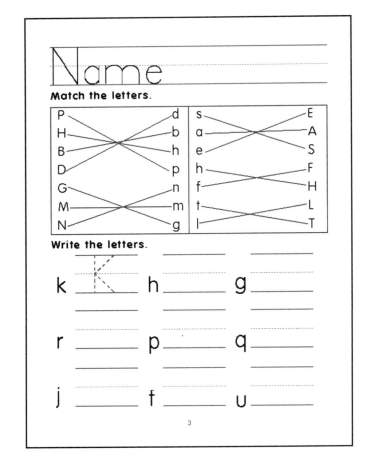

## OBJECTIVES:

1. To review basic shapes: *circle, square, triangle, rectangle,* and *oval.*

2. To review colors: *red, blue, yellow, green,* and *purple.*

3. To listen carefully.

4. To follow a direction given only once.

5. To recognize the meaning of position and direction words.

**MATERIALS:** pencils, crayons, basic shape and color objects and cards.

## TEACHING PAGES 4 AND 5:

1. Ask the children to look at the box on page 4. Have individual children name the shapes. Read the direction for the second activity. Tell the children who can to match the colored shapes to an object of the same color. Have them name the color and shape on the left and then name the red object. Ask them to trace the line between the *red* shape and the *red* object. Complete the page either independently or by following the procedure used for the *red* shape.

2. On page 5, tell the children that they will need to listen carefully to the sentence you read. Give the direction only once asking the children to *circle* the picture that goes with the sentence. Read:

*circle*:    The children are coming *out of* the door.

*star*:    The cat is *under* the table.

*cup*:    The bird is *in* the cage.

*triangle*:    The tree is *behind* the house.

*square*:    The boy is going *down* the stairs.

*flower*:    The kite is high above the ground. Check the work. Ask the children who missed the answer to explain both pictures to you. This will help determine whether the error was in the concept or in the listening.

## EXTENDED ACTIVITIES:

1. Create a small obstacle course for the children outside. Have them jump *over* something like a branch or low rock, stand *on* a stool or a flat stone, duck *under* a branch or low doorway, stand *inside* an old tire or circle drawn on the walk, and so on. Say the words as they walk the course.

2. Begin a booklet for Position and Direction words. Make a page for each concept: *in, out, over, under, up, down, high, low,* and so on.

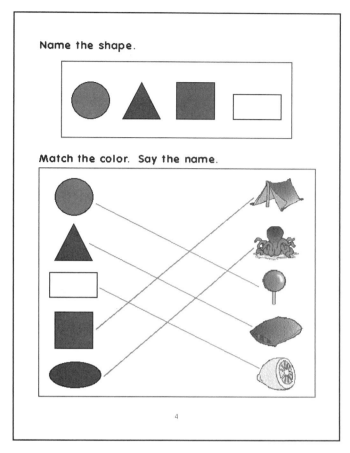

Name the shape.

Match the color. Say the name.

Circle the picture.

**SUGGESTED READING/ STORY IDEAS:**

1. Read and/or act out stories or rhymes which emphasize position words. Examples: "Jack Be Nimble" and "Hey Diddle Diddle" to illustrate the concept of over; "Twinkle, Twinkle Little Star" to show above; "Little Boy Blue" (under the haystack); and "Humpty Dumpty" (sat on a wall).

2. Make a cloth or felt story book with blank pages. Make several figures: people, trees, a house, table, shapes, animals, and other objects out of felt. Keep the book and the figures in a learning center setting. Have the children make up stories about people and animals going in and out of the house, putting things on or under the table, and any other story ideas the children may have.

**OBJECTIVES:**

1. To put letters in alphabetical order.
2. To recognize that a silent *e* at the end of a word gives the vowel a long sound.
3. To recognize short and long vowel words.

**MATERIALS:** pencils, chart paper or tagboard, alphabet letter cards.

**TEACHING PAGES 6 AND 7:**

1. To prepare for page 6, have the children look at their alphabet charts and say the alphabet pointing to each letter as they say it. Write the small letters of the alphabet on the board omitting several letters, for example:

a, _____, c, d, _____, f, g, h, _____, j, k, _____, m, n, o, _____, q, r, s, _____, u, v, w, _____, y, z. Have individual children tell which letters are missing and come forward to write in the missing letter. Read the directions on page 6. Explain to the children that they must write in the missing letters. They may use their alphabet charts, if needed. Check. Correct letter formation as needed.

2. To prepare for page 7, put the following words on the board, or on a sheet of chart paper, in a single column:

tap
tub
man
hat
pan
kit
not

Ask the children to sound them out, or say them and have the children repeat them. Ask what short vowel sound is heard in each. Tell the children that they will soon begin learning long vowel sounds, sounds in which the letters say their own names. Explain that some letters are silent, but they are used to help other vowels say their own names. One of these letters we call silent *e*. Demonstrate for the children what happens to the sound and to the word when a silent *e* is added to each of the letters above. Write these words in a separate parallel column (tape, tube, mane, hate, pane, kite, note).

| | | |
|---|---|---|
| tap + e = | tape |
| tub + e = | tube |
| man + e = | mane |
| hat + e = | hate |

Ask the children to repeat each new word after you emphasizing the vowel sound change. Talk about the new words and their meaning.

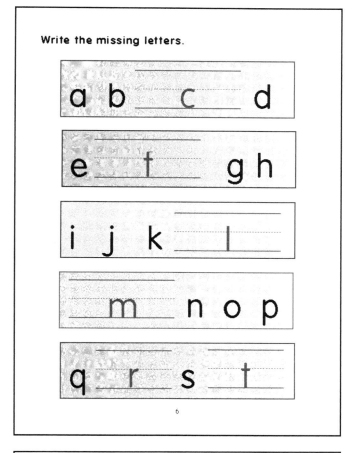

Write the missing letters.

a b c d

e f g h

i j k l

m n o p

q r s t

6

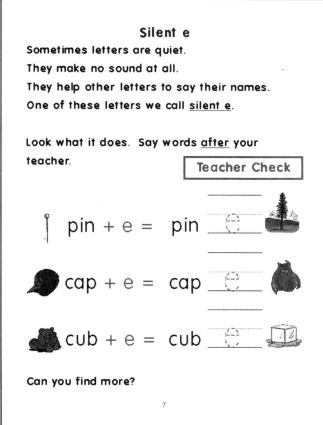

**Silent e**

Sometimes letters are quiet.

They make no sound at all.

They help other letters to say their names.

One of these letters we call <u>silent e</u>.

Look what it does. Say words <u>after</u> your teacher.

| Teacher Check |

pin + e = pin _e_

cap + e = cap _e_

cub + e = cub _e_

Can you find more?

7

151

3. Read page 7 to the children. Ask the children to look at the word *pin* and say it. Have them trace the silent *e* after the *pin* and read the new word. Finish the page in the same manner.

4. Have the children think of more short vowel words that can be changed to a long vowel by adding silent *e*. Make a list on chart paper showing the words they have found.

**EXTENDED ACTIVITIES:**

1. Have the children work with their alphabet letter cards. Have them copy the short vowel words from the board, page 7, or the chart. Ask them to place an *e* card after each word (more *e* cards may need to be made).

2. If children are having difficultly with alphabet sequences, do further practice on the board or using individual letter cards. Have an aide or an older student work individually with the child.

**SUGGESTED READING/ STORY IDEAS:**

1. Encourage children to begin creating stories about people and things around them. Help them to write a story about an older relative (grandparent, aunt, uncle, and so on). Have them give the name of the person, who they are, how they look, what they like, why the child likes them, how they help the child, and other details that will help the child remember that person and appreciate them. Write the story for them in the Story Book section at the back of this book.

2. Share stories. Read other stories about older people who are important in the lives of young children.

**OBJECTIVES:**

1. To recognize the long sound of *a*.
2. To find words and pictures for the long sound of *a*.

**MATERIALS:** pencils, crayons, Bible, magazines or newspapers, paste or glue, chart paper or tagboard, *a* flash cards.

**TEACHING PAGES 8 AND 9:**

1. Begin page 8 by asking the children to try to think of words in which the letter *a* says its name. Help if they cannot do this (make, rake, take, ape, cape, tape, lake, and so on). Look at the first picture on the page (*apron*). Ask the children to name the picture. What sound do they hear at the beginning of the word (long *a*). Have them trace the *a* on the lines under the picture. Repeat this procedure for the remaining pictures.

2. Read a list of words like the following. Ask the children to hold up an *a* card when they hear the long *a* sound. Examples: *cake, cute, stable, kite, tape*.

3. Page 9 is a long *a* review and reinforcement page. It gives the children an opportunity to work with you to find pictures and words which have the long *a* sound. Talk about the long *a* work done on page 8.

4. Have the children trace both the capital and small long *a* on the page.

5. Have the children look through magazines and catalogues to find pictures and words that have the long *a* sound. This page may be a collage of written words, drawings, cut and paste words and pictures. Help the children stress the long *a* sound when they find it. Help as needed with the writing, cutting, pasting to complete the page.

**EXTENDED ACTIVITIES:**

1. Make a long Aa chart.
2. Add long *Aa* to the alphabet Scrap Book.
3. Talk about names and words from the Bible that have the long *Aa* sound: *Abraham, Jacob, stable, angel, Amen*, and so on. Add these to the Bible list or booklet.

**SUGGESTED READING/ STORY IDEAS:**

1. Recall how God changed Abraham's name from Abram to Abraham (Genesis 17:5). Read the story of Abraham and Isaac (Genesis 22:1-19). Talk about God's test for Abraham and how God sent an angel to stop him.

2. Have the children illustrate or act out the story.

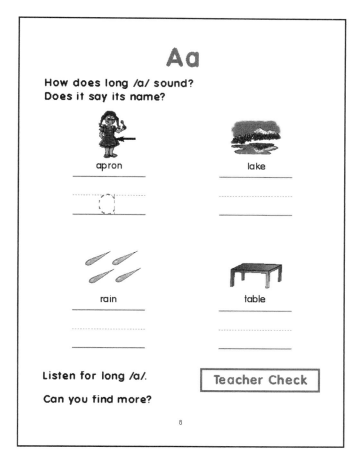

**OBJECTIVES:**
1. To write a story.
2. To recognize long a words.
3. To review initial consonants: *b, c, d,* and *f.*

**MATERIALS:** pencils and crayons, long *a* chart, charts or picture cards for *b, c, d,* and *f* as initial sounds.

**TEACHING PAGES 10 AND 11:**
1. Prepare for page 10, by playing a rhyming game with the children. Divide the children into groups. Give each group a long *a* word: Examples: cape, lake, rain, play. Ask the children in the group to find as many words as they can that rhyme with their words. Allow about five minutes. Ask the children to tell everyone the words they have found. Write the words on the board. Next, ask the children if they can group any of the words together. Begin working on ideas for a story that will use as many long *a* words as possible.

2. Work with the children to write a long *a* story. Write it on the board or on chart paper. Some children may be able to copy the story into their books. Others will need help. If the story is longer than the space in the book, have the children write the name of the story in their books and one sentence of the story. Ask them to draw a picture to accompany the story.

3. Write the letters *b, c, d,* and *f* on the board. Have children take turns giving you words that begin with each letter. Read the direction on page 11. Tell the children that they are to look at both pictures in each box, say the names, listen carefully to the beginning sound of each, and circle the one that begins with the same sound as the letter in the box at the beginning of each row. Ask the children to say the picture names aloud. At the bottom of the page, direct the children to write the letter for the beginning sound on the line under each picture. All letters are in the box at the top of the page.

**EXTENDED ACTIVITIES:**
1. Continue to encourage children who are able to use the alphabet letter cards to make new words. Use the *a* cards to make long a words: Examples: ate, cake, bake. Use the words in a sentence. Add to the list of words and names they can form. Help as needed. Remember: all children may not be ready for this activity.
2. Make a long *Aa* puppet.
3. ENRICHMENT activity for more advanced children. Look at the lists of long *a* words that the

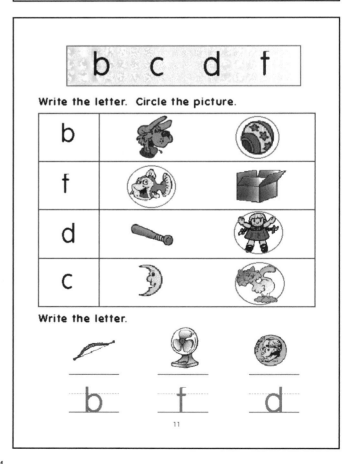

Long Aa Story.
Make a story with your long /a/ words.

Teacher Check

Draw a picture.

10

b   c   d   f

Write the letter. Circle the picture.

Write the letter.

b   f   d

11

children discovered for the story lesson. Ask the more advanced children to mark all of the words that use a silent *e* to help the vowel say its name. Ask them what they notice about the words that are not marked (they make the long *a* sound using a different silent vowel or letter combination, *ai, ay, ey*). Tell the children that the long *a* sound has more than one letter combinations. Have the children sort out the words that use *ai, ay,* and *ey*. Ask them to use these words in a sentence.

**SUGGESTED READING/ STORY IDEAS:**
　1. Read books or poems about rain and rainbows.
　2. Have the children write a poem about a rainbow.

**OBJECTIVES:**
1. To read the color words red and blue.
2. To review the colors red and blue.

**MATERIALS:** pencils, red and blue crayons, old magazines and catalogues, scissors, glue or paste, Bible, word cards for red and blue, other red and blue objects (blocks, bears, buttons, and so on).

**TEACHING PAGES 12 AND 13:**
1. The children have been seeing the words for the colors *red* and *blue* in many places over the last several months. On page 12, begin working with the children to sound out and read these words. The word *red* is not difficult to sound out. The word *blue*, however, has a *u* sound they have not yet learned. Discuss the pictures in the red section of the page. Ask the children to point to and read the word *red.* Have them trace it with their fingers. Finally, have them trace the word *red* on the lines. Introduce the blue section in the same way.

2. For page 13, have the children look through magazines and catalogues for pictures of things that are red and blue. They may also draw pictures. Check to make sure that they glue the *red* things on the side of the page which says *red* and the *blue* things on the *blue* side.

**EXTENDED ACTIVITIES:**
1. If you have not done so, begin a Color book. Use construction paper or chart paper to make a page for each color learned. Print the name of the color in large letters at the top of the page. Color or paste objects that are usually found in that color or which could be found in that color. Make a RED and a BLUE page to begin the book. You may also want to add words that are associated with the colors if the children know them (examples, baby blue, sky blue, rosy, fire red, scarlet, and so on).

2. Practice making red and blue patterns with shapes, blocks, bears, or buttons. Have the children copy your patterns and then invent their own.

3. Additional writing practice for all color words is found in the back of the book.

**SUGGESTED READING/ STORY IDEAS:**
1. Reread the story of Moses crossing the Red Sea (Exodus 14, 15). Use a map or globe to show the children where the Red Sea is located.

2. Read Exodus, Chapters 25 and 26 and tell or read to the children the verses about the colors of

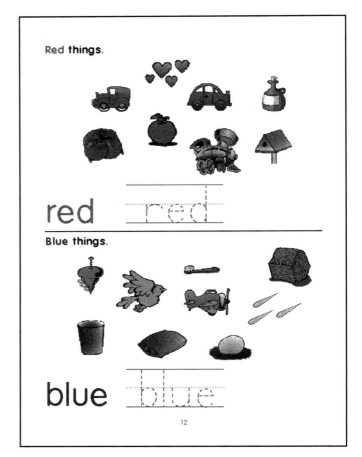

Red things.

red ̲r̲e̲d̲

Blue things.

blue ̲b̲l̲u̲e̲

12

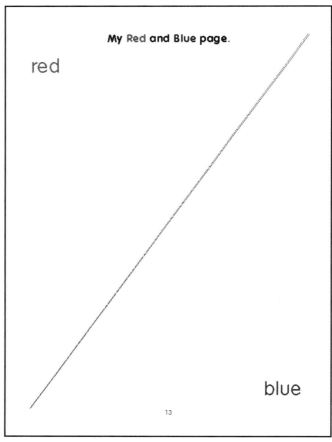

My Red and Blue page.

red

blue

13

the temple curtains "blue, and purple, and scarlet materials."

3. Begin a Color Poetry Book. Have the children think of as many things as they can for each color. Write the list on the board. Then work with the children to create a "color" poem. Begin with Red and Blue.

**OBJECTIVES:**
1. To recognize the long sound of *e*.
2. To find words and pictures for the long sound of *e*.

**MATERIALS:** pencils, crayons, Bible, magazines or newspapers, paste or glue, chart paper or tagboard, *e* flash cards.

**TEACHING PAGES 14 AND 15:**
1. Begin page 14 by asking the children to try to think of words in which the letter *e* says its name. Help if they cannot do this (see, green, dream, and so on). Look at the first picture on the page (bee). Ask the children to name the picture. What vowel sound do they hear (long *e*). Have them trace the *e* on the lines under the picture. Repeat this procedure for the remaining pictures.

2. Read a list of words like the following. Ask the children to hold up an *e* card when they hear the long *e* sound. Examples: street, make, reel, seen, whale, sea.

3. Page 15 is a long *e* review and reinforcement page. It gives the children an opportunity to work with you to find pictures and words which have the long *e* sound. Talk about the long *e* work done on page 14.

4. Have the children trace both the capital and small long *e* on the page.

5. Have the children look through magazines and catalogues to find pictures and words that have the long *e* sound. This page may be a collage of written words, drawings, cut and paste words and pictures. Help the children stress the long *e* sound when they find it. Help as needed with the writing, cutting, and pasting to complete the page.

**EXTENDED ACTIVITIES:**
1. Make a long *Ee* chart.
2. Add long *Ee* to the alphabet Scrap Book.
3. Talk about names and words from the Bible that have the long *Ee* sound: *Esau, Ezekiel, Eden, Egypt, Elizabeth, Elijah, Eve, and eternal.* Add these to your Bible list or booklet. Ask the children to think of all the Bible figures they know who have lived in Egypt at one time (Examples: Joseph; Jacob; Moses; Jesus, Mary, and Joseph, and so on). Use a map or globe to show the children where Egypt is located.

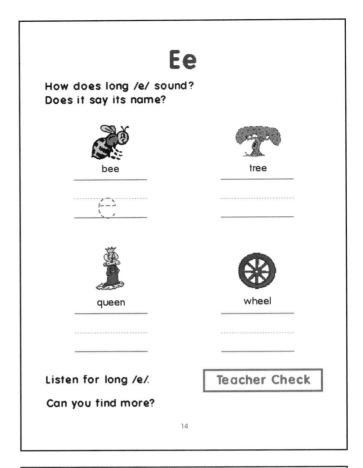

**Ee**

How does long /e/ sound?
Does it say its name?

bee

tree

queen

wheel

Listen for long /e/.

Can you find more?

Teacher Check

14

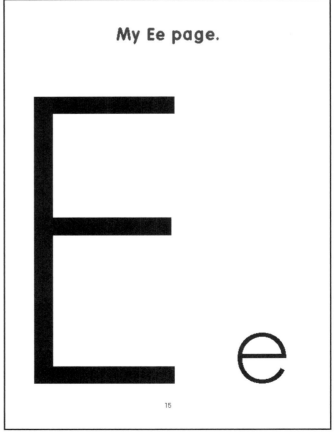

**My Ee page.**

15

**SUGGESTED READING/ STORY IDEAS:**

1. Read the story of Adam and Eve in the garden of Eden (Genesis 2:8-14). Have the children illustrate the story and retell it.

2. Recall the story of Elizabeth and the birth of John the Baptist, or the story of Mary's visit to Elizabeth. Let the children retell the story.

## OBJECTIVES:
1. To write a story.
2. To recognize long e words.
3. To review initial consonants: *g, h, j,* and *k.*

**MATERIALS:** pencils and crayons, long *e* chart, charts or picture cards for *g, h, j,* and *k* as initial sounds.

## TEACHING PAGES 16 AND 17:
1. Prepare for page 16, by playing a rhyming game with the children. Divide the children into groups. Give each group a long e word. Examples: see, dream, meal, green. Ask the children in the group to find as many words as they can that rhyme with their words. Allow about five minutes. Ask the children to tell everyone the words they have found. Write the words on the board. Next, ask the children if they can group any of the words together. Begin working on ideas for a story that will use as many long e words as possible.

2. Work with the children to write a long e story. Write it on the board or on chart paper. Some children may be able to copy the story into their books. Others will need help. If the story is longer than the space in the book, have the children write the name of the story in their books and one sentence of the story. Ask them to draw a picture to accompany the story.

3. Write the letters *g, h, j,* and *k* on the board. Have children take turns giving you words that begin with each letter. You may also distribute picture cards for these initial sounds and have the children bring their cards forward and place them under the correct letter. Read the direction on page 17. Tell the children that they are to look at the pictures in each box, say the names, listen carefully to the beginning sound of each, and circle the letter that they hear at the beginning of the picture. Ask the children to say the picture names aloud. At the bottom of the page, direct the children to write the letter for the beginning sound on the line under each picture. All letters are in the box at the top of the page.

## EXTENDED ACTIVITIES:
1. Continue to encourage children who are able to use the alphabet letter cards to make new words. Use the e cards to make long e words. Examples: see, meet, tree. Use the words in a sentence. Add to the list of words and names they can form. Help as needed.
2. Make a long *Ee* puppet.

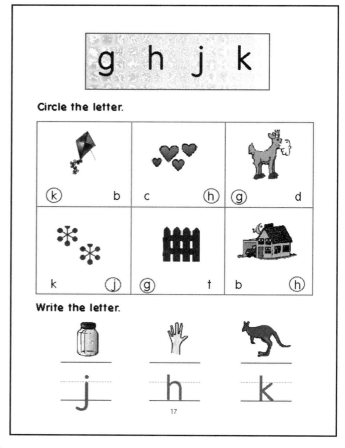

3. ENRICHMENT activity for more advanced children. Look at the lists of long *e* words that the children discovered for the story lesson. Ask the more advanced children to mark all of the words that have a double *e* used to say its name. Ask them what they notice about the words that are not marked (they make the long *e* sound using a different silent vowel or letter combinations, *ea, ie, y*). Sometimes the final long *e* sound is made by the letter *y* (puppy, funny, baby, daddy, and so on). Tell the children that the long *e* sound has more than one letter combination. Have the children sort out the words that use *ea, ie, y*. Ask them to use these words in a sentence.

**SUGGESTED READING/ STORY IDEAS:**
1. Read *The Very Hungry Caterpillar*, by Eric Carle. See how many long *e* pictures and words can be found (green, eat, hungry, and so on).
2. Retell the story using a stick caterpillar and butterfly puppets.

## OBJECTIVES:

1. To recognize simple words in both capital and small letters.
2. To recognize the color words *red* and *blue*.
3. To listen carefully.
4. To follow a direction given only once.
5. To comprehend words for size.

**MATERIALS:** pencils and crayons, word cards with words beginning with both capital and small letters, objects of different sizes and lengths.

## TEACHING PAGES 18 AND 19:

1. Display flash cards or write on the board several simple words (in, it, see, man, and so on). Write the words beginning with a small letter in one column. Write the same words, in a different order, beginning with a capital letter in a second column. Read the words in both columns with the children. Ask a child to come forward and to draw a line from first word in column one to the word which matches it in column two. Continue until all pairs have been matched.

2. Read the directions on page 18. Review the words with the children. It is not necessary at this time that the children be able to read all of the words. This activity is checking their recognition skills. Have the children do both boxes independently, if they are able. Work with the children who cannot do this independently.

3. On page 19, read the direction to the children. Tell them you will read a sentence once. Have them circle the picture that matches the sentence. Read:

*fish:* The boat is little.
*umbrella:* One person is very tall.
*apple:* The ball is small.
*teddy bear:* Mark the tallest person. Check. If children missed any, have them describe the pictures in the box to you. This will help determine if the problem may be conceptual or related to inattentive listening.

## EXTENDED ACTIVITIES:

1. Have those children who are able use the words on page 18 in sentences.

2. On page 18 have the children take a red crayon and circle the words for *red*. Then have them take a blue crayon and circle the words for *blue*.

3. Use three objects of different sizes to demonstrate tall, taller, tallest; small, medium, large; and any other comparative concepts which are not clear.

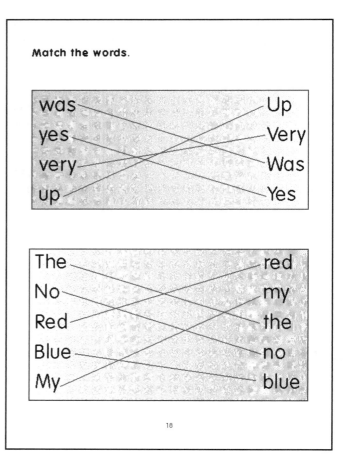

Match the words.

was — Up
yes — Very
very — Was
up — Yes

The — red
No — my
Red — the
Blue — no
My — blue

18

Put an **X** on the picture.

19

**SUGGESTED READING/ STORY IDEAS:**

1. Have the children think of a story about the tallest and smallest members of their families. This may include people and pets. Help them to write their stories on practice paper first and then copy them into the storybook at the back of this book. Help as needed. Check letter formation.

2. Ask the children to tell/read their stories to the class.

**OBJECTIVES:**
1. To read the color words green and yellow.
2. To review the colors green and yellow.

**MATERIALS:** pencils, green and yellow crayons, old magazines and catalogues, scissors, glue or paste, Bible, word cards for green and yellow, other green and yellow objects (blocks, bears, buttons, and so on).

**TEACHING PAGES 20 AND 21:**

1. The children have been seeing the words for the colors *green* and *yellow* in many places over the last several months. On page 20, begin working with the children to sound out and read these words. The word *green* is not difficult to sound out. The word *yellow*, however, has *ow* sound they have not yet learned. Discuss the pictures in the green section of the page. Ask the children to point to and read the word *green*. Have them trace it with their fingers. Finally, have them trace the word *green* on the lines. Introduce the yellow section in the same way.

2. For page 21, have the children look through magazines and catalogues for pictures of things that are green and yellow. They may also draw pictures. Check to make sure that they glue the *green* things on the side of the page which says *green* and the *yellow* things on the *yellow* side.

3. Additional writing practice for all color words is found in the back of the book.

**EXTENDED ACTIVITIES:**

1. Continue the Color book. Use construction paper or chart paper to make a page for each color learned. Print the name of the color in large letters at the top of the page. Color or paste objects that are usually found in that color or which could be found in that color. Add a GREEN and a YELLOW page to the book. You may also want to add words that are associated with the colors if the children know them (examples, emerald green, lime green, lemon yellow, and so on).

2. Practice making red, blue, green, and yellow patterns with shapes, blocks, bears, or buttons. Have the children copy your patterns and then invent their own.

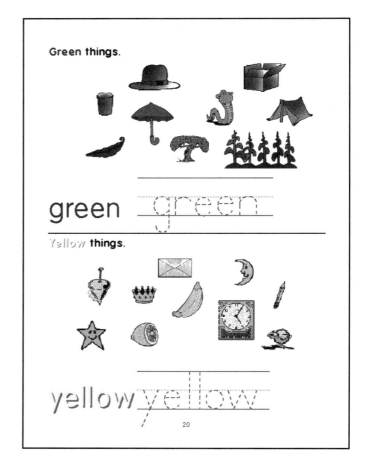

Green things.

green _green_

Yellow things.

yellow _yellow_

20

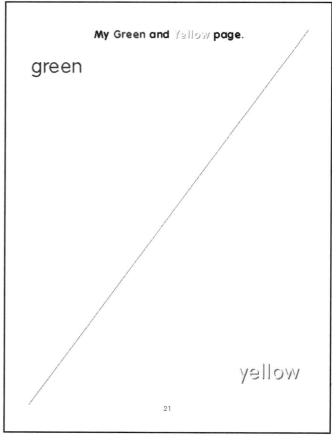

My Green and Yellow page.

green

yellow

21

**SUGGESTED READING/ STORY IDEAS:**

1. The Bible contains many references to green, especially with regard to trees and pastures. Read the Twenty-third Psalm to the children and ask them to close their eyes and listen as you read. Ask them to try to picture the places and scenes mentioned in the psalm.

2. Print or type the Twenty-third Psalm on a sheet of paper. Have the children illustrate portions of it. Display the pictures around the psalm. Help the children to memorize a few verses from the Psalm.

3. Add to the Color Poetry Book. Have the children think of as many things as they can for each color. Write the list on the board. Then work with the children to create a "color" poem for *Green* and *Yellow*.

**OBJECTIVES:**
1. To recognize long *a* and long *e* sounds.
2. To listen carefully.
3. To follow a direction given only once.
4. To put things in order.

**MATERIALS:** pencils, long *a* and long *e* charts, sequence cards.

**TEACHING PAGES 22 AND 23:**

1. Prepare for page 22 by reading a list of words which have both long *a* and long *e* sounds in them. Have the children raise their *a* cards when they hear the long *a* sound and their *e* cards when they hear the long *e* sound.

2. Read the direction on page 22. Tell the children that as they name each picture, they are to listen carefully for the long sound. Ask them to point to the first picture (bee). Have them say the name and tell what long sound they hear (*e*). Tell them to write an *e* on the line under the picture of the bee. Continue this procedure for the first two rows. If children are able, let them complete the third row on their own. Check. Correct any errors and any letter formation problems.

3. Prepare for page 23, by using the sequence cards and asking individual children to put them in order and tell the story. Put a simple sequence on the board out of order. Example: child holding a flower, flower in garden, flower in vase. Ask the children what picture comes first (flower in garden). Write a large numeral *1* under the picture of the flower in the garden. Ask the children what happened next (child holding flower). Write a large numeral *2* under this picture. Ask the children what happened last (flower in vase). Write a large numeral *3* under this picture. Ask the children to look at page 23. Talk about the pictures in the first row. Have the children describe what is happening in each. Ask which picture shows what happened first (planting seeds). Have them trace the numeral *1* under the picture. Ask them what picture shows what happened next (leaves sprouting). Have them trace the numeral *2* under the picture. Ask them what picture shows what happened last (tall plants). Have them trace the numeral *3* under the picture. Have the children study the second row of pictures carefully. Ask them to point to the picture that shows what came first (egg). Check. Tell them to write the numeral *1* under the picture that shows what came first. Ask them to point to the picture that shows what happened next (egg shell cracking). Check. Tell them to write the numeral *2*

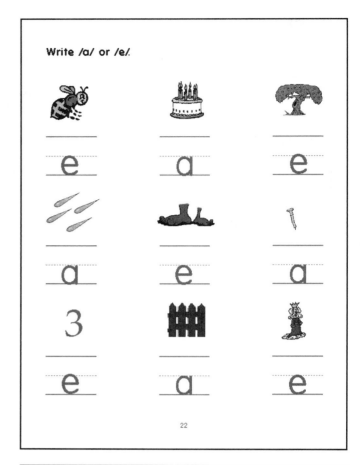

under the picture. Ask them to point to the picture that shows what happened last (chick hatches). Check. Tell them to write the numeral *3* under the picture. Check formation of numerals as well. Ask the children to look at the third row of pictures carefully. Proceed as above (*1* mixing bowl, *2* cookies being placed on sheet, *3* cookies going into oven). If children are able, allow them to do the third row on their own. Check.

**EXTENDED ACTIVITIES:**

1. Review long *a* and *e* sounds as needed.

2. Ask the children to give the beginning sounds of the pictures on page 22.

3. If children continue to have difficulty with sequencing, obtain some comic strips from the newspaper (two copies of each is better). Glue one copy to a piece of cardboard or tagboard. Cut the second copy into segments and place in an envelope taped to the back of the cardboard. Let the children work independently placing the cut pieces in order and checking them against the copy on the cardboard.

**SUGGESTED READING/ STORY IDEAS:**

1. Have the children tell a story for each of the sequences on page 23. Encourage them to add details. Examples: Who planted the seeds? Whose garden was it? How long did it take for them to come up? What kind of flowers were they? What color flowers? And so on.

2. Read the book *The Very Busy Spider* by Eric Carle. Have the children watch how the spider moves through the entire day.

**OBJECTIVES:**

   1. To recognize the long sound of *i*.

   2. To find words and pictures for the long sound of *i*.

**MATERIALS:** pencils, crayons, Bible, magazines or newspapers, paste or glue, chart paper or tagboard, *i* flash cards.

**TEACHING PAGES 24 AND 25:**

   1. Begin page 24 by asking the children to try to think of words in which the letter *i* says its name. Help if they cannot do this (like, high, dive, and so on). Look at the first picture on the page (bike). Ask the children to name the picture. What vowel sound do they hear (long *i*). Have them trace the *i* on the lines under the picture. Repeat this procedure for the remaining pictures.

   2. Read a list of words like the following. Ask the children to hold up an *i* card when they hear the long *i* sound. Examples: white, light, rain, hive, pie, sea.

   3. Page 25 is a long *i* review and reinforcement page. It gives the children an opportunity to work with you to find pictures and words which have the long *i* sound. Talk about the long *i* work done on page 24.

   4. Have the children trace both the capital and small long *i* on the page.

   5. Have the children look through magazines and catalogues to find pictures and words that have the long *i* sound. This page may be a collage of written words, drawings, cut and paste words and pictures. Help the children stress the long *i* sound when they find it. Help as needed with the writing, cutting, pasting to complete the page.

**EXTENDED ACTIVITIES:**

   1. Make a long *Ii* chart.

   2. Add long *Ii* to the alphabet Scrap Book.

   3. Talk about names and words from the Bible that have the long *Ii* sound: *Isaiah, Isaac, Bible, light,* and *life.* Add these to your Bible list or booklet.

**SUGGESTED READING/ STORY IDEAS:**

   1. Recall the story of Abraham and Isaac. Let the children tell it if they can.

   2. Read the story of Isaac and his two sons, Jacob and Esau (Genesis 25: 27-34). Have the children act out the story.

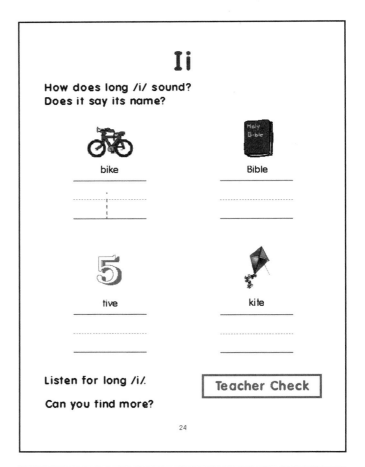

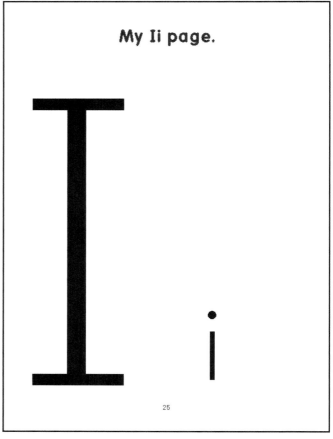

## OBJECTIVES:
1. To write a story.
2. To recognize long i words.
3. To review initial consonants: *l, m, n,* and *p.*

**MATERIALS:** pencils and crayons, long *i* chart, charts or picture cards for *l, m, n,* and *p* as initial sounds.

## TEACHING PAGES 26 AND 27:
1. Prepare for page 26, by playing a rhyming game with the children. Divide the children into groups. Give each group a long *i* word: Examples: high, light, like, line. Ask the children in the group to find as many words as they can that rhyme with their words. Allow about five minutes. Ask the children to tell everyone the words they have found. Write the words on the board. Next ask the children if they can group any of the words together. Begin working on ideas for a story that will use as many long *i* words as possible.

2. Work with the children to write a long *i* story. Write it on the board or on chart paper. Some children may be able to copy the story into their books. Others will need help. If the story is longer than the space in the book, have the children write the name of the story in their books and one sentence of the story. Ask them to draw a picture to accompany the story.

3. Write the letters *l, m, n,* and *p* on the board. Have children take turns giving you words that begin with each letter. You may also distribute picture cards for these initial sounds and have the children bring their cards forward and place them under the correct letter. Read the direction on page 27. Tell the children that they are to look at the pictures in each box, say the names, listen carefully to the beginning sound of each, and circle the letter that they hear at the beginning of the picture. Ask the children to say the picture names aloud. At the bottom of the page, direct the children to write the letter for the beginning sound on the line under each picture. All letters are in the box at the top of the page.

## EXTENDED ACTIVITIES:
1. Continue to encourage children who are able to use the alphabet letter cards to make new words. Use the *i* cards to make long *i* words: Examples: like, bike, time, fine. Use the words in a sentence. Add to the list of words and names they can form. Help as needed.
2. Make a long *li* puppet.

3. ENRICHMENT activity for more advanced children. Look at the lists of long *i* words that the children discovered for the story lesson. Ask the more advanced children to mark all of the words that have a silent *e* used to help the vowel say its name. Ask them what they notice about the words that are not marked (they make the long *i* sound using a different silent vowel or letter combinations, *igh, ie, y*). Sometimes the final long *i* sound is made by the letter *y* (cry, fly, my, sky, and so on). Tell the children that the long *i* sound has more than one letter combination. Have the children sort out the words that use *igh, ie, y*. Ask them to use these words in a sentence.

4. Review the initial consonants as needed.

5. Ask the children who are able, to identify the vowel sounds for each picture on page 27.

**SUGGESTED READING/ STORY IDEAS:**

1. Find long *i* words that can be grouped together and ask the children to write short poems. For example: fly, sky, high, kite; bike, ride, slide, like; write, night, light; and so on.

2. Have the children illustrate the poems and then recite them.

## OBJECTIVES:
1. To review the sound of short *a*.
2. To recognize the letters *i, l, T, m, z, y, u*.

**MATERIALS:** pencils, short a chart, flash cards, short *a* story.

## TEACHING PAGES 28 AND 29:
1. Review the short *a* chart and story before beginning page 28. Ask the children to find things around them that have the short *a* sound. Have the children look at the top of the page. Ask them what the first picture is (bat). Ask them what vowel sound they hear (short *a*). Have them trace the *a* under the picture. Finish the row in the same manner.

2. Read the direction at the middle of page 28. Ask the children to say the picture names aloud emphasizing the vowel sound. Have them circle the pictures independently. Check.

3. Page 29 is a letter recognition review. If children have difficulty with this do several practice exercises on the board similar to those on the page. Ask the children to point to the letter in the first box at the top of the page. Ask a child to say the name of the letter (*l*). Tell the children that they are to find the letter in the long box. Have them point to the letters that match. Tell them to circle the two *l*'s in the box. Complete the activity in the same manner or allow the children to do independently.

4. After making sure that the children identify the letters in the bottom boxes correctly, let them find and circle the word on their own.

## EXTENDED ACTIVITIES:
1. Have the children make sentences with the words in the last activity on page 29.

2. If any children have problems with letter recognition, continue to review those letters most frequently missed.

3. Add to the short *a* chart and story if the children have found additional words or pictures.

## SUGGESTED READING/ STORY IDEAS:
1. Review favorite short *a* stories like *The Cat in the Hat*, or *The Cat in the Hat Comes Back*.

2. Have the children create their own version of the story substituting other short *a* words and characters.

Write short /a/.

Circle short /a/ pictures.

Do you remember more?

28

Circle the letters.

| i | (i) | o | e | j | (i) |
|---|---|---|---|---|---|
| l | k | (l) | m | h | (l) |
| T | A | B | (T) | F | (T) |
| m | (m) | h | (m) | e | n |

| z | vest | (zoo) | who |
|---|---|---|---|
| y | (you) | very | we |
| u | no | (us) | vote |

29

**OBJECTIVES:**
1. To read the color words *purple* and *pink*.
2. To review the colors *purple* and *pink*.

**MATERIALS:** pencils, purple and pink crayons, old magazines and catalogues, scissors, glue or paste, Bible, word cards for purple and pink, other purple and pink objects (blocks, bears, buttons, and so on).

**TEACHING PAGES 30 AND 31:**
1. The children have been seeing the words for the colors *purple* and *pink* in many places over the last several months. On page 30, begin working with the children to sound out and read these words. The word *pink* is not difficult to sound out. The word *purple*, however, has *ur* sound they have not yet learned. Discuss the pictures in the purple section of the page. Ask the children to point to and read the word *purple*. Have them trace it with their fingers. Finally, have them trace the word *purple* on the lines. Introduce the *pink* section in the same way.

2. For page 31, have the children look through magazines and catalogues for pictures of things that are purple and pink. They may also draw pictures. Check to make sure that they glue the *purple* things on the side of the page which says *purple* and the *pink* things on the *pink* side.

3. Additional writing practice for all color words is found in the back of the book.

**EXTENDED ACTIVITIES:**
1. Continue the Color book. Use construction paper or chart paper to make a page for each color learned. Print the name of the color in large letters at the top of the page. Color or paste objects that are usually found in that color or which could be found in that color. Add a PURPLE and a PINK page to the book. You may also want to add words that are associated with the colors if the children know them (examples, violet, rose, and so on).

2. Practice making purple, pink, red, blue, green, and yellow patterns with shapes, blocks, bears, or buttons. Have the children copy your patterns and then invent their own.

**SUGGESTED READING/ STORY IDEAS:**
1. The color *purple* was considered a royal color in ancient times. The Bible has many references to the color *purple*. Select some and read them to the children. Examples: Exodus 25:4; 26:1; 26:31; 28: 5, 6, 8, 15, 33; 39:1, 2, 3, 5, 8, 24, 29;

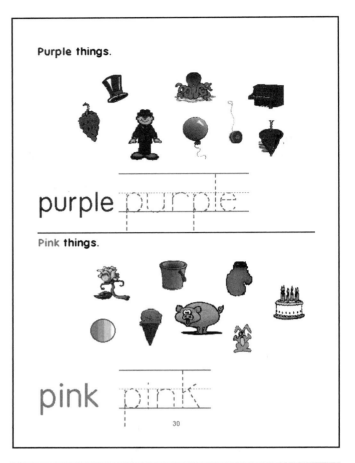

Purple things.

purple

Pink things.

pink

30

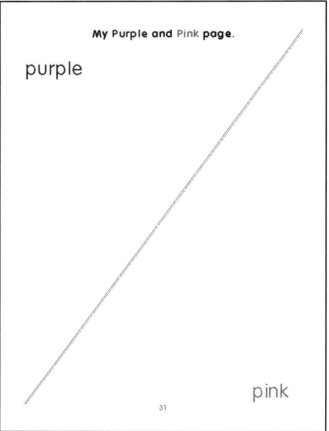

My Purple and Pink page.

purple

pink

31

Judges 8:26; Esther 8:15. Read Mark 15:17 and 20; John 19: 2 and 5 which talks about Jesus being clothed in a purple robe for the passion. Have the children select a passage to illustrate.

2. Add to the Color Poetry Book. List as many things on the board as the children can think of for each color. Then work with the children to create a "color" poem for PURPLE and PINK.

**OBJECTIVES:**
1. To recognize the long sound of *o*.
2. To find words and pictures for the long sound of *o*.

**MATERIALS:** pencils, crayons, Bible, magazines or newspapers, paste or glue, chart paper or tagboard, *o* flash cards.

**TEACHING PAGES 32 AND 33:**
1. Begin page 32 by asking the children to try to think of words in which the letter *o* says its name. Help if they cannot do this (boat, rope, no, hold, and so on). Look at the first picture on the page (rope). Ask the children to name the picture. What vowel sound do they hear (long *o*). Have them trace the *o* on the lines under the picture. Repeat this procedure for the remaining pictures.
2. Read a list of words like the following. Ask the children to hold up an *o* card when they hear the long *o* sound. Examples: home, take, glow, bike, know, boat, green.
3. Page 33 is a long *o* review and reinforcement page. It gives the children an opportunity to work with you to find pictures and words which have the long *o* sound. Talk about the long *o* work done on page 32.
4. Have the children trace both the capital and small long *o* on the page.
5. Have the children look through magazines and catalogues to find pictures and words that have the long *o* sound. This page may be a collage of written words, drawings, cut and paste words and pictures. Help the children stress the long *o* sound when they find it. Help as needed with the writing, cutting, and pasting to complete the page.

**EXTENDED ACTIVITIES:**
1. Make a long *Oo* chart.
2. Add long *Oo* to the alphabet Scrap Book.
3. Talk about names and words from the Bible that have the long *Oo* sound: *Jonah, Moses, Joseph, obedience*, and so on. Add these to your Bible list or booklet.

**SUGGESTED READING/ STORY IDEAS:**
1. Read the story of Jonah (Jonah 1:1-17). Have the children illustrate and act out the story.

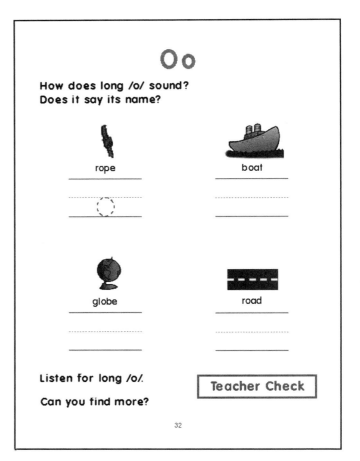

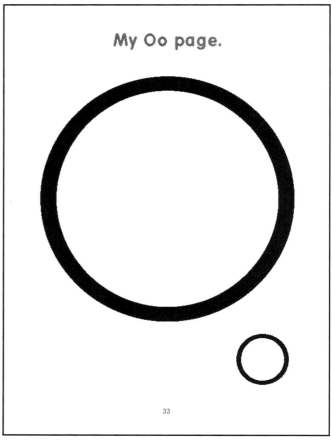

2. Review what the children know of Moses, Joseph and his brothers, and Joseph, Mary's husband. Reread the stories as needed.

**OBJECTIVES:**
1. To write a story.
2. To recognize long *o* words.
3. To review initial consonants: *qu, r, s,* and *t.*

**MATERIALS:** pencils and crayons, long *o* chart, charts or picture cards for *qu, r, s,* and *t* as initial sounds.

**TEACHING PAGES 34 AND 35:**

1. Prepare for page 34, by playing a rhyming game with the children. Divide the children into groups. Give each group a long *o* word. Examples: grow, goat, hope. Ask the children in the group to find as many words as they can that rhyme with their words. Allow about five minutes. Ask the children to tell everyone the words they have found. Write the words on the board. Next, ask the children if they can group any of the words together. Begin working on ideas for a story that will use as many long *o* words as possible.

2. Work with the children to write a long *o* story. Write it on the board or on chart paper. Some children may be able to copy the story into their books. Others will need help. If the story is longer than the space in the book, have the children write the name of the story in their books and one sentence of the story. Ask them to draw a picture to accompany the story.

3. Write the letters *qu, r, s,* and *t* on the board. Have children take turns giving you words that begin with each letter. You may also distribute picture cards for these initial sounds and have the children bring their cards forward and place them under the correct letter. Read the direction on page 35. Tell the children that they are to look at the pictures in each box, say the names, listen carefully to the beginning sound of each, and circle the letter that they hear at the beginning of the picture. Ask the children to say the picture names aloud. At the bottom of the page, direct the children to write the letter for the beginning sound on the line under each picture. All letters are in the box at the top of the page.

**EXTENDED ACTIVITIES:**

1. Continue to encourage children who are able to use the alphabet letter cards to make new words. Use the *o* cards to make long *o* words. Examples: home, no, and low. Use the words in a sentence. Add to the list of words and names they can form. Help as needed.

2. Make a long *Oo* puppet.

3. ENRICHMENT activity for more advanced children. Look at the lists of long *o* words that the children discovered for the story lesson. Ask the more advanced children to mark all of the words that have a silent *e* used to help the *o* say its name. Ask them what they notice about the words that are not marked (they make the long *o* sound using a different silent vowel or letter combinations, *ow, oa*). Tell the children that the long *o* sound has more than one letter combination. Have the children sort out the words that use *ow, oa*. Ask them to use these words in a sentence.

**SUGGESTED READING/ STORY IDEAS:**

1. Read Ezra Keats' *Snowy Day* to the children. Talk about snow and how it affects people's lives (cold, making snowmen, shoveling snow, and so on).

2. Have the children write a poem about snow. If children have never experienced snow, have them imagine what it would be like to play in the snow.

**OBJECTIVES:**

1. To recognize basic shapes in common objects.
2. To recognize basic colors and color words.
3. To listen carefully.
4. To follow a direction given only once.
5. To recognize position words: *in, on, under,* and *next to.*

**MATERIALS:** pencils and crayons (red, blue, yellow, purple, green), pictures and objects with basic shapes, color word cards, objects to demonstrate the concepts *in, on, under,* and *next to.*

**TEACHING PAGES 36 AND 37:**

1. Look at the picture on page 36. Ask the children to tell you what they see. (rocket ship) Review the shapes and the color words in the directions. Let the children complete the page independently. Walk around and check as they work.

2. Prepare for page 37 by placing several objects on a table or desk. Ask the children to come forward one at a time and select an object. Direct each child to place the object using the concepts for *in, on, under,* or *next to.* Examples: Place the block *in* the desk. Place the doll *under* the table. Place the ball *on* the window ledge. Place the box of crayons *next to* the book box. Continue until each child has a turn. If a child has a problem, help them and then return to that child later to reinforce the concept.

3. Read the direction on page 37. Tell the children you will read a sentence once. They will circle the picture which shows what the sentence describes. Ask the children to point to the red apple.
*Read:*
The mouse is *on* the box.
Move on to the blue plane.
*Read:*
The flowers are *next to* the box.
Move to the green tent.
*Read:*
The ball is *under* the table.
Check. Ask the children to describe all of the pictures in any box they have missed. This will give an indication whether the problem is a listening problem or a problem understanding the concepts.

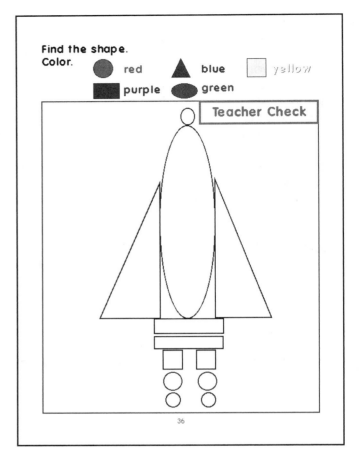

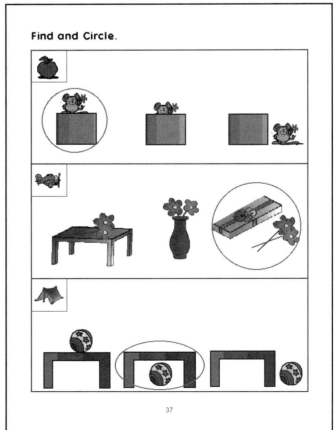

178

**EXTENDED ACTIVITIES:**

1. If any child had difficulty with the activity on page 37, use objects and play games to reinforce the concepts that are weak. Go back to the page and ask the child to do the following: Go to the red apple.

*Read:* The mouse is *in* the box.

Go to the blue plane.

*Read:* The flowers are on the table.

Go to the green tent.

*Read:* The ball is *next to* the table.

2. Let children who are more advanced create their own position word games including words such as *above, below, on top of, over, on/off, open/closed,* and *in/out.*

**SUGGESTED READING/ STORY IDEAS:**

1. Ask the children to create stories for each of the boxes on page 37 incorporating all three pictures into the story. Encourage them to add details: name the mouse, to whom does the mouse belong; what kind of flower, what color, who are the flowers for, is it a special occasion; whose ball is it, who might play with the ball, and so on.

2. Select one of the stories and write it for the children in the Story Book section of this book.

**OBJECTIVES:**
1. To read the color words *orange* and *black*.
2. To review the colors *orange* and *black*.

**MATERIALS:** pencils, orange and black crayons, old magazines and catalogues, scissors, glue or paste, word cards for orange and black, other orange and black objects (blocks, bears, buttons, and so on).

**TEACHING PAGES 38 AND 39:**
1. The children have been seeing the words for the colors *orange* and *black* in many places over the last several months. On page 38, begin working with the children to sound out and read these words. The word *black* is not difficult to sound out. The word *orange*, however, does not clearly use the *a* sound. Discuss the pictures in the orange section of the page. Ask the children to point to and read the word *orange*. Have them trace it with their fingers. Finally, have them trace the word *orange* on the lines.
Introduce the black section in the same way.

2. For page 39, have the children look through magazines and catalogues for pictures of things that are orange and black. They may also draw pictures. Check to make sure that they glue the *orange* things on the side of the page which says *orange* and the *black* things on the *black* side.

3. Additional writing practice for all color words is found in the back of the book.

**EXTENDED ACTIVITIES:**
1. Continue the Color book. Use construction paper or chart paper to make a page for each color learned. Print the name of the color in large letters at the top of the page. Color or paste objects that are usually found in that color or which could be found in that color. Add a ORANGE and a BLACK page to the book. You may also want to add words that are associated with the colors if the children know them (jet black and so on).

2. Practice making orange, black, purple, pink, red, blue, green, and yellow patterns, using three or four colors at a time. Use shapes, blocks, bears, or buttons. Have the children copy your patterns and then invent their own.

**SUGGESTED READING/ STORY IDEAS:**
1. Read stories and poems about night and stormy clouds.

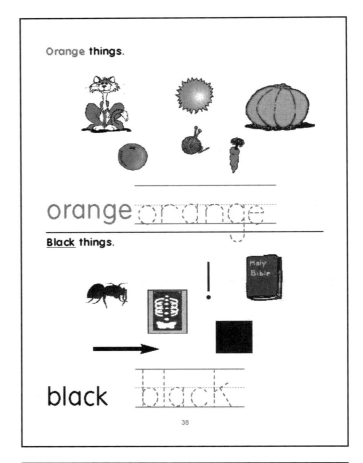

Orange **things.**

orange ~~orange~~

**Black things.**

black ~~black~~

38

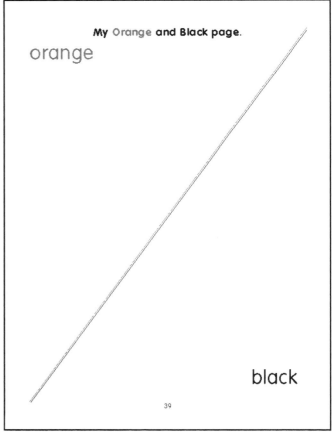

**My Orange and Black page.**

orange

black

39

2. Add to the Color Poetry Book. List as many things on the board as the children can think of for each color. Then work with the children to create a "color" poem for ORANGE and BLACK.

**OBJECTIVES:**

1. To review the sound of short *e*.
2. To listen carefully.
3. To follow a direction given only once.
4. To recognize concepts and words for size: big, little, large, small, tall.
5. To recognize comparative words for size: bigger, biggest, taller, tallest, smaller, smallest.
6. To review recognition of numerals 1–6.

**MATERIALS:** pencils, crayons, short *e* chart, stories, and flash cards; objects to use for size comparison.

**TEACHING PAGES 40 AND 41:**

1. Review the short *e* chart and story before beginning page 40. Ask the children to find things around them that have the short *e* sound. Have the children look at the top of the page. Ask them what the first picture is (bed). Ask them what vowel sound they hear (short *e*). Have them circle the pictures with the short *e* sound.

2. Read the direction at the middle of page 40. Ask the children to say the picture names aloud emphasizing the vowel sound. Have them write short *e* under the pictures. Check.

3. Prepare for page 41 by placing objects of different sizes on a table or desk. Have sets of objects which show the same object in different sizes (buttons, pencils, toys, pictures of large or tall objects, and so on). Line the objects up in sets of three and ask children to come forward individually and listen to your directions. Ask them to select the smallest from the set, or the biggest. Continue the procedure until each child has a turn. Use these concepts:
big/little, large/small, tall/taller/tallest, small/smaller/smallest, big/bigger/biggest.
If a child is uncertain, give the correct answer and then return to the concept later to reinforce it.

4. Ask the children to look at page 41. Tell them that you will read a sentence once. Have them mark an *X* on the object described in the sentence. Ask the children to find the numeral.
1. Read: Put an *X* on the smallest ball.
Continue with the remaining boxes:
2. Read: Put an *X* on the big snail.
3. Read: Put an *X* on the large flower.
4. Read: Put an *X* on the biggest fire hydrant.
5. Read: Put an *X* on the tallest cat.
6. Read: Put an *X* on the small bird.

Check. Ask the children to describe the pictures in any boxes that are incorrect. Retest or do further practice with objects.

**EXTENDED ACTIVITIES:**

1. Add to the short *e* chart and story if the children have found additional words or pictures.

2. Use additional objects or picture cards to review size concepts as needed. More advanced children can find examples of other size words: long/short, thick/thin, wide/narrow.

**SUGGESTED READING/ STORY IDEAS:**

1. Read stories such as Aesop's Fable about *The Lion and the Mouse* which emphasize different sizes. Talk about this story. Does bigger always mean more powerful than smaller?

2. Have the children write a story using one of the size opposites: big/little; tall/short; or others.

**OBJECTIVES:**
1. To recognize the long sound of *u*.
2. To find words and pictures for the long sound of *u*.

**MATERIALS:** pencils, crayons, Bible, magazines or newspapers, paste or glue, chart paper or tagboard, *u* flash cards.

**TEACHING PAGES 42 AND 43:**
1. Begin page 42 by asking the children to try to think of words in which the letter *u* says its name. Help if they cannot do this (you, fuse, cute, pew, and so on). Look at the first picture on the page (music). Ask the children to name the picture. What long vowel sound do they hear (long *u*). Have them trace the *u* on the lines under the picture. Repeat this procedure for the remaining pictures.
2. Read a list of words like the following. Ask the children to hold up a *u* card when they hear the long *u* sound. Examples: cue, fuel, goat, he, few, and cake.
3. Page 43 is a long *u* review and reinforcement page. It gives the children an opportunity to work with you to find pictures and words which have the long *u* sound. Talk about the long *u* work done on page 42.
4. Have the children trace both the capital and small *u* on the page.
5. Have the children look through magazines and catalogues to find pictures and words that have the long *u* sound. This page may be a collage of written words, drawings, cut and paste words and pictures. Help the children stress the long *u* sound when they find it. Help as needed with the writing, cutting, and pasting to complete the page.

**EXTENDED ACTIVITIES:**
1. Make a long *Uu* chart.
2. Add long *Uu* to the alphabet Scrap Book.
3. Talk about names and words from the Bible that have the long *Uu* sound: *tribute, Luke, Joshua, Ruth,* and so on. Add these to your Bible list or booklet.

**SUGGESTED READING/ STORY IDEAS:**
1. Choose one or two stories from the Gospel of Luke. Read them to the children.
2. Have the children illustrate the stories.

## OBJECTIVES:

1. To write a story.
2. To recognize long *u* words.
3. To review initial consonants: *v, w, x, y,* and *z.*

**MATERIALS:** pencils and crayons, long *u* chart, charts or picture cards for *v, w, x, y,* and *z* as initial sounds.

## TEACHING PAGES 44 AND 45:

1. Prepare for page 44, by playing a rhyming game with the children. Divide the children into groups. Give each group a long *u* word. Examples: you, cube. Ask the children in the group to find as many words as they can that rhyme with their words. Allow about five minutes. Ask the children to tell everyone the words they have found. Write the words on the board. Next, ask the children if they can group any of the words together. Begin working on ideas for a story that will use as many long *u* words as possible.

2. Work with the children to write a long *u* story. Write it on the board or on chart paper. Some children may be able to copy the story into their books. Others will need help. If the story is longer than the space in the book, have the children write the name of the story in their books and one sentence of the story. Ask them to draw a picture to accompany the story.

3. Write the letters *v, w, x, y,* and *z* on the board. Have children take turns giving you words that begin with each letter. You may also distribute picture cards for these initial sounds and have the children bring their cards forward and place them under the correct letter. Read the direction on page 45. Tell the children that they are to look at the pictures in each box, say the names, listen carefully to the beginning sound of each, and circle the letter that they hear at the beginning of the picture. Ask the children to say the picture names aloud. At the bottom of the page, direct the children to write the letter for the beginning sound on the line under each picture. All letters are in the box at the top of the page.

## EXTENDED ACTIVITIES:

1. Continue to encourage children who are able to use the alphabet letter cards to make new words. Use the *u* cards to make long *u* words. Examples: use, you. Use the words in a sentence. Add to the list of words and names they can form. Help as needed.

2. Make a long *Uu* puppet.

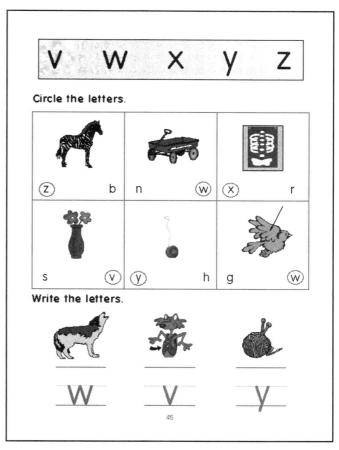

3. ENRICHMENT activity for more advanced children. Look at the lists of long *u* words that the children discovered for the story lesson. Ask the more advanced children to mark all of the words that have a silent *e* used to help the *u* say its name. Ask them what they notice about the words that are not marked (they make the long *u* sound using a different silent vowel or letter combinations, *ou, ew*). Tell the children that the long *u* sound has more than one letter combination. Have the children sort out the words that use *ou, ew*. Ask them to use these words in a sentence.

**SUGGESTED READING/ STORY IDEAS:**

1. Have the children create stories about a friend entitled: All About YOU! They can ask questions about family, friends, pets, favorite foods, colors, books, and so on. Help them write their stories.

2. Have the children decorate their stories and present them to the friend as a gift.

## OBJECTIVES:

1. To read the color words *white* and *brown*.
2. To review the colors *white* and *brown*.

**MATERIALS:** pencils, white and brown crayons, old magazines and catalogues, scissors, glue or paste, word cards for *white* and *brown*, other white and brown objects (blocks, bears, buttons, and so on).

## TEACHING PAGES 46 AND 47:

1. The children have been seeing the words for the colors *white* and *brown* in many places over the last several months. On page 46, begin working with the children to sound out and read these words. Both words are unusual: *white* uses the *wh* sound which the children have not yet learned and *brown* contains the *ow* sound. Discuss the pictures in the white section of the page. Ask the children to point to and read the word *white*. Have them trace it with their fingers. Finally, have them trace the word white on the lines. Introduce the brown section in the same way.

2. For page 47, have the children look through magazines and catalogues for pictures of things that are white and brown. They may also draw pictures. Check to make sure that they glue the *white* things on the side of the page which says *white* and the *brown* things on the *brown* side.

3. Additional writing practice for all color words is found in the back of the book.

## EXTENDED ACTIVITIES:

1. Continue the Color book. Use construction paper or chart paper to make a page for each color learned. Print the name of the color in large letters at the top of the page. Color or paste objects that are usually found in that color or which could be found in that color. Add a WHITE and a BROWN page to the book. You may also want to add words that are associated with the colors if the children know them (snow white, chocolate brown, and so on).

2. Add white and brown to the pattern activity along with the orange, black, purple, pink, red, blue, green, and yellow patterns. Use three or four colors at a time. Use shapes, blocks, bears, or buttons. Have the children copy your patterns and then invent their own.

White **things.**

white ┆white┆

Brown **things.**

brown ┆brown┆

46

**My** white **and brown page.**

white

brown

47

**SUGGESTED READING/ STORY IDEAS:**

1. Read the book *Brown Bear, Brown Bear, What do you see?* (Bill Martin). Have the children talk about the story.

2. Add to the Color Poetry Book. List as many things on the board as the children can think of for each color. Then work with the children to create a "color" poem for WHITE and BROWN.

## OBJECTIVES:

1. To review the sound of short *i*.
2. To put letters in alphabetical order.
3. To put pictures in order.

**MATERIALS:** pencils, crayons, short *i* chart, stories, and flash cards; sequence cards or pictures; alphabet chart.

## TEACHING PAGES 48 AND 49:

1. Review the short *i* chart and story before beginning page 48. Ask the children to find things around them that have the short *i* sound. Have the children look at the top of the page. Ask them what the first picture is (pig). Ask them what vowel sound they hear (short *i*). Have them circle the pictures independently. Check.

2. Read the direction at the middle of page 48. Ask the children to say the picture names aloud emphasizing the vowel sound. Have them write *i* under the picture. Finish the row in the same manner.

3. Prepare for page 49 by putting several letters of the alphabet on the board out of order (use groups of four or five at a time). Ask the children to help you put them in the correct order. Sing the alphabet song or say the alphabet to refresh their memories.

4. Ask the children to go to the first box at the top of page 49. Have them read the letters in the box. Ask if anyone can tell what letter is missing (*y*). If no one can, ask them to find the *w* on the alphabet chart and follow the letters until they reach the missing letter. Follow the same procedure for the remaining two boxes.

5. At the bottom of page 49, practice with sequence cards or draw a simple sequence on the board and demonstrate for the children that they are to write a *1* under the picture that shows what comes first; a *2* under the picture that shows what happened next; and a *3* under the picture that shows what happened last. Go to the pictures at the bottom of the page and ask the children to describe what is happening in each picture. Ask them to point to the picture that shows what happened first (child sleeping). Let them finish on their own. Check. Have the children act out the sequence, if necessary, for those who did not understand the correct sequence.

## EXTENDED ACTIVITIES:

1. Add to the short *i* chart and story if the children have found additional words or pictures.

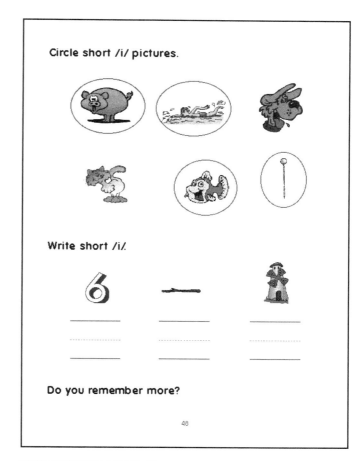

Circle short /i/ pictures.

Write short /i/.

Do you remember more?

48

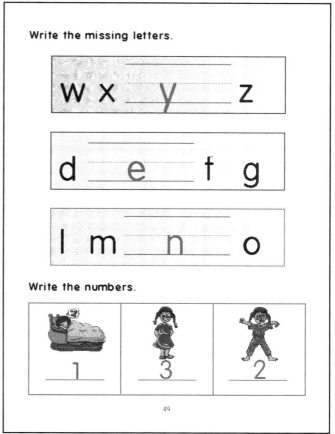

Write the missing letters.

w x ___ z

d ___ e ___ f g

l m ___ n ___ o

Write the numbers.

49

2. Continue to review alphabet and picture sequence as needed.

**SUGGESTED READING/ STORY IDEAS:**

1.  Read the story *The Little Engine That Could* to the children. Emphasize the short *i* sound in both *little* and *engine*. See if they can spot any other short *i* words in the story.

2.  Ask the children if they can think of something that seemed very hard for them to do, but that they accomplished with others encouraging them. Write down what they say and use for a story.

**OBJECTIVES:**
　　1. To recognize the consonant digraph *sh*.
　　2. To find words and pictures which begin with *sh*.

**MATERIALS:** pencils, crayons, Bible, magazines or newspapers, paste or glue, chart paper or tagboard, *sh* flash cards.

**TEACHING PAGES 50 AND 51:**
This lesson begins the study of the consonant digraphs: *sh, ch, th* and *wh*.

　　1. Prepare for page 50 by asking the children to say the *sh* sound. As the children say the sound, ask them to put their hand in front of their mouths. What do they feel? In what position are their teeth? Is this a quiet sound? Is this a sound they make when they want someone to be quiet? Ask the children to think of words that begin with the *sh* sound. Put those words on the board. Then have the children look at the first picture on the page (shell). Ask the children to name the picture. What sound do they hear at the beginning (*sh*). Have them write *sh* on the lines under the picture. Repeat this procedure for the remaining pictures.

　　2. Read a list of words like the following. Ask the children to hold up an *sh* card when they hear the sound. Examples: shine, church, shiver, she, chicken.

　　3. Page 51 is a review and reinforcement page for *sh*. It gives the children an opportunity to work with you to find pictures and words which have the *sh* sound. Talk about the work done on page 50.

　　4. Have the children trace the large *Sh* on the page.

　　5. Have the children look through magazines and catalogues to find pictures and words that begin with the *sh* sound. This page may be a collage of written words, drawings, cut and paste words and pictures. Help the children stress the *sh* sound when they find it. Help as needed with the writing, cutting, pasting to complete the page.

**EXTENDED ACTIVITIES:**
　　1. Make an *Sh* chart.
　　2. Add *Sh* to the alphabet scrapbook.
　　3. Talk about names and words from the Bible that have the *sh* sound: *shepherd, Shadrach, shadow, sheep, shine, shore,* and so on. Add these to your Bible list or booklet.

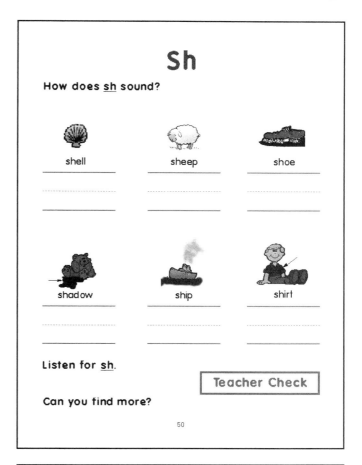

**SUGGESTED READING/ STORY IDEAS:**

1. Read the story of the Good Shepherd (John 10). Talk about what a shepherd does, about how he cares for his sheep. Let the children talk about how Jesus is a Good Shepherd to them and their families.

2. Pray Psalm 23 with the children.

## OBJECTIVES:

1. To write a story.
2. To recognize *sh* words.
3. To recognize the sound of *b* at the end of words.
4. To review the sound *ck* at the end of words.

**MATERIALS:** pencils and crayons, *sh* chart, pictures charts of objects that end in the __*b* sound and the __*ck* sound.

## TEACHING PAGES 52 AND 53:

1. Prepare for page 52 by dividing the children into groups. Ask them to find as many words or objects in the room as they can that begin with the *sh* sound. Allow about five minutes. Ask the children to tell everyone the words they have found. Write the words on the board. Next, ask the children if they can group any of the words together. Begin working on ideas for a story that will use as many *sh* words as possible.

2. Work with the children to write the *sh* story. Write it on the board or on chart paper. Some children may be able to copy the story into their books. Others will need help. If the story is longer than the space in the book, have the children write the name of the story in their books and one sentence of the story. Ask them to draw a picture to accompany the story.

3. Write the letter *b* on the board. Have children take turns giving you words that begin with the letter. Tell the children that today you will begin looking at the sounds found at the end of words. Ask them if they can think of any words that end with the *b* sound. Tell the children that they are to look at the pictures in the top section, say the names, listen carefully to the ending sound of each, and circle the letter *b* under the picture. Ask the children to say the picture names aloud.

4. Proceed in the same fashion for the __*ck* ending sounds (see Lesson 44, page 89). Invite the children to try to think of more words for each.

## EXTENDED ACTIVITIES:

1. Continue to encourage children who are able to use the alphabet letter cards to make new words. Use the __*b* and __*ck* cards to make new words. Examples: tub, job, duck. Use the words in a sentence. Add to the list of words and names they can form. Help as needed.

Write a story. Use <u>sh</u> words.

Teacher Check

52

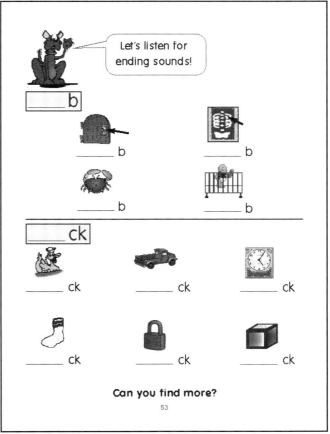

Let's listen for ending sounds!

b

_____ b      _____ b

_____ b      _____ b

ck

_____ ck      _____ ck      _____ ck

_____ ck      _____ ck      _____ ck

**Can you find more?**

53

2. Make an *sh* puppet.

3. ENRICHMENT activity for more advanced children. Use the list of *sh* words that the children discovered for the story lesson. Ask the more advanced children to find words that have the *sh* sound in the middle of a word (worship, fellowship). Tell them that in some words the *sh* sound is spelled *ti* or *ci* (direction, conscious). Have them also try to find words or pictures of things which have the *b* sound in the middle.

**SUGGESTED READING/ STORY IDEAS:**

1. Tell the children the story of Job in the Bible. Talk about his love for God in spite of all the trials he was sent.

2. Find books about ships, sheep, shepherds and other topics that use the *sh* sound.

## OBJECTIVES:
1. To read the number words *one* and *two*.
2. To find things that come in one's and two's.

**MATERIALS:** pencils, crayons, old magazines and catalogues, scissors, glue or paste, word cards for *one* and *two*, single objects and objects in pairs.

## TEACHING PAGES 54 AND 55:
1. The children have been seeing the words for the numbers *one* and *two* in many places over the last several months. On page 54, begin working with the children to sound out and read these words. Both words are unusual: *one* sounds like *won* and *two* contains a silent *w*. Discuss the pictures in the *one* section of the page. Ask the children to point to and read the word *one*. Have them trace it with their fingers. Finally, have them trace the word *one* on the lines. Talk about things that are "one of a kind".
Introduce the *two* section in the same way.

2. For page 55, have the children look through magazines and catalogues for pictures of things that come in *one* and *two*. They may also draw pictures. Check to make sure that they glue the *one* things on the side of the page which says *one* and the *two* things on the *two* side.

3. Additional writing practice for all number words is found in the back of the book.

## EXTENDED ACTIVITIES:
1. Begin a Number Book. Use construction paper or chart paper to make a page for each number learned. Print the number word in large letters at the top of the page. Color or paste pictures of objects that are usually found in one's or two's on the page.

2. Begin to work with number patterns alternating objects single and double objects (1, 2, 2, 1; 2, 1, 2, 1; and so on). Use shapes, blocks, bears, buttons, or other objects. Have the children copy your patterns and then invent their own.

## SUGGESTED READING/ STORY IDEAS:
1. Read books such as *One Fish, Two Fish, Red Fish, Blue Fish* to reinforce the concept.
2. Have the children create their own One _____, Two _____ story or poem.

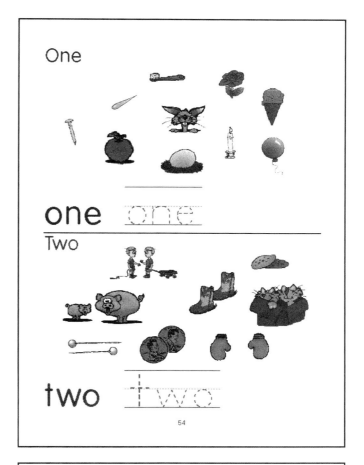

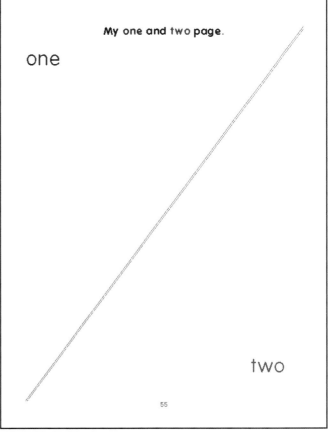

My one and two page.

one

two

## OBJECTIVES:
1. To review the sound of short *o*.
2. To review the sound of short *u*.
3. To copy a shape pattern.
4. To copy a color pattern.

**MATERIALS:** pencils, crayons, short *o* and short *u* charts, stories, and flash cards; pattern blocks and cards.

## TEACHING PAGES 56 AND 57:

1. Review the short *o* chart and story before beginning page 56. Ask the children to find things around them that have the short *o* sound. Have the children look at the top of the page. Ask them what the first picture is (top). Ask them what vowel sound they hear (short *o*). Have them name all of the pictures emphasizing the vowel sound in each. Ask them to circle all of the short *o* pictures. Check.

2. Follow the same procedures for the short *u* review at the bottom of the page.

3. Prepare for page 57 by using the pattern cards created for the color and number word lessons. Put some simple shape patterns on the board and ask a child to come forward and complete the pattern. Give all children a turn at this.

4. Ask the children to go to the first box at the top of page 57. Have them tell what shapes and colors they see. Ask if anyone can tell what shape and color comes next (blue triangle). Have them trace the triangle with a blue crayon. Ask what follows the blue triangle (red circle). Tell them to add a red circle after the blue triangle. Follow the same procedure for the remaining three boxes. For children who have difficulty, concentrate on the shape pattern separately from the color pattern.

## EXTENDED ACTIVITIES:

1. Add to the short *o* and *u* charts and stories if the children have found additional words or pictures.

2. Continue pattern practice with children who have difficulty.

## SUGGESTED READING/ STORY IDEAS:

1. Review stories which have used short *o* and short *u* words.

2. Read a story like Laura Simms' book *The Squeaky Door* which emphasize a repeated pattern in the telling of the story.

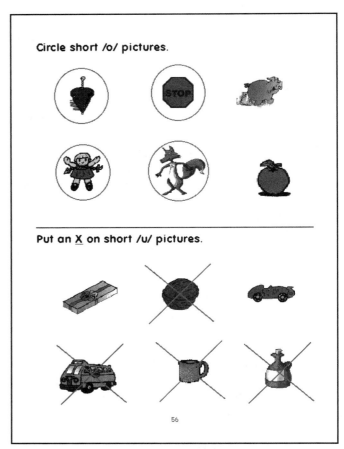

Circle short /o/ pictures.

Put an **X** on short /u/ pictures.

56

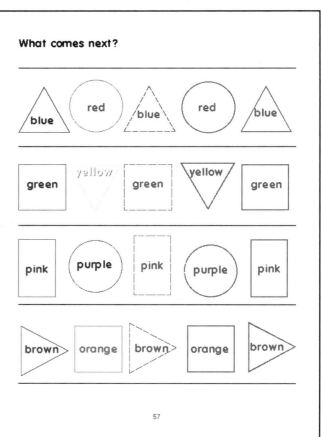

**What comes next?**

57

## OBJECTIVES:
1. To review the shape of a circle.
2. To recognize and read the word *circle*.
3. To find pictures of things that have circles.

**MATERIALS:** pencils, crayons, magazines, catalogues, paste or glue, word card for circle, drawing paper, circles of various sizes and colors cut from construction paper.

## TEACHING PAGES 58 AND 59:
1. The children have seen the word for *circle* through the year. Now they will learn to read the word and recognize that it stands for one of the shapes they have been studying. The word is not one that they can sound out with the sounds they have already learned. They have not had the *s* sound of the letter *c* or the *ir* sound. To prepare for page 58, write the word *circle* on the board. Say the word and ask the children to repeat it as you point to it. Ask them what sound they hear at the beginning of the word (*s*). Ask what letter is making that sound (*c*). Point out the *ir* sound in the middle of the word.

2. Read page 58. Ask the children to identify all the circles in the picture. How many did they find? Ask the children how many times they see the word circle on the page. Have them trace the word *circle* at the bottom of the page with their fingers and then write it with their pencils.

3. For page 59, have the children look through magazines and catalogues for pictures of things that are circular or round in shape. They may also draw pictures.

4. Additional writing practice for all shape words is found in the back of the book.

## EXTENDED ACTIVITIES:
1. If you have not done so, begin a Shape Book. Use construction paper or chart paper to make a page for each shape learned. Print the word CIRCLE in large letters at the top of the page. Color or paste pictures of objects that contain circles.

2. Give the children circles cut from construction paper in various sizes and colors. Ask the children to lay out a picture using the circles on a sheet of drawing paper. When they are satisfied with their pictures, let them glue the circles down and draw a background for the picture.

3. ENRICHMENT for more advanced students. Write the following on the board: *ir, er, ur.* Explain to the children that these three combinations

Circle

**We see circles everywhere.**

circle

58

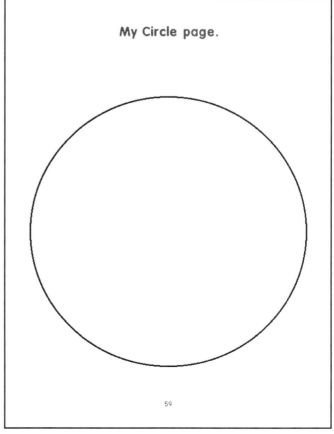

**My Circle page.**

59

have the same sound. Help them to think of things with this sound. Write the words on the board in columns under each combination.

**SUGGESTED READING/ STORY IDEAS:**

1. Ask the children to tell stories about their circle pictures.

2. If they like, help them write the stories and display them along with the pictures.

3. After they are displayed, place the stories and pictures in individual folders to form a shape story and picture book that will be added to as new shape words are introduced.

**OBJECTIVES:**

 1. To recognize the consonant digraph *ch.*

 2. To find words and pictures which begin with the soft sound of *ch.*

**MATERIALS:** pencils, crayons, Bible, magazines or newspapers, paste or glue, chart paper or tagboard, *ch* flash cards.

**TEACHING PAGES 60 AND 61:**

 1. Prepare for page 60 by asking the children to say the *ch* sound. As the children say the sound, ask them to put their hand in front of their mouths. What do they feel? In what position are their teeth? Is this a quiet sound? How is it different from *sh.* Is this a sound they make when they imitate a train? Ask the children to think of words that begin with the *ch* sound. Put those words on the board. Then have the children look at the first picture on the page (church). Ask the children to name the picture. What sound do they hear at the beginning (*ch*). What sound do they hear at the end (*ch*). Have them write *ch* on the lines under the picture. Repeat this procedure for the remaining pictures.

 2. Read a list of words like the following. Ask the children to hold up a *ch* card when they hear the sound. Examples: chipmunk, sheep, choke, shine, chunk. Have children practice the <u>sh</u> and <u>ch</u> sounds until they clearly hear and feel the difference.

 3. Page 61 is a review and reinforcement page for *ch.* It gives the children an opportunity to work with you to find pictures and words which have the *ch* sound. Talk about the work done on page 60.

 4. Have the children trace the large *Ch* on the page.

 5. Have the children look through magazines and catalogues to find pictures and words that begin with the *ch* sound. This page may be a collage of written words, drawings, cut and paste words and pictures. Help the children stress the *ch* sound when they find it. Help as needed with the writing, cutting, pasting to complete the page.

**EXTENDED ACTIVITIES:**

 1. Make an *ch* chart.

 2. Add *ch* to the alphabet Scrap Book.

 3. Talk about names and words from the Bible that have the *ch* sound: *children, child, chosen, church,* and so on. Add these to your Bible list or booklet.

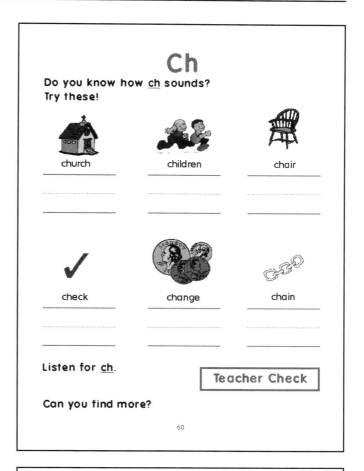

## Ch

**Do you know how <u>ch</u> sounds? Try these!**

| | | |
|---|---|---|
| church | children | chair |
| check | change | chain |

**Listen for <u>ch</u>.**

     Teacher Check

**Can you find more?**

60

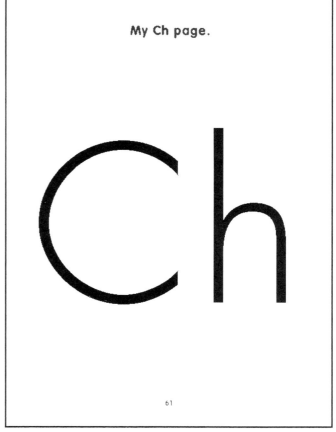

**My Ch page.**

61

**SUGGESTED READING/ STORY IDEAS:**

1. Read some of the stories in the Acts of the Apostles which tell about the difficulties the Apostles had in the early Church especially some of those which tell of Peter's miraculous escape from prison, or the conversion of Paul. Have the children act out one or two of them.

2. Read sections of the Gospels which show Jesus' love for little children (Matthew 19:4; Mark 10:14; Luke 18:16).

**OBJECTIVES:**

1. To write a story.
2. To recognize words that begin with the soft sound of *ch*.
3. To recognize the sound *d* at the end of words.
4. To recognize the sound *g* at the end of words.

**MATERIALS:** pencils and crayons, *ch* chart, pictures charts of objects that end in the _*d* sound and the _*g* sound.

**TEACHING PAGES 62 AND 63:**

1. Prepare for page 62 by dividing the children into groups. Ask the children to find as many words or objects in the room as they can that begin with the *ch* sound. Allow about five minutes. Ask the children to tell everyone the words they have found. Write the words on the board. Next, ask the children if they can group any of the words together. Begin working on ideas for a story that will use as many *ch* words as possible.

2. Work with the children to write the *ch* story. Write it on the board or on chart paper. Some children may be able to copy the story into their books. Others will need help. If the story is longer than the space in the book, have the children write the name of the story in their books and one sentence of the story. Ask them to draw a picture to accompany the story.

3. Write the letter *d* on the board. Have children take turns giving you words that begin with the letter. Tell the children that today they will be looking for this sound at the end of words. Ask them if they can think of any words that end with the *d* sound. Tell the children that they are to look at the pictures in the top section, say the names, listen carefully to the ending sound of each, and circle the letter *d* under the picture. Ask the children to say the picture names aloud.

4. Proceed in the same fashion for the _*g* ending sounds. Invite the children to try to think of more words for each.

**EXTENDED ACTIVITIES:**

1. Continue to encourage children who are able to use the alphabet letter cards to make new words. Use the _*d* and _*g* cards to make new words. Examples: wed, dog, log. Use the words in a sentence. Add to the list of words and names they can form. Help as needed.

2. Make an *ch* puppet.

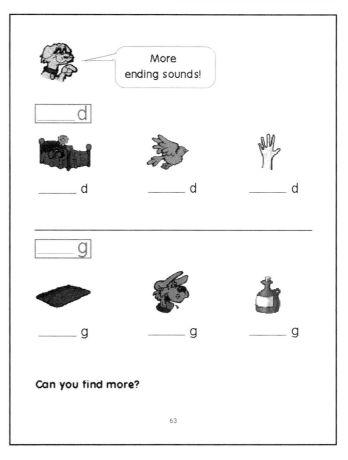

3. ENRICHMENT activity for more advanced children. Use the list of *ch* words that the children discovered for the story lesson. Ask the more advanced children to find words that have the *ch* sound at the end of a word (such, much, match). Tell them that in some words the *ch* has a hard sound like a *k* (Christ, Christian, Christopher, Christmas). Have them also try to find words or pictures of things which have the *d* or *g* sound in the middle.

**SUGGESTED READING/ STORY IDEAS:**

1. Read some of the books about *Clifford, the Big Red Dog.* Point out that *Clifford,* and *red* both end in *d* and *big* and *dog* both end in *g.* Look for other words.

2. Have the children write or tell stories about the children in their families. Illustrate and share with the class.

**OBJECTIVES:**
1. To read the number words *three* and *four*.
2. To find things that come in three's and four's.

**MATERIALS:** pencils, crayons, old magazines and catalogues, scissors, glue or paste, word cards for *three* and *four*.

**TEACHING PAGES 64 AND 65:**

1. The children have been seeing the words for the numbers *three* and *four* in many places over the last several months. On page 64, begin working with the children to sound out and read these words. Both words are unusual: *three* has the digraph *th* which the children will learn shortly and *four* contains the *or* sound. Discuss the pictures in the three section of the page. Ask the children to point to and read the word three. Have them trace it with their fingers. Finally, have them trace the word *three* on the lines. Talk about things that come in three's (triplets, wheels on a tricycle, sides of a triangle).

Introduce the four section in the same way.

2. For page 65, have the children look through magazines and catalogues for pictures of things that come in *three* and *four*. They may also draw pictures. Check to make sure that they glue the *three* things on the side of the page which says *three* and the *four* things on the *four* side.

3. Additional writing practice for all number words is found in the back of the book.

**EXTENDED ACTIVITIES:**

1. Add to the Number Book. Use construction paper or chart paper to make a page for each number learned. Print the number word in large letters at the top of the page. Color or paste pictures of objects that are usually found in three's or four's on the page.

2. Begin to work with number patterns alternating objects single and double objects (1, 2, 3, 1; 3, 4, 2, 1; and so on). Use shapes, blocks, bears, buttons, or other objects. Have the children copy your patterns and then invent their own.

**SUGGESTED READING/ STORY IDEAS:**

1. Read books such as *The Three Little Pigs*, *The Three Javelinas*, and other stories that reinforce the concept.

2. Have the children create their own Three _____, Four _____ story or poem.

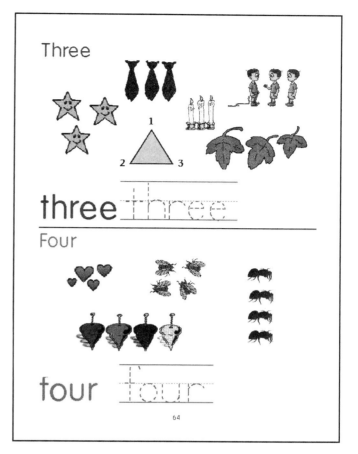

Three

three ~~three~~

Four

four ~~four~~

64

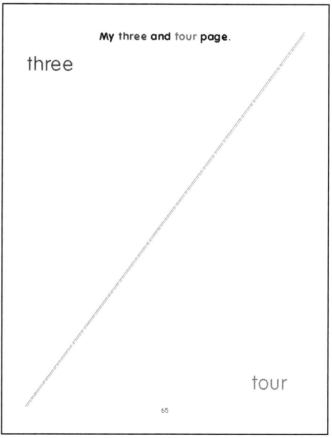

**My three and four page.**

three

four

65

**OBJECTIVES:**
1. To review long *o* and long *e* sounds.
2. To put letters in order.
3. To put pictures in order.

**MATERIALS:** pencils, long *o* and long *e* charts, stories, and flash cards, alphabet chart and cards, sequence cards.

**TEACHING PAGES 66 AND 67:**

1. Write the letters *Oo* and *Ee* on the board. Ask the children to try to remember or to find words that have the long *o* and long *e* sounds. Write the words under the appropriate letter as the children say them. Read the directions for page 66. Ask the children to say the name of the first picture (boat). Ask a child to tell what long vowel sound is heard in the word *boat*. Tell the children to write an *o* on the lines under the picture. Finish the first row with the children. Have them say the names of the remaining pictures emphasizing the vowel sound. Let them finish the page independently, if they are able.

2. Have the children take out their alphabet charts and cards. Ask them to find the cards that match the first five letters of the alphabet. Have them put the cards in order as they say the letters. Continue doing this with several other sequences of letters. Help those children who need it. When they have finished, read the direction on page 67. Ask the children to look at the four letters at the top of the first box and say them. Tell them that they will need to put the letters in order. Let them do this with their individual cards if needed. Have them write the letters in the correct order on the lines provided. Proceed to the second box in the same manner.

3. Ask the children to look at the three boxes on the bottom of the page. Have them explain what is happening in each picture. Then ask them which picture shows what happened first (glass on edge of table). Tell them to write the numeral *1* under the picture. Ask them what happened next (glass breaking). Have them write the numeral *2* under the second picture. Finally, have them tell what happened last (sweeping up the glass). Ask them to write the numeral *3* under the final picture.

**EXTENDED ACTIVITIES:**
1. Review the long vowel sounds as needed.
2. Review alphabet and picture sequence as needed.

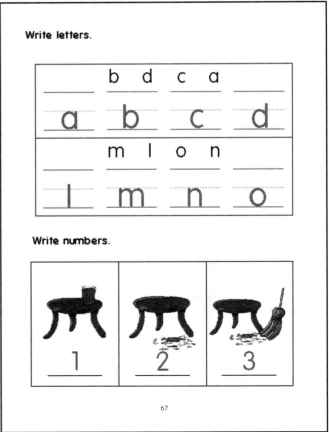

3. For more advanced students, have them give the beginning and ending sounds for each picture on page 66. Ask them to use each word in a sentence. Ask them to make letter puzzles for the other students and to create some sequence stories of their own.

**SUGGESTED READING/ STORY IDEAS:**

1. Read the book *Polar Bear, Polar Bear, What Do I Hear* (Bill Martin) and see how many long vowel words the children can find.

2. Have the children act out the story.

**OBJECTIVES:**
1. To review the shape of a square.
2. To recognize and read the word square.
3. To find pictures of things that have squares.

**MATERIALS:** pencils, crayons, magazines, catalogues, paste or glue, word card for square, drawing paper, squares and circles of various sizes and colors cut from construction paper.

**TEACHING PAGES 68 AND 69:**
1. The children have seen the word for *square* through the year. Now they will learn to read the word and recognize that it stands for one of the shapes they have been studying. The word is not one that they can sound out with the sounds they have already learned. To prepare for page 68, write the word *square* on the board. Say the word and ask the children to repeat it as you point to it. Ask them what sound they hear at the beginning of the word (*s*).

2. Read page 68. Ask the children to identify all the squares in the picture. How many did they find? Ask the children how many times they see the word *square* on the page. Have them trace the word *square* at the bottom of the page with their fingers and then write it with their pencils.

3. For page 69, have the children talk about all the things they have found that are square or have a square as part of their shape. Make a list on the board. Try to group the items. Help the children to write a story about something exciting that is square. Write it first on the board or chart paper. Have the children copy it into their books and illustrate.

4. Additional writing practice for all shape words is found in the back of the book.

**EXTENDED ACTIVITIES:**
1. Add to the Shape Book. Use construction paper or chart paper to make a page for each shape learned. Print the word SQUARE in large letters at the top of the page. Color or paste pictures of objects that contain squares.

2. Give the children circles and squares cut from construction paper in various sizes and colors. Ask the children to lay out a picture using the circles and squares on a sheet of drawing paper. When they are satisfied with their pictures, let them glue the shapes down and draw a background for the picture.

Square

square square

68

---

**My Square Story.**

**Write a story.**

| Teacher Check |

**Draw a picture.**

69

**SUGGESTED READING/ STORY IDEAS:**

1. Ask the children to tell stories about their pictures.

2. If they like, help them write the stories and display them along with the pictures.

3. After they are displayed, place the stories and pictures in individual folders for the shape story and picture book.

**OBJECTIVES:**
1. To recognize the consonant digraph *th*.
2. To find words and pictures which begin with the soft sound of *th*.

**MATERIALS:** pencils, crayons, Bible, magazines or newspapers, paste or glue, chart paper or tagboard, *th* flash cards.

**TEACHING PAGES 70 AND 71:**
1. Prepare for page 70 by asking the children to say the *th* sound. Tell them that they often hear two sounds for *th*, a soft sound as in the word *think* and a hard sound as in the word *this* or *that*. On page 70 they will look for the soft sound of *th*. As the children say the sound, ask them to put their hand in front of their mouths. What do they feel? Where are their tongues? In what position are their teeth? Is this a quiet sound? How is it different from *sh*. Ask the children to think of words that begin with the soft *th* sound. Put those words on the board. Then have the children look at the first picture on the page (three). Ask the children to name the picture. What sound do they hear at the beginning (*th*). Have them write *th* on the lines under the picture. Repeat this procedure for the remaining pictures.

2. Read a list of words like the following. Ask the children to hold up a *th* card when they hear the sound. Examples: thimble, thought, shiver, thing, cherry.

3. Page 71 is a review and reinforcement page for *th*. It gives the children an opportunity to work with you to find pictures and words which have the soft *th* sound. Talk about the work done on page 70.

4. Have the children trace the large *Th* on the page.

5. Have the children look through magazines and catalogues to find pictures and words that begin with the soft *th* sound. This page may be a collage of written words, drawings, cut and paste words and pictures. Help the children stress the soft *th* sound when they find it. Help as needed with the writing, cutting, and pasting to complete the page.

**EXTENDED ACTIVITIES:**
1. Make a soft *th* chart.
2. Add soft *th* to the alphabet scrapbook.
3. Make a *th* puppet.

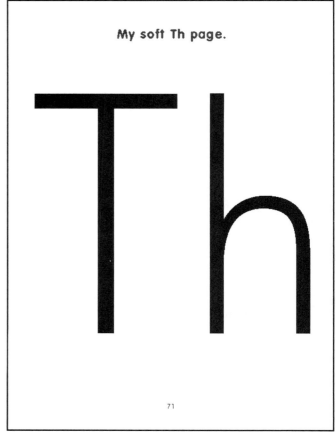

4. Talk about names and words from the Bible that have the soft *th* sound: *Thanksgiving, thanks, three, thousand, thrones,* and so on. Add these to your Bible list or booklet.

## SUGGESTED READING/ STORY IDEAS:

1. Read one or more of the Psalms that give thanks to the Lord. Talk about thanking people and thanking God for all the good done to us.

2. Have the children pick a favorite psalm. Copy it for the child, if a copier is available. Mount it and let the child decorate around it. Help the child to memorize at least one or two verses of the psalm.

**OBJECTIVES:**
1. To recognize the consonant digraph *th*.
2. To find words and pictures which begin with the hard sound of *th*.

**MATERIALS:** pencils, crayons, Bible, magazines or newspapers, paste or glue, chart paper or tagboard, *th* flash cards.

**TEACHING PAGES 72 AND 73:**
1. Prepare for page 72 by asking the children to say the hard *th* sound as in the word *the*. As the children say the sound, ask them to put their hand in front of their mouths. What do they feel? Where are their tongues? In what position are their teeth? This is not a quiet sound. Does it "tickle" their tongues? How is it different from the soft *th*? Ask the children to think of words that begin with the hard *th* sound. (this, that, these, those, them, and so on). Put those words on the board. Then have the children look at the first picture on the page (the). Ask the children to say the word. What sound do they hear at the beginning (*th*). Have them write *th* on the lines under the picture. Repeat this procedure for the remaining pictures emphasizing that the hard <u>th</u> is often found in the middle of words.

2. Read a list of words like the following. Ask the children to hold up a *th* card when they hear the hard sound. Examples: this, think, children, there, them, thing, ship.

3. Page 73 is a review and reinforcement page for hard *th*. It gives the children an opportunity to work with you to find pictures and words which have the hard *th* sound. Talk about the work done on page 72.

4. Have the children trace the large *Th* on the page.

5. Have the children look through magazines and catalogues to find pictures and words that begin with the hard *th* sound. This page may be a collage of written words, drawings, cut and paste words and pictures. Help the children stress the hard *th* sound when they find it. Help as needed with the writing, cutting, pasting to complete the page.

**EXTENDED ACTIVITIES:**
1. Make a hard *th* chart.
2. Add hard *th* to the alphabet scrapbook.
3. Talk about names and words from the Bible that have the hard *th* sound: *Thee, Thou, Thy, Thine, mother, Father, brother*, and so on. Add these to your Bible list or booklet.

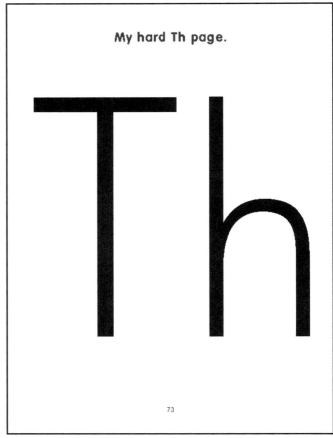

**SUGGESTED READING/ STORY IDEAS:**

1. Read the Lord's Prayer again to the children. Emphasize words with digraphs (some will depend on the translation): (hard) Father, Thy, this, (soft) earth.

2. Have the children tell or write stories about their Mother and Father. Write for the children in the storybook section at the back of their books.

**OBJECTIVES:**

1. To write a story.
2. To recognize words that begin with both soft and hard sounds of *th*.
3. To recognize the sound *k* at the end of words.
4. To recognize the sound *l* at the end of words.

**MATERIALS:** pencils and crayons, *th* charts, pictures charts of objects that end in the ___*k* sound and the ___*l* sound.

**TEACHING PAGES 74 AND 75:**

1. Prepare for page 74 by dividing the children into groups. Ask the children to find as many words or objects in the room as they can that begin with the *th* sound. Give some groups the soft *th* sound and others, the hard sound. Allow about five minutes. Ask the children to tell everyone the words they have found. Write the words on the board. Next ask the children if they can group any of the words together. Begin working on ideas for a story that will use as many *th* words as possible.

2. Work with the children to write the *th* story. Write it on the board or on chart paper. Some children may be able to copy the story into their books. Others will need help. If the story is longer than the space in the book, have the children write the name of the story in their books and one sentence of the story. Ask them to draw a picture to accompany the story.

3. Write the letter *k* on the board. Have children take turns giving you words that begin with the letter. Tell the children that today they will be looking for this sound at the end of words. Ask them if they can think of any words that end with the *k* sound. Tell the children that they are to look at the pictures in the top section, say the names, listen carefully to the ending sound of each, and circle the letter *k* under the picture. Ask the children to say the picture names aloud.

4. Proceed in the same fashion for the ___*l* ending sounds. Invite the children to try to think of more words for each.

**EXTENDED ACTIVITIES:**

1. Continue to encourage children who are able to use the alphabet letter cards to make new words. Use the ___*k* and ___*l* cards to make new words. Examples: ball, doll, pink. Use the words in a sentence. Add to the list of words and names they can form. Help as needed.

2. ENRICHMENT activity for more advanced children. Use the list of *th* words that the children

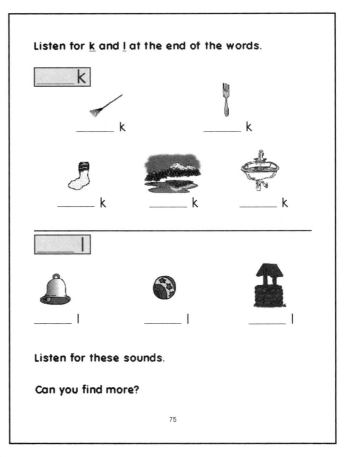

212

discovered for the story lesson. Ask the more advanced children to find words that have the *th* sound in the middle of the word (mother, brother, other). Have them also try to find words or pictures of things which have the *k* or *l* sound in the middle.

**SUGGESTED READING/ STORY IDEAS:**
1. Choose rhyming words that end in *k* and *l*.

Examples:
    hark, lark, bark, dark, mark, Mark, park,

    lake, bake, cake, make, take, wake, fake, Jake, quake, rake, sake,

    ball, tall, fall, hall, mall, call, Paul, wall,

    bell, fell, hell, sell, tell, well, yell.

Choose a set of words and create a nonsense rhyme with the children. For more advanced children, give each a set of words and let them create their own rhymes. Help with the writing.
2. Recite the nonsense rhymes for another class, or a family member.

**OBJECTIVES:**
1. To read the number words *five* and *six*.
2. To find things that come in five's and six's.

**MATERIALS:** pencils, crayons, old magazines and catalogues, scissors, glue or paste, word cards for *five* and *six*.

**TEACHING PAGES 76 AND 77:**
1. The children have been seeing the words for the numbers *five* and *six* in many places over the last several months. On page 76, begin working with the children to sound out and read these words. Both words can be easily sounded out. Discuss the pictures in the *five* section of the page. Ask the children to point to and read the word *five*. Have them trace it with their fingers. Finally, have them trace the word *five* on the lines. Talk about things that come in five's (quintuplets). Introduce the *six* section in the same way.

2. For page 77, have the children look through magazines and catalogues for pictures of things that come in five and six. They may also draw pictures. Check to make sure that they glue the *five* things on the side of the page which says *five* and the *six* things on the *six* side.

3. Additional writing practice for all number words is found in the back of the book.

**EXTENDED ACTIVITIES:**
1. Add to the Number Book. Use construction paper or chart paper to make a page for each number learned. Print the number word in large letters at the top of the page. Color or paste pictures of objects that are usually found in five's or six's on the page.

2. Begin to work with number patterns alternating objects (5, 4, 3, 2; 4, 3, 4, 5; and so on). Use shapes, blocks, bears, buttons, or other objects. Have the children copy your patterns and then invent their own.

**SUGGESTED READING/ STORY IDEAS:**
1. Read poems from A. A. Milne's book *Now We Are Six*.
2. Most of the children will be either five or six years old. Have them write a story entitled: *What It's Like to be Five (Six)*.

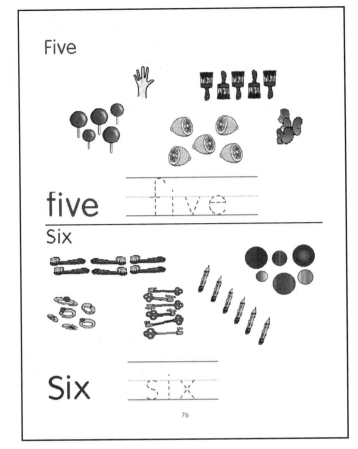

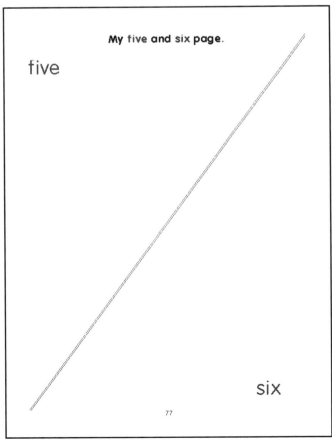

**OBJECTIVES:**

1. To review long *i*, long *u*, and long *a* sounds.
2. To read number words *one, two, three, four, five,* and *six.*
3. To recognize the numerals that go with the number words.

**MATERIALS:** pencils, long *i* , long *a* and long *u* charts, stories, and flash cards, number word cards, objects in groups up to six.

**TEACHING PAGES 78 AND 79:**

1. Write the letters *Ii, Uu,* and *Aa* on the board. Ask the children to try to remember or to find words that have the long *Ii,* long *Uu,* and long *Aa* sounds. Write the words under the appropriate letter as the children say them. Read the directions for page 78. Ask the children to say the name of the first picture (pie). Ask a child to tell what long vowel sound is heard in the word pie. Tell the children to write an *i* on the lines under the picture. Finish the first row with the children. Have them say the names of the remaining pictures emphasizing the vowel sound. Let them finish the page independently, if they are able.

2. Prepare for page 79 by reviewing the number words *one* through *six.* Put the numerals 1 through 6 on the board. Have each child come forward, take a word card, and match it to the correct numeral on the board. Go to page 79 and read the direction. Ask the children to put their fingers on the numeral *1.* Have them trace the line between the numeral and the number word one. Finish the top box in the same manner. If children are able, let them finish the bottom box independently. Check and review any that are missed.

**EXTENDED ACTIVITIES:**

1. Review the long vowel sounds as needed.
2. Give the children individual sets of number word cards. Ask one child to put out a set of objects (any number 1 through 6). Ask another child to find the correct number word to describe how many are in the set. Children who know their words can work with those who do not.
3. For more advanced students, have them give the beginning and ending sounds for each picture on page 78. Ask them to use each word in a sentence.

**Write /i/ or /u/ or /a/.**

| pie | rake | bike |
|-----|------|------|
| i | a | i |

| music | tie | cake |
|-------|-----|------|
| U | i | a |

| kite | suit | five |
|------|------|------|
| i | U | i |

78

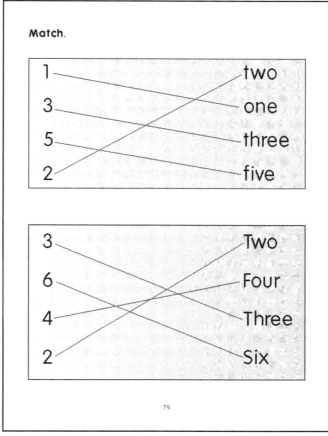

**Match.**

| 1 | two |
| 3 | one |
| 5 | three |
| 2 | five |

| 3 | Two |
| 6 | Four |
| 4 | Three |
| 2 | Six |

79

**SUGGESTED READING/ STORY IDEAS:**

1. Reread the story of *The Lion and the Mouse* from Aesop's Fables. Ask the children what other stories they know in which a lion or lions play a part (Examples: Daniel in the Lion's Den; The Lion King; Aslan, the lion in the *Chronicles of Narnia*). Are these lion's good, bad, frightening?

2. Have the children create their own lion character and make up a story or stories about it. If children do many different stories, combine them into a book entitled *Lion Stories*.

## OBJECTIVES:
1. To review the shape of a triangle.
2. To recognize and read the word triangle.
3. To find pictures of things that have triangles.

**MATERIALS:** pencils, crayons, magazines, catalogues, paste or glue, word card for square, drawing paper, triangles, squares and circles of various sizes and colors cut from construction paper.

## TEACHING PAGES 80 AND 81:
1. The children have seen the word for *triangle* through the year. Now they will learn to read the word and recognize that it stands for one of the shapes they have been studying. The word is not one that they can sound out with the sounds they have already learned. To prepare for page 80, write the word *triangle* on the board. Say the word and ask the children to repeat it as you point to it. Ask them what sound they hear at the beginning of the word (*f*).

2. Read page 80. Ask the children to identify all the triangles in the picture. How many did they find? Ask the children how many times they see the word *triangle* on the page. Have them trace the word *triangle* at the bottom of the page with their fingers and then write it with their pencils.

3. For page 81, have the children look through magazines and catalogues for pictures of things that are triangular in shape. They may also draw pictures. Make a list on the board of things they found. Try to group the items. Help the children to write a story about something exciting that is triangle. Write it first on the board or chart paper. Have the children copy it into their books and illustrate.

4. Additional writing practice for all shape words is found in the back of the book.

## EXTENDED ACTIVITIES:
1. Add to the Shape Book. Use construction paper or chart paper to make a page for each shape learned. Print the word TRIANGLE in large letters at the top of the page. Color or paste pictures of objects that contain triangles.

2. Give the children triangles, circles, and squares cut from construction paper in various sizes and colors. Ask the children to lay out a picture using the triangles, circles, and squares on a sheet of drawing paper. When they are satisfied with their pictures, let them glue the shapes down and draw a background for the picture.

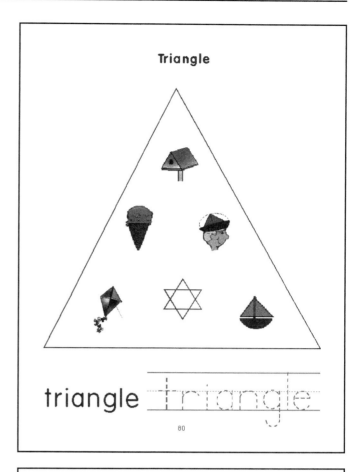

**Triangle**

triangle

80

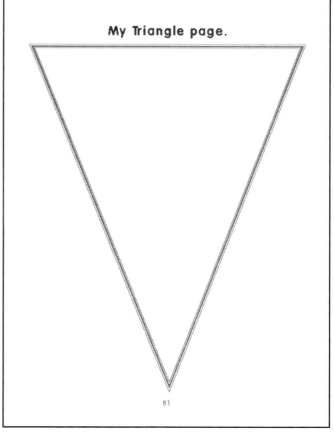

**My Triangle page.**

81

**SUGGESTED READING/ STORY IDEAS:**

1. Ask the children to tell stories about their pictures.

2. If they like, help them write the stories and display them along with the pictures.

3. After they are displayed, place the stories and pictures in individual folders for the shape story picture book.

**OBJECTIVES:**
   1. To recognize the consonant digraph *wh*.
   2. To find words and pictures which begin with the sound of *wh*.

**MATERIALS:** pencils, crayons, Bible, magazines or newspapers, paste or glue, chart paper or tagboard, *wh* flash cards.

**TEACHING PAGES 82 AND 83:**
   1. Prepare for page 82 by asking the children to say the *wh* sound as in the word *where*. As the children say the sound, ask them to put their hand in front of their mouths. What do they feel? In what position are their lips? This is a quiet sound. How is it different from the *w* sound? Ask the children to think of words that begin with the *wh* sound. Put those words on the board. Then have the children look at the first picture on the page (whale). Ask the children to say the word. What sound do they hear at the beginning (*wh*). Have them write *wh* on the lines under the picture. Repeat this procedure for the remaining picture.
   2. Read a list of words like the following. Ask the children to hold up a *wh* card when they hear the sound. Examples: what, why, this, children, when, them, whistle, shop, white.
   3. Page 83 is a review and reinforcement page for *wh*. It gives the children an opportunity to work with you to find pictures and words which have the hard *wh* sound. Talk about the work done on page 82.
   4. Have the children trace the large *Wh* on the page.
   5. Have the children look through magazines and catalogues to find pictures and words that begin with the *wh* sound. This page may be a collage of written words, drawings, cut and paste words and pictures. Help the children stress the *wh* sound when they find it. Help as needed with the writing, cutting, pasting to complete the page.

**EXTENDED ACTIVITIES:**
   1. Make a *wh* chart.
   2. Add *wh* to the alphabet scrapbook.
   3. Talk about names and words from the Bible that have the hard *wh* sound: *whale, wheat,* and so on. Add these to your Bible list or booklet.

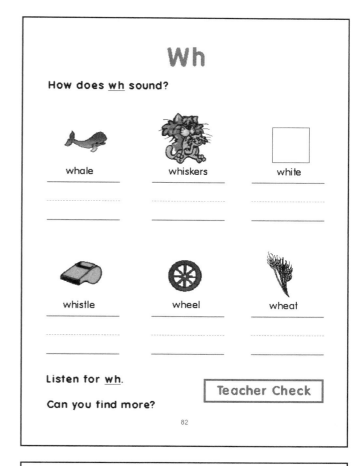

**SUGGESTED READING/ STORY IDEAS:**

1. Recall the story of Jonah and the whale. Have the children tell it if possible.

2. Many references to wheat can be found in the Bible (Example: Matthew 13). Choose one of the parables and read or tell the story to the children. Have them retell or act it out when you have finished explaining it.

**OBJECTIVES:**

1. To write a story.
2. To recognize *wh* words.
3. To recognize the sound *m* at the end of words.
4. To recognize the sound *p* at the end of words.

**MATERIALS:** pencils and crayons, *wh* chart, pictures of objects that end in the _*m* sound and the _*p* sound.

**TEACHING PAGES 84 AND 85:**

1. Prepare for page 84 by dividing the children into groups. Ask the children to find as many words or objects in the room as they can that begin with the *wh* sound. Allow about five minutes. Ask the children to tell everyone the words they have found. Write the words on the board. Next ask the children if they can group any of the words together. Begin working on ideas for a story that will use as many *wh* words as possible.

2. Work with the children to write the *wh* story. Write it on the board or on chart paper. Some children may be able to copy the story into their books. Others will need help. If the story is longer than the space in the book, have the children write the name of the story in their books and one sentence of the story. Ask them to draw a picture to accompany the story.

3. Write the letter *m* on the board. Have the children take turns giving you words that begin with the letter. Tell the children that today you will begin looking at the sounds found at the end of words. Ask them if they can think of any words that end with the _*m* sound. Tell the children that they are to look at the pictures in the top section, say the names, listen carefully to the ending sound of each, and circle the letter *m* under the picture. Ask the children to say the picture names aloud.

4. Proceed in the same fashion for the _*p* ending sounds. Invite the children to try to think of more words for each.

**EXTENDED ACTIVITIES:**

1. Continue to encourage children who are able to use the alphabet letter cards to make new words. Use the _*m* and _*p* cards to make new words. Examples: cup, up, ham, am. Use the words in a sentence. Add to the list of words and names they can form. Help as needed.

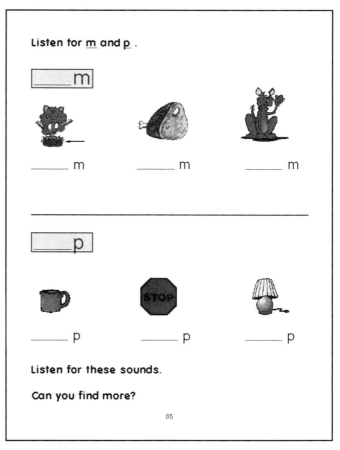

2. Make an *Wh* puppet.

3. ENRICHMENT activity for more advanced children. Use the list of _*m* and _*p* words that the children discovered for the story lesson. Have them also try to find words or pictures of things which have these sounds in the middle.

## SUGGESTED READING/ STORY IDEAS:

1. Read books such as *Hop on Pop*, or *Green Eggs and Ham* and emphasize the words that end in _*m* and _*p*.

2. Choose several groups of rhyming words that end in _*m* and _*p*.

Examples:

    hop, pop, mop, drop, top, stop, shop, flop,

    dip, hip, lip, nip, pip, quip, rip, sip, tip, whip, ship, chip, yip, zip,

    am, dam, ham, lam(b), Pam, ram, Sam, tam, yam.

Choose a set of words and create a nonsense rhyme with the children. For more advanced children, give each a set of words and let them create their own rhymes. Help with the writing.

**OBJECTIVES:**

1. To read the number words *seven* and *eight*.
2. To find things that come in seven's and eight's.

**MATERIALS:** pencils, crayons, old magazines and catalogues, scissors, glue or paste, word cards for *seven* and *eight* as well as those for the numbers one through six.

**TEACHING PAGES 86 AND 87:**

1. The children have been seeing the words for the numbers *seven* and *eight* in many places over the last several months. On page 86, begin working with the children to sound out and read these words. The word *eight* is unusual because it uses the letter group *eigh* for the *a* sound. Discuss the pictures in the *seven* section of the page. Ask the children to point to and read the word *seven*. Have them trace it with their fingers. Finally, have them trace the word *seven* on the lines. Introduce the eight section in the same way.

2. For page 87, have the children look through magazines and catalogues for pictures of things that come in seven and eight. They may also draw pictures. Check to make sure that they glue the *seven* things on the side of the page which says *seven* and the *eight* things on the *eight* side.

3. Additional writing practice for all number words is found in the back of the book.

**EXTENDED ACTIVITIES:**

1. Add to the Number Book. Use construction paper or chart paper to make a page for each number learned. Print the number word in large letters at the top of the page. Color or paste pictures of objects that are usually found in seven's or eight's on the page.

2. Continue to work with number patterns alternating sets of objects (a group of 4, a group of 2, a group of 7; groups of 3, 5, 1). Use shapes, blocks, bears, buttons, or other objects. Have the children copy your patterns and then invent their own.

**SUGGESTED READING/ STORY IDEAS:**

1. Read the story of the multiplication of the seven loaves (Mark 8:1-9). Have the children act out the story.

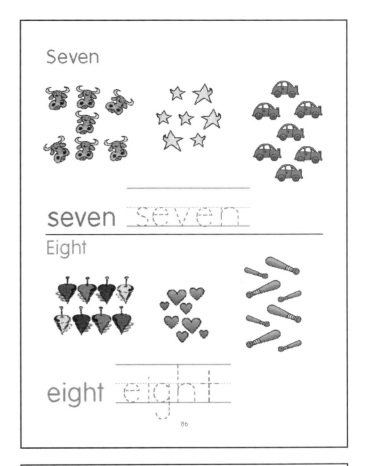

Seven

seven seven

Eight

eight eight

86

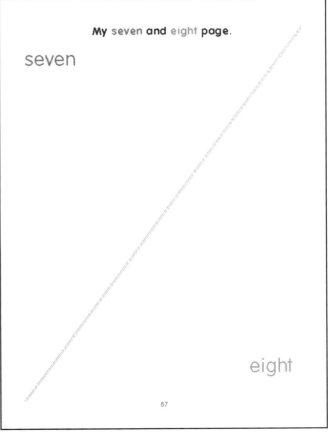

My seven and eight page.

seven

eight

87

2. Read what Jesus had to say about forgiveness (Matthew 18:21-22). Talk about what it means to forgive someone else.

3. Review the Creation story and have the children illustrate each of the seven days.

**OBJECTIVES:**
1. To recognize the sound of *ch*.
2. To recognize the sound of soft *th*.
3. To listen carefully.
4. To follow a direction given only once.
5. To recognize and apply position and direction words.

**MATERIALS:** pencils, crayons, *ch* and *th* charts, objects to reinforce position and direction words.

**TEACHING PAGES 88 AND 89:**
1. Divide the class into two groups. Ask one group to find as many *ch* pictures and words as they can in five minutes. Ask the other to find soft *th* pictures and words in the same time. Allow each group time to present their findings to the class. Ask the class to add more to each group if they are able.

2. Ask the children to look at the box at the top of page 88. Read the directions. Have the children say the names of all the pictures in the *ch* box. Ask them to circle all of the pictures that begin with the *ch* sound. Give help if needed. Check together. Note any children with difficulty distinguishing between the *ch* and *sh* sounds.

3. Proceed with the *th* box in the same manner.

4. To prepare for page 89, ask a child to come forward and pick an object from the table. Ask the children in the class to take turns giving directions to the child such as: Put the object *under* a desk. Put the object *inside* the box of folders. Put the object *on top* of the teacher's desk. Rotate after three or four questions giving another child a turn. Lead the children to include a variety of position and direction words.

5. Read the direction on page 89. Tell the children that you will read a sentence once. They are to do what the sentence asks. Tell them that they will do three things in each box. This is more complicated than earlier listening activities. Read slowly and clearly. Allow enough time for each direction before moving on to the next direction. If the children do not have a very long attention span, divide this activity into sections with a break either in between boxes or by giving just one direction for each box and returning to it another time to give a second and third direction. Have them put their fingers on the box marked.

1. Read: Draw a red square on top of the table. Wait for the children to finish. Continue in the first box.

Read: Draw a blue ball under the table.
Wait and then continue.

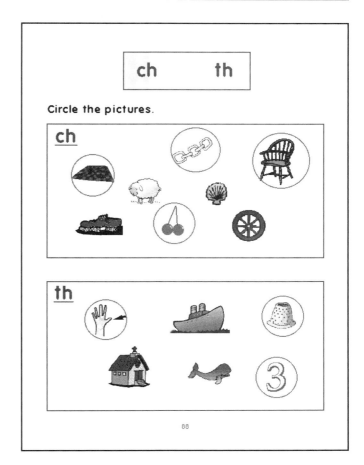

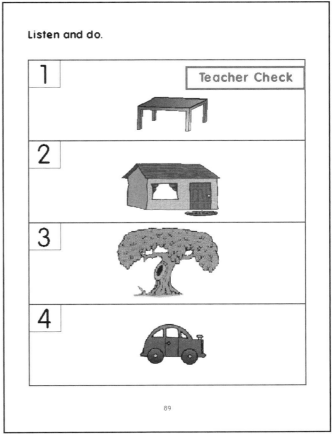

Read:　Draw a green triangle next to the table.
Wait and then continue.
2. Read:　Draw a yellow sun above the house.
Read:　Draw a street in front of the house.
Read:　Draw a brown rectangle on the roof of the house.
3. Read:　Draw a red bird in the tree.
Read:　Draw an orange box under the tree.
Read:　Draw three yellow flowers on the tree.
4. Read:　Draw one person next to the car.
Read:　Draw a purple oval on top of the car.
Read:　Draw a blue bird flying over the car.
Check the activity and clarify any problems.

## EXTENDED ACTIVITIES:

1. Review *ch* and *th* sounds as needed.

2. Work individually with children having problems with listening or with position and direction words. Have more advanced students create activities similar to those on page 89. Have them draw a simple object on a large sheet of drawing paper. Then, have them give directions to another student similar to those used above.

## SUGGESTED READING/ STORY IDEAS:

1. Have the children give story ideas for the completed boxes on page 89.

2. Select individual children to tell the stories.

## OBJECTIVES:

1. To review the shape of a rectangle.
2. To recognize and read the word *rectangle*.
3. To find pictures of things that have rectangles.

**MATERIALS:** pencils, crayons, magazines, catalogues, paste or glue, word card for rectangle, drawing paper, rectangles, triangles, squares, and circles of various sizes and colors cut from construction paper.

## TEACHING PAGES 90 AND 91:

1. The children have seen the word for *rectangle* through the year. Now they will learn to read the word and recognize that it stands for one of the shapes they have been studying. The word is not one that they can sound out with the sounds they have already learned. To prepare for page 90, write the word *rectangle* on the board. Say the word and ask the children to repeat it as you point to it. Ask them what sound they hear at the beginning of the word (*r*).

2. Read page 90. Ask the children to identify all the rectangles in the picture. How many did they find? Ask the children how many times they see the word rectangle on the page. Have them trace the word rectangle at the bottom of the page with their fingers and then write it with their pencils. This is a very long word. Urge the children to take their time. Check letter formation.

3. For page 91, have the children look through magazines and catalogues for pictures of rectangular shapes. They may also draw pictures. Make a list on the board of the pictures they found. Try to group the items. Help the children to write a story about something exciting that is rectangle. Write it first on the board or chart paper. Have the children copy it into their books and illustrate.

4. Additional writing practice for all shape words is found in the back of the book.

## EXTENDED ACTIVITIES:

1. Add to the Shape Book. Use construction paper or chart paper to make a page for each shape learned. Print the word RECTANGLE in large letters at the top of the page. Color or paste pictures of objects that contain rectangles.

2. Give the children rectangles, triangles, circles, and squares cut from construction paper in various sizes and colors. Ask the children to lay out a picture on a sheet of drawing paper using all of the shapes. When they are satisfied with their

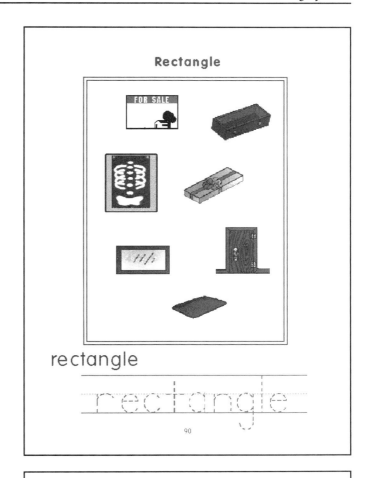

pictures, let them glue the shapes down and draw a background for the picture.

**SUGGESTED READING/ STORY IDEAS:**
1. Ask the children to tell stories about their pictures.
2. If they like, help them write the stories and display them along with the pictures.
3. After they are displayed, place the stories and pictures in individual folders for the shape picture book.

## OBJECTIVES:
1. To put numerals in order: 1 through 10.
2. To put letters in order.
3. To recognize color words.
4. To follow directions.

**MATERIALS:** pencils, crayons, alphabet cards and chart, number cards and chart.

## TEACHING PAGES 92 AND 93:
1. Prepare for page 92 by asking 10 children to come forward. Give each child a numeral card (1 through 10) with a large numeral on it. Have the children line up "out of order" in the front of the room. Ask the other children to help you arrange the 10 children in the correct order. (If you have a small class, line the numeral cards up on a table, desk, carpet, or other area where they can be spread out and rearranged. Have the children help you order them.) Repeat the activity if any children are having difficulty.

2. Read the direction at the top of page 92. Tell the children that they are to write in the numeral that is missing in each line. Do the first line together and allow the children to finish independently if they are able.

3. Read the direction at the bottom of page 92. Review the alphabet beforehand as needed. Ask the children to do the line on their own. They may use an alphabet chart.

4. Review the color words for page 93. Tell the children that they will need to color the large egg following the directions at the bottom of the page. Ask them to find a section of the egg with the numeral *1* in it. When they have done that, ask them to look at the bottom of the page and see what color the numeral *1* section should be. Have the children take their crayon and very carefully color the numeral *1* section. Repeat this process for each of the other numerals.

## EXTENDED ACTIVITIES:
1. Review number and letter sequence as needed.
2. Do more "color by number" exercises.

## SUGGESTED READING/ STORY IDEAS:
1. Ask the children what they think might be inside of the egg on page 93. List all of their ideas on the board. Using the ideas create a story or poem about the egg.
2. Read the story *The Mysterious Tadpole* by Stephen Kellogg. Ask the children what they think will happen with the egg at the end of the book.

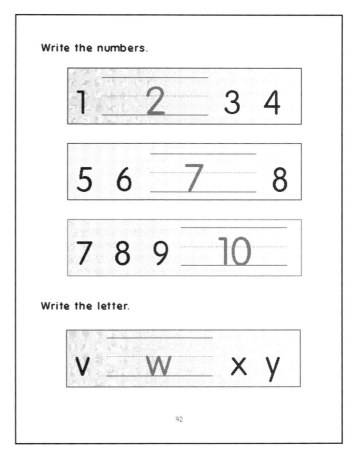

**Write the numbers.**

1  2  3  4

5  6  7  8

7  8  9  10

**Write the letter.**

v  w  x  y

92

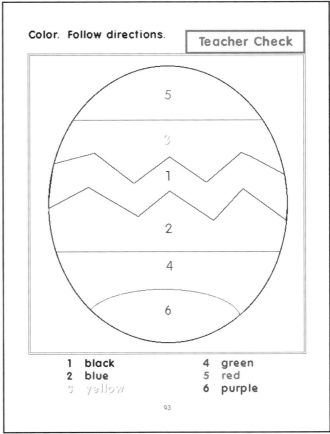

**Color. Follow directions.**          Teacher Check

| 1 | black | 4 | green |
| 2 | blue | 5 | red |
| 3 | yellow | 6 | purple |

93

229

## OBJECTIVES:
1. To recognize the sound of *sh*.
2. To recognize the sound of *wh*.
3. To recognize the sound *n* at the end of words.
4. To recognize the sound *r* at the end of words.

**MATERIALS:** pencils, crayons, *sh* and *wh* charts.

## TEACHING PAGES 94 AND 95:
1. Divide the class into two groups. Ask one group to find as many *sh* pictures and words as they can in five minutes. Ask the other to find *wh* pictures and words in the same time. Allow each group time to present their findings to the class. Ask the class to add more to each group if they are able.

2. Ask the children to look at the box at the top of page 94. Read the directions. Have the children say the names of all the pictures in the *sh* box. Ask them to circle all of the pictures that begin with the *sh* sound. Give help if needed. Check together. Note any children with difficulty distinguishing between the *sh* and *ch* sounds.

3. Proceed with the *wh* box in the same manner.

4. Write the letter *n* on the board. Have children take turns giving you words that begin with the letter. Tell the children that today you will begin looking at the sounds found at the end of words. Ask them if they can think of any words that end with the *n* sound. Tell the children that they are to look at the pictures in the top section, say the names, listen carefully to the ending sound of each, and circle the letter *n* under the picture. Ask the children to say the picture names aloud.

5. Proceed in the same fashion for the __*r* ending sounds. Invite the children to try to think of more words for each.

## EXTENDED ACTIVITIES:
1. Continue to encourage children who are able to use the alphabet letter cards to make new words. Use the __*n* and __*r* cards to make new words. Examples: can, man, car. Use the words in a sentence. Add to the list of words and names they can form. Help as needed.

2. Review *sh* and *wh* as needed.

3. ENRICHMENT activity for more advanced children. Have them find words that end in *sh*. Write them out and ask them to use the words in sentences. Use the list of __*n* and __*r* words that the children discovered for the story lesson. Have

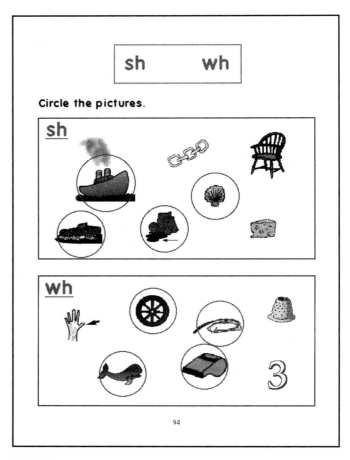

sh     wh

**Circle the pictures.**

sh

wh

94

**Listen for n and r at the end of words.**

n

_____ n        _____ n        _____ n

r

_____ r        _____ r        _____ r

**Listen for these sounds.**

**Can you find more?**

95

them also try to find words or pictures of things which have these sounds in the middle.

**SUGGESTED READING/ STORY IDEAS:**
1.  Choose several groups of rhyming words that end in _n_ and _r_.
Examples:
    can, ban, Dan, fan, Jan, man, Nan, pan, ran, tan, van,

    Ben, den, hen, Jen, Ken, men, pen, ten, when,

    car, far, jar, tar,

    chair, fair, dare, hair, lair, mare, pair, rare, stare.

Choose a set of words and create a nonsense rhyme with the children. For more advanced children, give each a set of words and let them create their own rhymes. Help with the writing.
2.  Have the children illustrate the rhymes.

## OBJECTIVES:
1. To read the number words *nine* and *ten*.
2. To find things that come in nine's and ten's.

**MATERIALS:** pencils, crayons, old magazines and catalogues, scissors, glue or paste, word cards for *nine* and *ten* as well as those for the numbers one through eight.

## TEACHING PAGES 96 AND 97:
1. The children have been seeing the words for the numbers *nine* and *ten* in many places over the last several months. On page 96, begin working with the children to sound out and read these words. Discuss the pictures in the *nine* section of the page. Ask the children to point to and read the word *nine*. Have them trace it with their fingers. Finally, have them trace the word nine on the lines. Introduce the *ten* section in the same way.

2. For page 97, have the children look through magazines and catalogues for pictures of things that come in *nine* and *ten*. They may also draw pictures. Check to make sure that they glue the *nine* things on the side of the page which says *nine* and the *ten* things on the *ten* side.

3. Additional writing practice for all number words is found in the back of the book.

## EXTENDED ACTIVITIES:
1. Add to the Number Book. Use construction paper or chart paper to make a page for each number learned. Print the number word in large letters at the top of the page. Color or paste pictures of objects that are usually found in nine's or ten's on the page.

2. Continue to work with number patterns alternating sets of objects (a group of 6, a group of 3, a group of 5; groups of 9, 2, 4). Use shapes, blocks, bears, buttons, or other objects. Have the children copy your patterns and then invent their own.

## SUGGESTED READING/ STORY IDEAS:
1. Read the story of the ten lepers that Jesus cured (Luke 17:12-19). Talk with the children about being thankful for the gifts God gives us.

2. Have the children illustrate and/or act out the story.

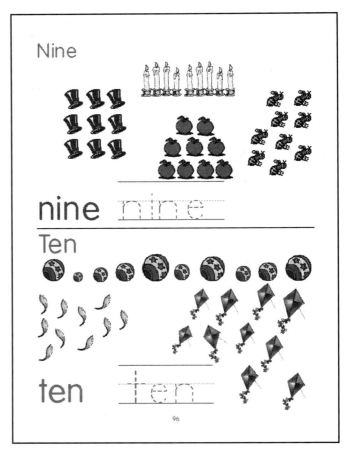

Nine

nine

Ten

ten

96

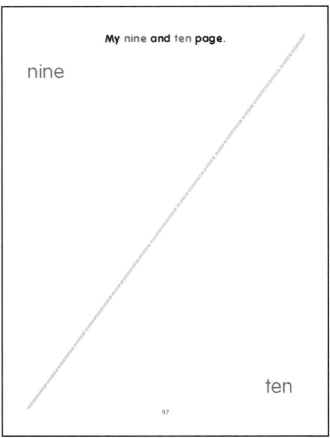

My nine and ten page.

nine

ten

97

## OBJECTIVES:

1. To review the ending sounds: *m, p, n,* and *r.*
2. To review the alphabet.
3. To put letters in order.

**MATERIALS:** pencils, crayons, charts for ending sounds *m, p, n,* and *r,* alphabet chart.

## TEACHING PAGES 98 AND 99:

1. Prepare for page 98 by putting _*m,* _*p,* _*n,* and _*r* on the board. Ask the children to help you find words for things that end in these letters. Each time they say a word and you write the word, emphasize the ending sound. Go to page 98. Ask the children to look at the box at the top of the page and say the ending sounds they see in the box. Read the direction. Ask the children to point to the picture in the first box (swim). Have them say the name emphasizing the ending sound (*m*). Ask them to put their finger on the letter that shows the ending sound. Tell them to draw a circle around the letter. Check. Note any child who checks the beginning rather than the ending sound and redo the box. Complete the page in the same manner. If any children are able, allow them to complete the page on their own.

2. On page 99 ask the children to say or sing the alphabet. On the bottom of the page, have them put the letters in order and write them on the line.

## EXTENDED ACTIVITIES:

1. Begin a card file or book of pictures and words for the ending sounds learned thus far.

2. Ask the children to give the initial consonants for each picture on page 98.

3. If you have games which drill the initial sounds of words, use them as well to reinforce ending sounds.

## SUGGESTED READING/ STORY IDEAS:

1. Take the time to go back over the stories and poems written by the children. Let them share one or two of their favorites.

2. For the daily story time, invite the children to bring a favorite book from home to share with the class. Assign one child for each day until each has had an opportunity to share.

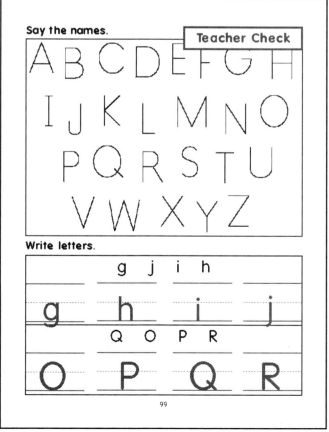

**OBJECTIVES:**
1. To review the shape of an *oval*.
2. To recognize and read the word *oval*.
3. To find pictures of things that have oval.

**MATERIALS:** pencils, crayons, magazines, catalogues, paste or glue, word card for *oval*, drawing paper, oval, rectangles, triangles, squares, and circles of various sizes and colors cut from construction paper.

**TEACHING PAGES 100 AND 101:**
1. The children have seen the word for *oval* through the year. Now they will learn to read the word and recognize that it stands for one of the shapes they have been studying. The word is not one that they can sound out with the sounds they have already learned. To prepare for page 100, write the word *oval* on the board. Say the word and ask the children to repeat it as you point to it. Ask them what sound they hear at the beginning of the word (long *o*).

2. Read page 100. Ask the children to identify all the ovals in the picture. How many did they find? Ask the children how many times they see the word *oval* on the page. Have them trace the word *oval* at the bottom of the page with their fingers and then write it with their pencils.

3. For page 101, have the children look through magazines and catalogues for pictures of things that have the oval shape. Make a list on the board of the pictures they found. Try to group the items. Help the children to write a story about something exciting that is oval. Write it first on the board or chart paper. Have the children copy it into their books and illustrate.

4. Additional writing practice for all shape words is found in the back of the book.

**EXTENDED ACTIVITIES:**
1. Add to the Shape Book. Use construction paper or chart paper to make a page for each shape learned. Print the word OVAL in large letters at the top of the page. Color or paste pictures of objects that contain ovals.

2. Give the children ovals, rectangles, triangles, circles, and squares cut from construction paper in various sizes and colors. Ask the children to lay out a picture on a sheet of drawing paper using all of the shapes. When they are satisfied with their pictures, let them glue the shapes down and draw a background for the picture.

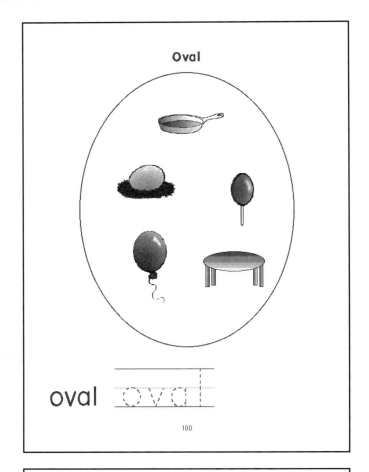

Oval

oval

100

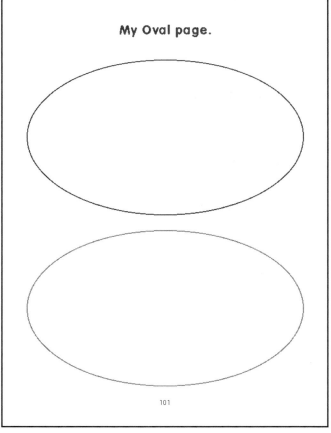

**My Oval page.**

101

**SUGGESTED READING/ STORY IDEAS:**

1. Ask the children to tell stories about their pictures.

2. If they like, help them write the stories and display them along with the pictures.

3. After they are displayed, place the stories and pictures in individual folders for the shape picture book.

**OBJECTIVES:**
1. To review the sound of short *a*.
2. To read short *a* words and sentences.
3. To write sentences.

**MATERIALS:** pencils, short a chart and stories, chart paper.

**TEACHING PAGES 102 AND 103:**
1. Review briefly short *a* words and pictures that the children know. Read the directions on page 102. Tell the children that they are to circle only those pictures which have a short *a* sound. Ask the children to name each of the pictures emphasizing the vowel sound. Have them circle the short *a* pictures. Check and note those children who need extra help.

2. Read the direction at the bottom of page 102. Tell the children that they are to write the letter *a* under each picture that has a short *a* sound. Ask the children to say the names of the three pictures. Have them write the letter *a* under each picture as they sound it out.

3. Prepare for page 103 by reviewing short a words from the list of words which the children have been forming with their letter cards throughout the year. Some of the children may already be reading books. Others may be very close to this stage. Some will not be ready for several months.

This page gives the children a wider range of words and word formation. It also introduces more sentences for the children to read and encourages them to write sentences. Essentially this is what they have been learning throughout the year with all of the story writing activities. Now the focus is on learning how to put sentences together with words they can read.

Read what Jip is saying at the top of the page. Look at the word box. Ask the children if they see any words that they can sound out. Let them pick any words from the box and try them. When they pick a word, ask them to use it in a sentence. After they have finished all the words they can read, help them with any remaining words, showing them how to sound them out.

Proceed to the sentences at the bottom. Ask if anyone can read the first sentence. Help if no one can. Have the children find the words in the sentence in the word box above and circle them.

Circle the short /a/ pictures.

Write short /a/.

102

I can read new words, too.
How about you?

**Teacher Check**

Try these.

| Short /a/ words | | | | |
|---|---|---|---|---|
| an | at | add | and | am |
| tan | rat | bad | band | Sam |
| man | mat | sad | sand | ram |
| ran | sat | mad | | |
| Nan | bat | Dad | | |
| Dan | | | | |
| Ann | | | | |

**Ann and Dan ran.**

**A tan rat ran.**

**Make your own sentence.**

103

236

Continue in the same manner with the second sentence.

Talk about sentences. Tell the children that a sentence tells about someone or something and what happens to that person or thing. Demonstrate this with the two sentences they have read. Finally, ask the children if they can use the words in the box to make their own sentence at the bottom of the page.

**EXTENDED ACTIVITIES:**

1. Review short *a* words and pictures with those who need help.

2. Practice making sentences by giving the children each a set of word cards based on words they already know and can sound out. Make sure they have cards which include both nouns and verbs. Have them make sentences by arranging the words into complete thoughts. If some children are having difficulty, have a child who can do this work with them. If any child is not ready for this activity, come back to it in a few weeks or months.

**SUGGESTED READING/ STORY IDEAS:**

1. Go back to books like *The Cat in the Hat*, or *Green Eggs and Ham*. Look for the short vowel sounds. Point out individual sentences.

2. If some are able, have them read the books with you.

**OBJECTIVES:**
1. To recognize the sound *s* at the end of words.
2. To recognize the sound *t* at the end of words.
3. To recognize number words: two–ten.

**MATERIALS:** pencils, crayons, chart paper, number chart with both numerals and words, number word cards.

**TEACHING PAGES 104 AND 105:**
1. Write the letter *s* on the board. Have the children take turns giving you words that begin with the letter. Tell the children that today you will begin looking at the sounds found at the end of words. Ask them if they can think of any words that end with the *s* sound. Read the direction on page 104. Tell the children that they are to look at the pictures in the top section, say the names, listen carefully to the ending sound of each, and circle the letter *s* under the picture. Ask the children to say the picture names aloud.
2. Proceed in the same fashion for the _*t* ending sounds. Invite the children to try to think of more words for each.
3. To prepare for page 105, write the numerals *1* through *10* across the board. Spread the number word cards at random on a table or desk. Ask individual children to come forward, take a word card and hold it under the matching numeral. Repeat as needed until all number words have been reviewed. Read the direction on page 105. Ask the children to read the first number word (ten). Have them trace the *10* on the lines under the word. Continue in this fashion with the first two rows. If children are able, let them do the third row on their own. Check.

**EXTENDED ACTIVITIES:**
1. Continue to encourage children who are able to use the alphabet letter cards to make new words. Use the _*s* and _*t* cards to make new words. Examples: cat, mat, caps, cups. Use the words in a sentence. Add to the list of words and names they can form. Help as needed.
2. Review number words as needed. If children need additional practice, make or purchase a number word "Bingo" or "Lotto" game.
3. ENRICHMENT activity for more advanced children. Use the list of _*s* and _*t* words that the children discovered for the story lesson. Have them try to find words or pictures of things which have these sounds in the middle.

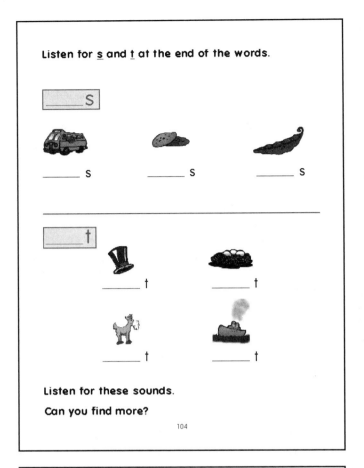

Listen for <u>s</u> and <u>t</u> at the end of the words.

Listen for these sounds.

Can you find more?

104

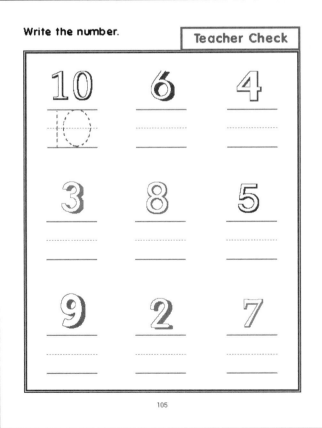

Write the number.　　　Teacher Check

105

**SUGGESTED READING/ STORY IDEAS:**
   1.  Choose several groups of rhyming words that end in __*s* and __*t*.
Examples:

   cat, bat, fat, mat, gnat, pat, rat, tat, vat, sat, hat,

   bet, debt, get, jet, met, net, pet, set, vet, wet, yet,

   bit, fit, hit, kit, lit, mitt, knit, pit, quit, sit, wit,

   class, glass, mass, sass, lass, bass, grass, pass.

Choose a set of words and create a nonsense rhyme with the children.  For more advanced children, give each a set of words and let them create their own rhymes. Help with the writing.
   2.  Have the children illustrate the rhymes.

## OBJECTIVES:

1. To read the direction words *up* and *down*.
2. To find things that go *up* and *down*.

**MATERIALS:** pencils, crayons, old magazines and catalogues, scissors, glue or paste, word cards for *up* and *down*.

## TEACHING PAGES 106 AND 107:

1. The children have been hearing the words *up* and *down* in many activities over the last several months. On page 106, begin working with the children to sound out and read these words. The word *down* is unusual because it uses the *ow* sound which they have not had. Ask the children to name places where they go *up* and *down*. Have them talk about things that go *up* and *down* (make a list). Discuss the pictures in the *up* section of the page. Ask the children to point to and read the word *up*. Have them trace it with their fingers. Finally, have them trace the word *up* on the lines. Introduce the *down* section in the same way.

2. For page 107, have the children look through magazines and catalogues for pictures of things that go *up* and *down*. They may also draw pictures. Check to make sure that they glue the things that go *up* on the side of the page which says *up* and the *down* things on the *down* side.

3. Additional writing practice for all number words is found in the back of the book.

## EXTENDED ACTIVITIES:

1. Begin a Position/Direction Book. Use construction paper or chart paper to make a page for each concept learned. Print the word in large letters at the top of the page. Color or paste pictures of objects that go *up* on one page and *down* on another page.

2. Ask the children about their experience with elevators, escalators, and stairs. How is each the same? How is each different? How do they know which direction an elevator is going?

3. Look at the list of things that go *up* and *down*. Ask the children if any of the things on that list only go *down* (examples: rain, snow). Ask them what things on the list can be tossed in the air (ball, rock, small object). What happens to them? Do they stay in the air? Do they come down? Why?

4. If you have the space or have a park nearby, make a kite with the children and fly it.

106

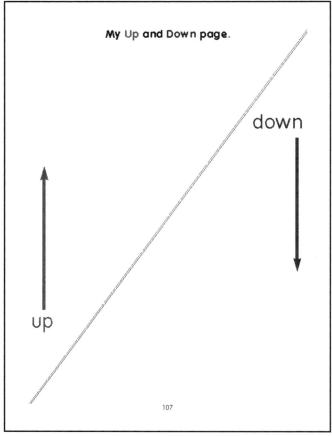

My Up and Down page.

107

**SUGGESTED READING/ STORY IDEAS:**

1. Read stories or rhymes which use *up* and *down*. Examples: *Eentsy, Weentsy Spider; Jack and Jill; Hickory, Dickory, Dock; Jack and the Beanstalk.*

2. Read the end of Mark's Gospel to the children. Talk about Jesus being taken up into heaven to return to His Father.

## OBJECTIVES:

1. To read short *e* words and sentences.
2. To write sentences.
3. To recognize the sound *v* at the end of words.
4. To recognize the sound *w* at the end of words.
5. To recognize the sound *x* at the end of words.
6. To recognize the sound *z* at the end of words.

**MATERIALS:** pencils, crayons, short *e* pictures and word charts or stories, objects or pictures of things with the ending sounds: *v, w, x, z.*

## TEACHING PAGES 108 AND 109:

1. Prepare for page 108 by reviewing short *e* words from the list of words which the children have been forming with their letter cards throughout the year. Some of the children may already be reading books. Others may be very close to this stage. Some will not be ready for several months.

This page gives the children a wider range of words and word formation. It also introduces more sentences for the children to read and encourages them to write sentences. Essentially this is what they have been learning throughout the year with all of the story writing activities. Now the focus is on learning how to put sentences together with words they can read.

Read what Sam is saying at the top of the page. Look at the word box. Ask the children if they see any words that they can sound out. Let them pick any words from the box and try them. When they pick a word, ask them to use it in a sentence.

After they have finished all the words they can read, help them with any remaining words, showing them how to sound them out.

Proceed to the sentences at the bottom. Ask if anyone can read the first sentence. Help if no one can. Have the children find the words in the sentence in the word box above and circle them. Continue in the same manner with the second sentence.

Talk about sentences. Tell the children that a sentence tells about someone or something and what happens to that person or thing.

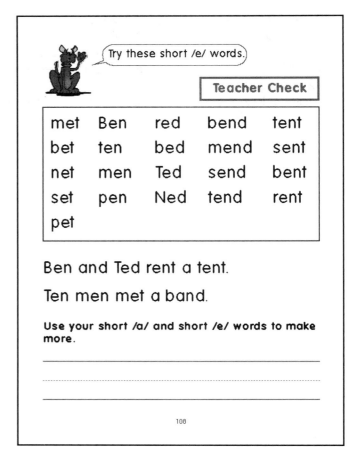

Try these short /e/ words.

**Teacher Check**

| met | Ben | red | bend | tent |
| bet | ten | bed | mend | sent |
| net | men | Ted | send | bent |
| set | pen | Ned | tend | rent |
| pet | | | | |

Ben and Ted rent a tent.

Ten men met a band.

**Use your short /a/ and short /e/ words to make more.**

108

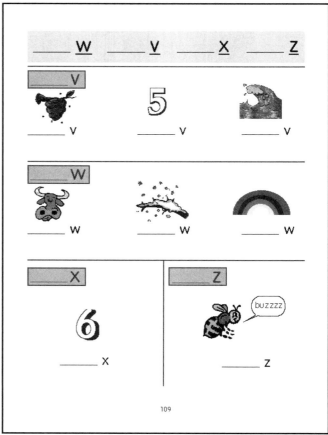

___ W ___ V ___ X ___ Z

V
___ v      ___ v      ___ v

W
___ w      ___ w      ___ w

X                    Z
___ x                ___ z

buzzzz

109

Demonstrate this with the two sentences they have read. Finally, ask the children if they can use the words in the box to make their own sentence at the bottom of the page.

2. Write the letter *v* on the board. Have children take turns giving you words that begin with the letter. Tell the children that today you will begin looking at the sounds found at the end of words. Ask them if they can think of any words that end with the *v* sound. On page 109 tell the children that they are to look at the pictures in the top box, say the names, listen carefully to the ending sound of each, and circle the letter *v* under the picture. Ask the children to say the picture names aloud.

3. Proceed in the same fashion for the __*w*, __*x*, and __*z* ending sounds. Invite the children to try to think of more words for each.

**EXTENDED ACTIVITIES:**

1. Review short *e* words and pictures with those who need help.

2. Practice making sentences by giving the children each a set of word cards based on words they already know and can sound out. Make sure they have cards which include both nouns and verbs. Have them make sentences by arranging the words into complete thoughts. If some children are having difficulty, have a child who can do this work with them. If any child is not ready for this activity, come back to it in a few weeks or months.

3. Continue to encourage children who are able to use the alphabet letter cards to make new words. Use the __*v*, __*w*, __*x* and __*z* cards to make new words. Use the words in a sentence. Add to the list of words and names they can form. Help as needed.

4. ENRICHMENT activity for more advanced children. Use the list of __*v*, __*w*, __*x*, and __*z* words that the children discovered for the story lesson. Have them try to find words or pictures of things which have these sounds in the middle.

**SUGGESTED READING/ STORY IDEAS:**

1. Read the stories of *The Little Red Hen*, and *Henny Penny*. See how many short *e* words can be found.

2. Act out either story with illustrations for background.

**OBJECTIVES:**

1. To recognize basic shapes.
2. To recognize and read the shape words: *rectangle, oval, square, circle, triangle.*
3. To review the initial consonant digraphs: *ch, wh, th,* and *sh.*

**MATERIALS:** pencils, word cards for shape names, basic shape blocks, charts for *ch, th, wh,* and *sh.*

**TEACHING PAGES 110 AND 111:**

1. Review the names of the basic shapes with the children before beginning page 110. Use word cards, charts, stories, and shape pictures. Say the name of a shape and have a child pick the word card and a shape block that match what you have said. Continue until all the shapes have been covered.

2. Read the direction on page 110. Have the children put their fingers on the square. Ask them to find the word square in the second column. Draw a line from the shape to the word. Check. Complete the activity in the same manner.

3. At the bottom of the page, ask the children to circle the word in each row that matches.

4. Review *ch, th, wh,* and *sh* by writing each digraph on the board. Ask the children to think of things which begin with these sounds. Review the charts for each sound. Ask the children to look at the box on the top of page 111. Have them say each sound as they point to it. Read the direction for the first activity. Have the children say the name of each picture. Tell them that they will circle the letters that they hear at the beginning of each. If children are able, let them work independently. If they are not, do each box together checking as you go.

5. Read the direction at the bottom of the page. Tell the children to use the letters in the box at the top of the page to find the beginning sound for each picture. Have them write the beginning sound on the line below each picture.

**EXTENDED ACTIVITIES:**

1. Review basic shapes and words as needed. Have the children work in groups with shape blocks to create a group picture. Ask each group to explain their picture to the others.

2. If you have geoboards available, give the children rubber bands, yarn, or string and have them make simple shapes or simple pictures on the geoboard. When they have finished, have them select the word cards for all the shapes used.

3. Review individual digraphs as needed.

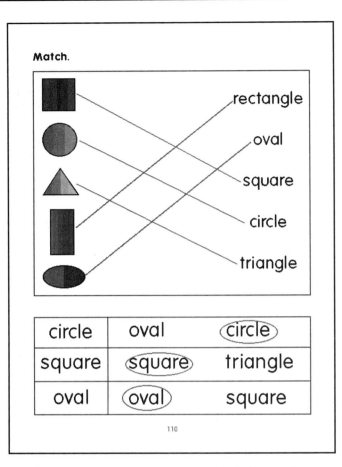

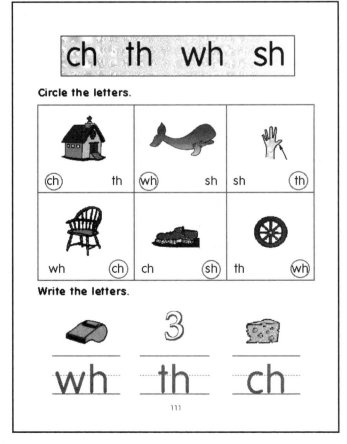

**SUGGESTED READING/ STORY IDEAS:**

1. Read the story of the *Three Bears*. Note any words that begin with digraphs (three, chairs). Note size comparison words.

2. Have the children draw their favorite part. Act out the story using the pictures.

**OBJECTIVES:**

1. To review initial consonants: *b, z, d, y, f, x, g, w.*
2. To follow directions.
3. To listen carefully.
4. To order events in a sequence.

**MATERIALS:** pencils, sequence cards, charts and stories for *b, z, d, y, f, x, g,* and *w.*

**TEACHING PAGES 112 AND 113:**

1. Give each child one of the following letters: *b, d, f, g, w, y,* or *z.* Ask anyone who has the same letter to work together. Have the children try to find things or find people whose names begin with their letter. Limit the search to the room and what can be seen from the window. Have the children report their findings to the class. If nothing can be found, allow the children time to think of other items to present that are not in the room.

2. Read the direction on page 112. Ask the children what picture they see in the first box (ball). Ask them to look at the two letters in the box (*b, l*) and tell which sound they hear at the beginning of the word (*b*). Complete the first row in the same manner. If children are able allow them to complete the page independently after making sure they know what each picture is.

3. Prepare for page 113 by putting sets of sequence cards out on desk or table. Mix the cards and sequences so that the children will have to select the cards and the sequence that go together. Ask individual children to come up and select three cards that go together. Have them put the cards in order. Then ask them to tell what they did and why. Put a simple sequence on the board such as a carved pumpkin, a child picking the pumpkin, and a pumpkin on the vine. Draw a line under each picture and ask the children to look carefully and tell which picture came first (pumpkin on the vine). Ask a child to come forward and write the numeral *1* under the picture of the pumpkin on the vine. Ask another child to tell what came next (picking the pumpkin). Have that child come forward and write the numeral *2* under the second picture. Finish the last picture in the same manner.

4. Go to page 113. Tell the children that in each row they must look at the pictures and decide what happen first, second, and last. Do the first set together. Ask the children which picture shows what happened first (clean child with ice cream cone). Have them write a *1* under the picture. Ask what happened next (child with dripping cone). Have them write a *2* under the picture. Ask them

Circle the letters.

112

Write the numbers.

113

what happened last (sticky child).   Have them write a *3* under the picture. Do the next two sets in the same manner.   If some children are able to finish the page independently, allow them to do so.

**EXTENDED ACTIVITIES:**
   1.  Review any initial sounds that are a problem.
   2.  Ask the children to give the ending sound for the pictures on page 112.
   3.  Review sequence with children continuing to have problems.

**SUGGESTED READING/ STORY IDEAS:**
   1.  Have the children make up stories for each of the sets of pictures on page 113.  Give details: names of children, flavor of ice cream, type of cookies, who will live in the house, and so on.
   2.  Have the children make up sentences for the pictures on page 112.

## OBJECTIVES:

1. To read the direction words *high* and *low*.
2. To find things that are *high* and *low*.
3. To understand the concepts of *high* and *low*

**MATERIALS:** pencils, crayons, old magazines and catalogues, scissors, glue or paste, word cards for *high* and *low*.

## TEACHING PAGES 114 AND 115:

1. The children have been hearing the words *high* and *low* in many activities over the last several months. On page 114, begin working with the children to sound out and read these words. The word *high* is unusual because it uses the *igh* sound for long *i* and *low* has the *ow* sound for long *o*. Ask the children to name places where they go *up* and *down*. Have them talk about things that are *high* and *low* (make a list). Discuss the pictures in the high section of the page. Ask the children to point to and read the word *high*. Have them trace it with their fingers. Finally, have them trace the word *high* on the lines. Introduce the *low* section in the same way.

2. For page 115, have the children look through magazines and catalogues for pictures of things that go *high* and *low*. They may also draw pictures. Check to make sure that they glue the things that go *high* on the side of the page which says *high* and the *low* things on the *low* side.

3. Additional writing practice for all number words is found in the back of the book.

## EXTENDED ACTIVITIES:

1. Add to the Position/Direction Book. Use construction paper or chart paper to make a page for each concept learned. Print the word in large letters at the top of the page. Color or paste pictures of objects that are *high* on one page and *low* on another page.

2. Ask the children about their experience with being in a high place. Where was it? Was it fun or was it a little scary?

3. Go on a walk outside with the children. Take a note pad along and record all of the things they see high above them (sun, airplanes, birds, sky, clouds, tall trees, and so on). What things do they see that are lower than their knees (ground, valley, ditch, flowers, pets, insects, and so on).

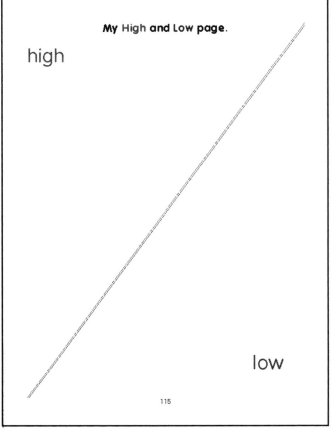

4. Experiment with song as well. Sing a high pitch and have the children copy it. Sing a low pitch and have them copy it. Fill glasses or glass bottles with different levels of water and strike gently with a spoon. What is high (more water or less)? What is low?

**SUGGESTED READING/ STORY IDEAS:**

1. Write a story about the things the children saw on their walk.

2. Get library books on airplanes, hot air balloons, and other things that fly.

## OBJECTIVES:
1. To recognize and read short *i* words.
2. To review the short sound of *a, i,* and *e*.
3. To review final sounds: *ck, g, l,* and *k*.

**MATERIALS:** pencils, crayons, short *i* charts and stories, pictures and objects that end in *ck, g, l,* and *k*.

## TEACHING PAGES 116 AND 117:
1. Prepare for page 116 by reviewing short *i* words from the list of words which the children have been forming with their letter cards throughout the year. Some of the children may already be reading books. Others may be very close to this stage. Some will not be ready for several months. This page gives the children a wider range of words and word formation. It also introduces more sentences for the children to read and encourages them to write sentences. Essentially this is what they have been learning throughout the year with all of the story writing activities. Now the focus is on learning how to put sentences together with words they can read. Look at the word box. Ask the children if they see any words that they can sound out. Let them pick any words from the box and try them. When they pick a word, ask them to use it in a sentence. After they have finished all the words they can read, help them with any remaining words, showing them how to sound them out. At the bottom of the page, ask the children to say the name for each picture. Ask them to tell you which vowel sound they hear in each one. Have them write the letter for the short vowel sound on the lines under each picture.

2. After reviewing the ending sounds needed for page 117 (*ck, g, l,* and *k*), read the directions. Have the children name the first two pictures (duck, ball). Ask which picture ends with the *ck* sound (duck). Have the children circle the picture of the duck. Complete the others in the same manner. Let children work independently if they are able.
Check.

## EXTENDED ACTIVITIES:
1. Use the short *i* words to make sentences. Mix them with the short *a* and *e* words already learned.
2. Review initial consonants as needed.
3. Ask the children to give you the ending sound for the pictures on page 117.

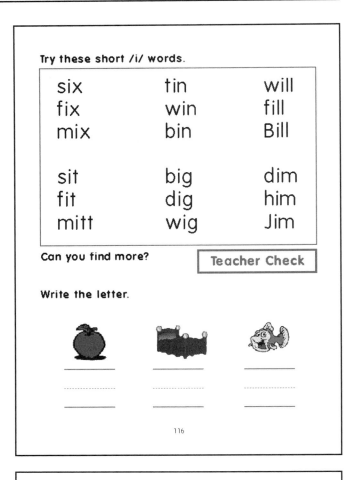

Try these short /i/ words.

| six | tin | will |
| fix | win | fill |
| mix | bin | Bill |
| | | |
| sit | big | dim |
| fit | dig | him |
| mitt | wig | Jim |

**Can you find more?**     **Teacher Check**

**Write the letter.**

116

**Circle the picture.**

| \_\_\_ck | | |
| \_\_\_g | | |
| \_\_\_l | | |
| \_\_\_k | | |

117

**SUGGESTED READING/ STORY IDEAS:**

1. Read some *Winnie the Pooh* stories (see: A. A. Milne, the *House at Pooh Corner* and *Winnie the Pooh*). Note the short *i* names: *Winnie, Piglet, Tigger.*

2. Have the children talk about their favorite characters.

**OBJECTIVES:**
1. To listen carefully.
2. To follow a direction given only once.
3. To recognize parts of the body.
4. To review colors.
5. To review the words *up, down, high,* and *low.*

**MATERIALS:** pencils, crayons, pictures and objects to review up, down, high, and low.

**TEACHING PAGES 118 AND 119:**
1. Ask the children to look at the outline drawing on page 118. Tell them that you will give them directions on what to add to the outline. Remind them that you will read the direction only once so they must listen carefully. Read the following directions slowly and clearly. Make sure they have their crayons out and ready.
*Read:*
Take your brown crayon. (Pause so that they can find crayon.) Color the hair on top of the child's head.

Take a blue crayon. (Pause.) Draw two eyes on the child's face.

Take a green crayon. (Pause.) Draw grass under the child's feet.

Take a red crayon. (Pause.) Draw a mouth on the child's face.

Take a yellow crayon. (Pause.) Color the T-shirt on the child.

Take a blue crayon. (Pause.) Color the jeans on the child.

Take a purple crayon. (Pause.) Draw a purple balloon up over the child's head.

Take a orange crayon. (Pause.) Draw an orange ball on the ground next to the　　　　　child's foot. (Accept either foot.)

Take a black crayon. (Pause.) Draw a black bird sitting on the child's shoulder. (Accept either shoulder.)

Check the picture noting any errors in color, position, or parts of the body.

**Listen and do.**

118

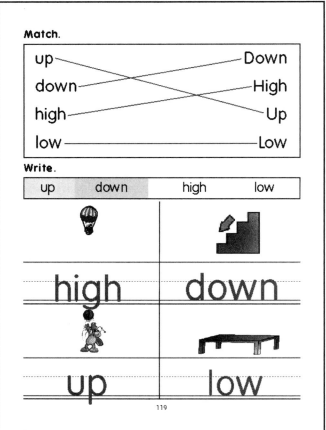

**Match.**

up ——— Down
down ——— High
high ——— Up
low ——— Low

**Write.**

| up | down | high | low |

high　　down

up　　low

119

2. Review the concepts of up, down, high, and low, by playing a game of "Simon Says". Ask the children to reach up to touch something, to stoop down low, to stretch for the clouds high in the sky, and so on. Review the words by having one child hold a word card and asking the other children to show what direction they must move.

3. Read the direction on the top of page 119. Tell the children they are to say and then match to words in the first column to the words in the second column. Ask the children to point to the word *up* in the first column. Have them find the word *Up* in the second column. Tell them to draw a line from up to Up. Finish the box in the same manner. Read the direction at the middle of the page. Ask the children to read the words in the long box. Tell them to look at the pictures in the four boxes. Ask them to look at the first picture and tell you which of the four words best tells what is happening in the box (high). Have them write the word *high* on the lines under the picture. Finish the other three boxes in the same manner.

**EXTENDED ACTIVITIES:**

1. Have the children look at the picture on page 118. What parts of the child can still be added (nose, eyebrows, ears, fingers, and so on). Have them add these to the picture and finish the picture adding as many other things as they wish.

2. If any children had difficulty identifying different parts of the body, work with them.

3. Review the words for *up*, *down*, *high*, and *low* as needed.

**SUGGESTED READING/ STORY IDEAS:**

1. Have the children create a story or poem about the child in the picture on page 118. Include details: name, age, family, pets, house, and so on.

2. Share the stories with the class.

## OBJECTIVES:

1. To review number words one through nine.
2. To match number words, numerals, and sets.
3. To review long *e* and long *a* sounds.

**MATERIALS:** pencils, crayons, manipulatives for sets, number word cards, charts and stories for long *e* and *a*.

## TEACHING PAGES 120 AND 121:

1. Write the numerals *1–10* on the board. Place the number word cards and sets of objects (1–10) on a table. Point to a numeral on the board. Ask a child to come forward and select the word card that matches the numeral. Ask a second child to come forward and point to the set of objects that shows how many are in the set that matches your numeral and the card. Example: Point to the numeral *5*. Have a child come and select the *five* card. Have the second child select the set with 5 objects in it. When this is completed, return the number card to the table and go on to another numeral. Go back to any number words or sets that caused difficulty.

2. Read the direction on page 120. Tell the children that they are to match the numeral to the set and then match the set to the number word. Ask them to find the numeral *1*. Have them trace the line from the *1* to the set of one dot. Then have them find the number word for *1* and trace the line from the set to the word. Complete this box together.

3. Read the direction at the middle of the page. Ask the children to read the first number word. (They may use a number chart if they need to.) Have the children write the numeral for the word on the line next to the word. Check numeral formation.

4. Review both long *e* and long *a* sounds with the children. Ask the children to look at the top box on page 121. Tell them that they will be looking for pictures with the long vowel sound of *e*. Have the children say the name of each picture emphasizing the vowel sounds. Tell them to circle all those pictures in which *e* says its own name. Check. Complete the long *a* box in a similar manner.

## EXTENDED ACTIVITIES:

1. Review number words one through ten as needed.

2. If children need more practice matching numeral to set to number word, have them work in two's with three sets of cards: one with the

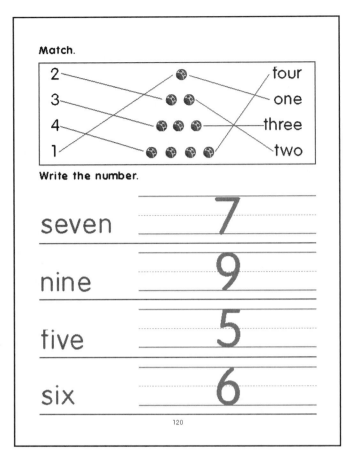

Match.

Write the number.

| seven | 7 |
| nine | 9 |
| five | 5 |
| six | 6 |

120

Circle long /e/ pictures.

Circle long /a/ pictures.

121

numerals *1–10,* one with number words *one* through *ten,* and one showing sets of objects for each number word.

3. Review long *e* and *a* as needed.

**SUGGESTED READING/ STORY IDEAS:**

1. Read the story of the first Easter in the Bible (Luke 24: 1-12; Matthew 28: 1-10; Mark 16: 1 -12; John 20:1-21). Talk about the different reactions to Jesus after He rose from the dead.

2. Illustrate or act out one of these accounts.

**OBJECTIVES:**
1. To read the position words *in* and *inside*.
2. To read the position words *out* and *outside*.
3. To find things that go *in* and *out*.

**MATERIALS:** pencils, crayons, old magazines and catalogues, scissors, glue or paste, word cards for *in, inside, out,* and *outside*, objects and containers that can be used to demonstrate *inside, outside, in* and *out*.

**TEACHING PAGES 122 AND 123:**
1. The children have been hearing the words *in* and *out* in many activities over the last several months. On page 122, begin working with the children to sound out and read these words. Ask the children to name times where they go *in* and *out*. Have them talk about things that go *in* and *out* (make a list). Discuss the pictures in the *in* section of the page. Ask the children to point to and read the word *in*. Have them trace it with their fingers. Finally, have them trace the word *in* on the lines. Introduce the *out* section in the same way.
2. Once someone or something has gone in or come out, we talk about them as being inside or outside. Use containers and objects to demonstrate inside a box or outside a jar. Go back to page 122 and discuss the *inside* and *outside* sections. Find the words and trace as above.
3. For page 123, have the children look through magazines and catalogues for pictures of things that go *in* and *out*. They may also draw pictures. Check to make sure that they glue the things that go *in* on the side of the page which says *in* and the *out* things on the *out* side. Additional writing practice for all number words is found in the back of the book.

**EXTENDED ACTIVITIES:**
1. Add to the Position/Direction Book. Use construction paper or chart paper to make a page for each concept learned. Print the word in large letters at the top of the page. Color or paste pictures of objects that go *in* on one page and *out* on another page.
2. Add pages for *inside* and *outside* as well.
3. Look at the list of things that go in and out. What kinds of places are there? (Doors, houses, stores, church, the shower, the bathtub, and so on.)

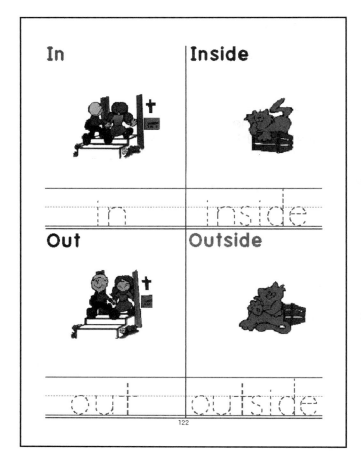

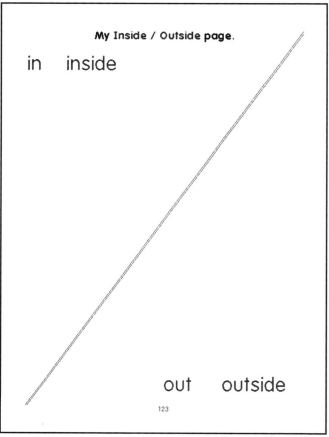

My Inside / Outside page.

in    inside

out    outside

123

256

4. Make a collage of things that can be found inside the home or classroom. Contrast it with a collage of things which are found outside the house or school.

5. Ask the children what happens when you turn something inside out. Demonstrate.

**SUGGESTED READING/ STORY IDEAS:**

1. Reread the book *Inside, Outside, Upside Down.* If you have a large box available, experiment with it.

2. Divide the class in two groups. Ask the first group to write a story about a child who can only live inside the house and can never go out. Ask the second group to write a story about a child who lives only outside and has no house. Have an aide help to write the stories as the children create them.

**OBJECTIVES:**
1. To recognize and read short *o* words.
2. To review initial consonants: *h, v, j, t, k, s, l, r, d.*

**MATERIALS:** pencils, crayons, short *o* charts and stories, pictures and charts for initial consonants: *h, v, j, t, k, s, l, r, d.*

**TEACHING PAGES 124 AND 125:**
1. Prepare for page 124 by reviewing short *o* words from the list of words which the children have been forming with their letter cards throughout the year. Some of the children may already be reading books. Others may be very close to this stage. Some will not be ready for several months. This page gives the children a wider range of words and word formation. Read what Sam is saying at the top of the page. Look at the word box. Ask the children if they see any words that they can sound out. Let them pick any words from the box and try them. When they pick a word, ask them to use it in a sentence. After they have finished all the words they can read, help them with any remaining words, showing them how to sound them out.

2. Give each child one of the following letters: *h, d, v, j, t, k, l,* or *r.* Ask anyone who has the same letter to work together. Have the children try to find things or people whose names begin with their letter. Limit the search to the room and what can be seen from the window. Have the children report their findings to the class. If nothing can be found, allow the children to think of other items to present that are not in the room.

3. Read the directions on page 125. Ask the children what picture they see in the first box (hand). Ask them to look at the two letters in the box (*h, d*) and tell which sound they hear at the beginning of the word (*h*). Complete the first row in the same manner. If children are able allow them to complete the page independently after making sure they know what each picture is.

**EXTENDED ACTIVITIES:**
1. Use the short *o* words to make sentences. Mix them with the short *a, i,* and *e* words already learned.
2. Review initial consonants as needed.

Can you say them?

| God | got | pop |
| rod | hot | hop |
| pod | not | top |
| sod | pot | mop |
| cob | fox | lock |
| Bob | box | clock |

Listen.

Can you find more?

124

Circle the letters.

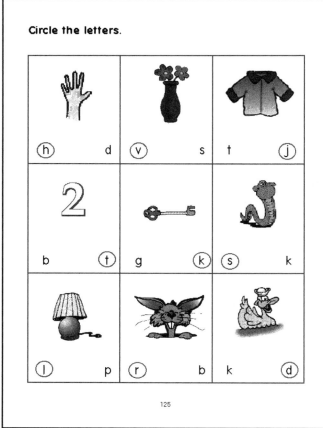

125

3. Ask the children to give you the ending sound for the pictures on page 125.

**SUGGESTED READING/ STORY IDEAS:**

1. God is very good to us. Have the children write a poem beginning each line with:
God is . . . .

2. Recite the poem for another class or for parents.

**OBJECTIVES:**
1. To predict the outcome of a story.
2. To review long *a, e, i,* and *o.*
3. To make and read rhyming words.

**MATERIALS:** pencils and crayons, sequence cards, long vowel charts and picture cards.

**TEACHING PAGES 126 AND 127:**
1. Put several sequence card sets out on the table WITHOUT the final card OR draw a simple sequence on the board without the concluding scene. Example: 1. Picture of a pie cut in four pieces. 2. Picture of four plates on a table. 3. NO PICTURE. Ask the children to look at the first picture and tell what they see. Look at the second picture and tell what they see. What do they think will happen in the next picture? Ask a child to come to the board and draw what they think will happen next (four plates with pie OR an empty pie pan would both be acceptable). With the sequence cards have the children pick the conclusion from a set of cards to complete the sequence.

2. On page 126 read the directions. Ask the children to tell what they see in the first picture (caterpillar). Have them tell what they see in picture *2* (cocoon cracking). Ask them what they expect to happen next (butterfly hatches from cocoon). Have them take their crayons and draw a butterfly in the space for picture *3.*
Repeat this process for the next two rows. (cookie dough on sheet, sheet in oven, cookies on plate or being eaten; bowl of cereal, child eating, empty bowl). Accept any logical conclusion.

3. Prepare for page 127 by putting the word *bike* on the board. Ask the children if they can think of any words to rhyme with it (hike, like, Mike, pike, strike). Write the words on the board as they say them. Point out that most rhyming words have the same endings and change the beginning sounds. Tell them that on page 127 they will be making some rhyming words of their own. Read what Sam and Jip have to say at the top of the page. Read the directions. Accept any words that are reasonable and demonstrate correct spelling. Examples: cake, rake, bake, take, make, fake, lake, sake, wake; bee, she, he, see; pie, tie, lie; goat, boat, coat.

**EXTENDED ACTIVITIES:**
1. Give the children more opportunities to predict the outcome of a sequence of events. Use everyday examples: If it's supper time and

your Mother forgot to go shopping, what happens?  If you are on your way to school and you drop your book into a puddle, what will happen? If you plant a garden and water it well, what do you expect to happen?

2. Practice more rhyming words.  Give more advanced students the opportunity to find rhyming words that sound the same but are spelled differently.

**SUGGESTED READING/ STORY IDEAS:**

1.  Have the children make up oral stories for the three sets of pictures on page 126.  Encourage them to add details.

2.  Tell those stories to a friend.

3.  Find a book in the library about caterpillars, cocoons, and butterflies and read it to the children.

4.  Reread the book *The Very Hungry Caterpillar* by Eric Carle.

## OBJECTIVES:

1. To recognize the consonant digraphs *ch, th,* and *sh* as ending sounds.
2. To review the lower case letters of the alphabet.
3. To write the alphabet in order.

**MATERIALS:** pencils, crayons, alphabet charts, chart paper, magazines and catalogues, scissors, glue or paste.

## TEACHING PAGES 128 AND 129:

1. Write the letter *ch* on the board. Have children take turns giving you words that begin with the letters. Tell the children that today you will begin looking at the sounds found at the end of words. Ask them if they can think of any words that end with the *ch* sound. Look at the box at the top of page 128. Tell the children that they are to look at the pictures in the top section, say the names, listen carefully to the ending sound of each, and circle the letter *ch* under the picture. Ask the children to say the picture names aloud.

2. Proceed in the same fashion for the __*th,* and __*sh* ending sounds. Invite the children to try to think of more words for each.

3. Review the alphabet with the children using songs or rhymes. Read the directions on page 129. Ask the children to write in the missing letters. They may use an alphabet chart if needed. Many children should be able to do this independently. Some will need help. Check letter formation.

## EXTENDED ACTIVITIES:

1. Make a chart for each of the ending sounds __*ch,* __*th,* and __*sh.* See how many more words and pictures the children can find.

2. Have the children practice any letters that are not correctly formed.

3. Review the alphabet with those who are having difficulty. Use tactile letters or magnetic letters and have the children order them as they say the alphabet.

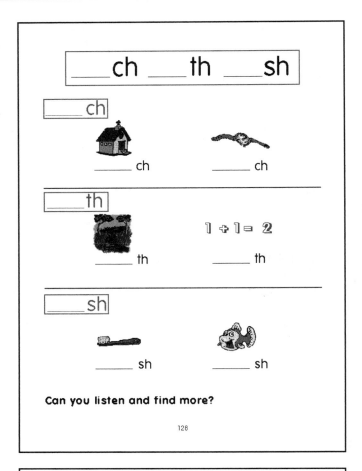

**Can you listen and find more?**

128

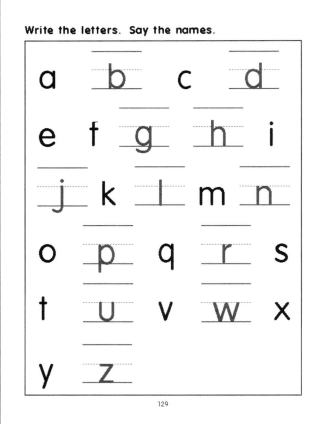

**Write the letters. Say the names.**

129

**SUGGESTED READING/ STORY IDEAS:**

1. Fish are often refered to in the New Testament. Find stories about the apostles fishing (Luke 5; 1-11; John 21: 1-9), about Jesus multiplying the loaves and fishes (Luke 9: 13- 17; John 6: 1-13), and about Jesus preparing fish for the apostles by the sea shore (John 21: 9-13). Read them to the children. Look at a map of the Holy Land and find the Sea of Galilee where these fish were caught.

2. Have the children select one of these stories to illustrate or act out.

**OBJECTIVES:**
1. To read the direction words *top* and *bottom*.
2. To find things that have a *top* and *bottom*.

**MATERIALS:** pencils, crayons, old magazines and catalogues, scissors, glue or paste, word cards for *top* and *bottom*.

**TEACHING PAGES 130 AND 131:**
1. The children have been hearing the words *top* and *bottom* in many activities over the last several months. On page 130, begin working with the children to sound out and read these words. Ask the children to name things that have a top and a bottom (boxes, stairs, furniture, and so on). List these things. Discuss the pictures in the *top* section of the page. Ask the children to point to and read the word *top*. Have them trace it with their fingers. Finally, have them trace the word *top* on the lines. Introduce the *bottom* section in the same way.

2. For page 131, have the children look through magazines and catalogues for pictures of things that have a *top* and a *bottom*. They may also draw pictures. Check to make sure that they glue the things that go *top* on the side of the page which says *top* and the *bottom* things on the *bottom* side.

3. Additional writing practice for all number words is found in the back of the book.

**EXTENDED ACTIVITIES:**
1. Add to the Position/Direction Book. Use construction paper or chart paper to make a page for each concept learned. Print the word in large letters at the top of the page. Color or paste pictures of objects that show the *top* of things on one page and the *bottom* of things on another page.

2. Recall the children's experiences with elevators, escalators, and stairs. How did it feel to be at the top of the stairs or escalator? How did it feel to be at the bottom looking up? How did they feel as the elevator went quickly to the top of the building? How did their stomachs feel when the elevator went quickly down to the bottom floor?

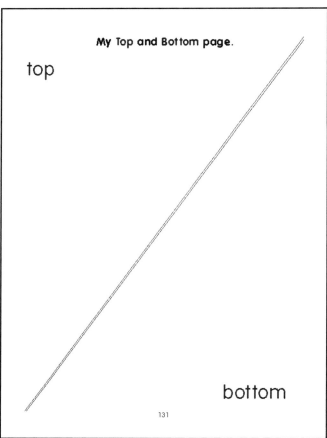

**SUGGESTED READING/ STORY IDEAS:**

1. Have the children think about what it would be like to live at the very top of a mountain. Have them make a list of things they think about (weather, clothes, getting around, and so on). When they have finished talking about it, have them write a story about it. Write it for them or have an aide help.

2. Have the children reverse the process above and think about what it would be like to live at the very bottom of the sea.

**OBJECTIVES:**
1. To recognize and read short *u* words.
2. To review the ending sounds: *d, t, n, r, b,* and *s.*

**MATERIALS:** pencils, crayons, short *u* charts and stories, charts and pictures for the ending sounds: *d, t, n, r, b,* and *s.*

**TEACHING PAGES 132 AND 133:**
1. Prepare for page 132 by reviewing short *u* words from the list of words which the children have been forming with their letter cards throughout the year. This page gives the children a wider range of words and word formation. Read what Jip is saying at the top of the page. Look at the word box. Ask the children if they see any words that they can sound out. Let them pick any words from the box and try them. When they pick a word, ask them to use it in a sentence. After they have finished all the words they can read, help them with any remaining words, showing them how to sound them out.

2. To prepare for page 133 either say a word ending in *d* or hold up a picture of something that has a name ending in *d.* Ask the children to tell you what sound they hear at the end of the word. Do this kind of review with all the ending sounds reviewed on this page: *d, t, n, r, b,* and *s.* Be careful not to include the pictures on page 133. Go to the page and read the direction. Ask the children to name all of the pictures and to listen carefully to the ending sound. Ask the children to point to the first __*d* on the page. Have them trace the line to the picture of the bed. Ask them if they hear the *d* sound at the end of the word *bed.* Go on to the remaining letters and pictures on the page.

**EXTENDED ACTIVITIES:**
1. Use the short *u* words to make sentences. Mix them with the short *a, i, o,* and *e* words already learned. Encourage the children to begin putting sentences together to make paragraphs.
2. Review ending consonants as needed.
3. Ask the children to give you the beginning sound for the pictures on page 133.

I can say these short /u/ words. Can you?

| | | |
|---|---|---|
| tun | cut | bug |
| sun | hut | dug |
| run | nut | rug |
| pup | huff | cub |
| cup | puff | tub |

**Listen.**

**Find more.**

132

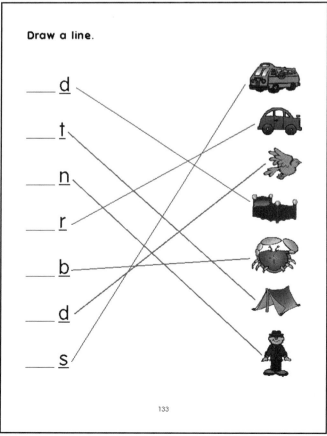

**Draw a line.**

___ d

___ t

___ n

___ r

___ b

___ d

___ s

133

**SUGGESTED READING/ STORY IDEAS:**

1. Read the story *The Grouchy Ladybug* by Eric Carle. Have the children notice how she moves through her day. See if they can find the little clock on each page that tells what time it is.

2. Have the children keep a log of what they do for a single day. Begin in the morning when they rise and finish when they go to bed. Parents can help write what is done at home. Share with the class on the following day.

**OBJECTIVES:**
1. To learn a new shape *star*.
2. To recognize and read the word *star*.
3. To write a story about a star.
4. To learn to draw a star.

**MATERIALS:** pencils, crayons, Bible, magazines, catalogues, paste or glue, word card for *star*, drawing paper, stars of various sizes and colors cut from construction paper.

**TEACHING PAGES 134 AND 135:**

1. The children have seen stars in many places. They have not seen the word for *star* through the year. Introduce the word by saying it, sounding it out, repeating it, and having the children read it with you. Make each child a word card for *star*. Give the children little star stickers to place around the edges. They will learn to read the word and recognize that it stands for a shape.

2. Look at page 134. Ask the children to connect the dots by following the letters in order. What picture have they made (star)? Answer the questions at the bottom of the page.

3. For page 135, have the children talk about things they have thought of that have stars or have a star as part of their shape. Make a list on the board. Help the children to write a story about a star. Write it first on the board or chart paper. Have the children copy it into their books and illustrate.

4. Additional writing practice for all shape words is found in the back of the book.

**EXTENDED ACTIVITIES:**

1. Add to the Shape Book. Use construction paper or chart paper to make a page for each shape learned. Print the word STAR in large letters at the top of the page. Color or paste pictures of objects that contain stars.

2. Give the children stars cut from construction paper in various sizes and colors. Ask the children to lay out a picture on a sheet of drawing paper using the stars. When they are satisfied with their pictures, let them glue them down and draw a background for the picture.

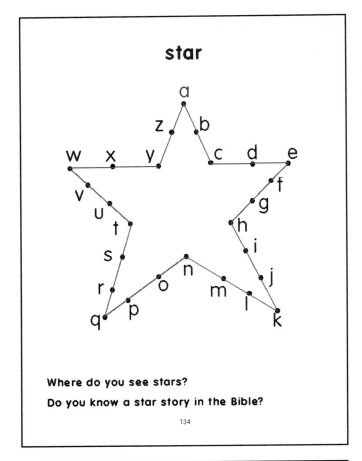

**star**

Where do you see stars?

Do you know a star story in the Bible?

134

**My Star page.**

**Pictures of stars.**

**A star story.**

Teacher Check

135

**SUGGESTED READING/ STORY IDEAS:**

1. Read Matthew 2:1-12 to the children and talk about the wise men following a star to find Jesus. Have them act out the story.

2. Ask the children to tell stories about their pictures.

3. If they like, help them write the stories and display them along with the pictures.

4. After they are displayed, place the stories and pictures in individual folders for the shape story and picture book.

5. Check the library for books about stars.

## OBJECTIVES:

1. To make new words.
2. To put numerals in order.

**MATERIALS:** pencils, letter cards, numeral cards from *1–10*.

## TEACHING PAGES 136 AND 137:

1. On page 136 have the children look at the picture and tell what is happening. The boy's name is Jake. The sentences next to the picture describe what is happening in the picture. Tell the children that they will fill in letters from the box to make words that describe the scene in the picture. Ask if anyone can read the first sentence. Ask what letter from the box could be placed before _ake to make a word that describes the picture (*l* – lake). Have them print an *l* on the line. Ask a child to read the second sentence. Ask what letter(s) would make the correct word here (*sn* – snake). Have the children write *sn* on the line. Complete the last two sentences in the same manner (*r* – rake; *sn* – snake). Follow the same procedure for the second picture and sentence group.

2. Page 137 is a number sequence review. Give each child a set of numeral cards which are not in order. Ask them to arrange them in order from 1 to 10. Help as needed. Read the directions on page 137. Tell the children that the numerals in each box are out of order. Ask them to look at the first box. Which numeral is the smallest (4)? Have them trace the *4* on the first line. Ask what numeral comes after 4. Have them write *5* on the next line. Complete the box in this manner. The final two boxes may be done independently. Help children who need it.

## EXTENDED ACTIVITIES:

1. Have the children review long vowel rhyming words. See if they can create more short stories like those on page 136.

2. Check numeral formation. Have each child practice where needed.

3. Review number sequencing with those who have difficulty.

## SUGGESTED READING/ STORY IDEAS:

1. Begin reviewing stories written throughout the year. Have the children select favorites that could be put together in a special Story Book to remember this year.

2. Have the children pick favorite library books. Read one each day.

---

**Find a word. Write a letter.**

Jake sat by a ⎵ake.
He saw a sⁿake.
He took a ⎵ake.
The sⁿake ran away.

| r | l | sn |

---

Sam had a ⎵ose.
He watered the ⎵ose.
He hit his ⎵ose.

| r | h | n |

136

---

**Write the numbers.**

| 7 5 4 6 | | | |
|---|---|---|---|
| 4 | 5 | 6 | 7 |

| 2 4 3 1 | | | |
|---|---|---|---|
| 1 | 2 | 3 | 4 |

| 10 8 9 7 | | | |
|---|---|---|---|
| 7 | 8 | 9 | 10 |

137

**OBJECTIVES:**

1. To recognize words beginning with capital and small letters.
2. To write last names.
3. To recognize consonants and vowels.

**MATERIALS:** pencils, name cards, alphabet chart.

**TEACHING PAGES 138 AND 139:**

1. Page 138 checks word and letter recognition skills. Have the children look at the first word in the box at the top of the page. Ask who can read the word. Have the children find the matching word in the second column. Have them trace the line between the two words. Move to the second word (Six) and follow the same procedure for the remaining words.

2. Read the directions for the bottom box. Tell the children that they are to find and circle the two words in each box that begin with the letter in the small box. Have the children work independently. Check.

3. The children have been practicing their names for most of the year. On page 139 have them write their last name on the top line. Ask them to count the number of letters in their last names. Have them write that number on the second line. Ask them to see how many vowels are in their last names. Remind them that the vowels are: *a, e, i, o,* and *u.* Have them write the vowels on the third line. Tell them, if they do not know, that consonants are the remaining letters of the alphabet, those that are not vowels. Have them write the consonants on the last line.

**EXTENDED ACTIVITIES:**

1. Check letter formation on page 139. Give further practice as needed.
2. Give additional word and letter recognition practice if necessary.
3. Do additional vowel/consonant practice using words the children know.

**SUGGESTED READING/ STORY IDEAS:**

1. Review stories read throughout the year on Biblical names. See what names the children remember. How much of their stories can they recall.

2. Ask the children about their own names. If they could choose another name, what would it be? Why? Have them make a rhyme: If my name were _____, I'd be _____.

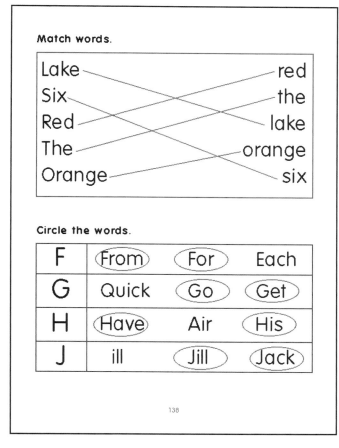

**Match words.**

Lake — red
Six — the
Red — lake
The — orange
Orange — six

**Circle the words.**

| F | From | For | Each |
| G | Quick | Go | Get |
| H | Have | Air | His |
| J | ill | Jill | Jack |

138

**Write your last name.**

**How many letters?**

**Write the vowels.**

**Write the consonants.**

**Teacher Check**

139

271

## OBJECTIVES:

1. To listen carefully.
2. To follow directions given only once.
3. To recognize shapes.
4. To recognize colors.
5. To review words and concepts for: *in, out, top,* and *bottom.*

**MATERIALS:** pencils, crayons, word cards for *in, out, top,* and *bottom*, objects to use for review of these concepts.

## TEACHING PAGES 140 AND 141:

1. To prepare for page 140, put a series of shapes on the board (square, triangle, square, square). Ask the children which shape is not like the others (triangle). Have a child come forward and put an *X* on the triangle. Ask the children what shape remains (squares). Have a child come forward and number the squares *1, 2, 3*. This can be repeated until all children have a turn. Go to page 140. Tell the children that you will give two instructions for each box. They are to listen carefully because you will say each instruction only once. Say: Look at the first box. Put an *X* on the shape that is not like the others. (Pause) Number the shapes that are the same. (Pause and check to see that the children are numbering the remaining shapes correctly.) Repeat this procedure for each box.

2. Review the words *in, out, top,* and *bottom* with the children. Use the objects to show different positions and have the children select the appropriate word. Read the first direction on page 141. Have the children match the word in the first column with the capitalized word in the second column. Let children work individually if they are able.

3. Have the children look at the pictures on the bottom of the page. Tell them you will read a sentence only once. Have them circle the picture that matches the sentence. Read: Put your finger on the *1.* Circle the toy that is *out* of the box. Put your finger on the *2.* Circle the bird at the *bottom* of the tree. Put your finger on the *3.* Circle the bird that is on *top* of the tree. Put your finger on the *4.* Circle the toy that is *in* the box. Check. Have the children explain the pictures in any box that was missed.

## EXTENDED ACTIVITIES:

1. Do additional shape activities with anyone having difficulty.

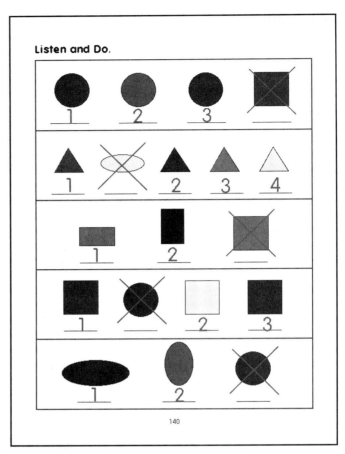

2. Reinforce the concepts for *in, out, top,* and *bottom* as needed.

**SUGGESTED READING/ STORY IDEAS:**
1. Continue reviewing and selecting favorite stories and poems with the children.
2. Have the children select their favorite Bible stories to retell or act out for others.

## OBJECTIVES:

1. To review all long vowel sounds.
2. To recognize patterns.
3. To complete patterns.

**MATERIALS:** pencils, crayons, long vowel charts and stories, pattern cards, objects to make patterns.

## TEACHING PAGES 142 AND 143:

The lessons from this point on are primarily review lessons. They will include all of the major concepts covered in this program. This curriculum does not include "tests" as such. These pages may be used to check skills learned in previous lessons. Activities and procedures for all of these lessons can be drawn from previous lessons as well. Please feel free to go back to activities that the children liked and found helpful.

1. Page 142 can be used as a review to check recognition of long vowel sounds. Review the vowel sounds briefly with the children. Read the direction on page 142. Have the children say the names of all the pictures to make sure they understand what they are. Do the first box with the children. Let them complete the page on their own. Check.

2. Put some simple patterns on the board: 2 3 2 3 __ __ __ __; oval, square, triangle, oval, square, __, __, __. Ask the children to help you finish the patterns. Use both numeral and shape patterns. Read the direction on page 143. Ask the children to read the pattern in the first box: 1 2 1 __ __ __. Have the children tell you what numeral comes after the 1 (2). Tell them to write the 2 on the first line. Ask what comes next (1). Have them write a 1 on the second line. Ask what numeral will complete the pattern (2). Have them write a 2 on the final line. Complete the remaining boxes in the same manner.

## EXTENDED ACTIVITIES:

1. Review vowel sounds as needed.
2. Ask the children to give the beginning and the ending sounds for the pictures on page 142.
3. Have children work in pairs for additional pattern practice.

## SUGGESTED READING/ STORY IDEAS:

1. Begin preparing the children's favorite original stories to be duplicated and illustrated for their class Story Book.
2. Continue reading favorite library books and Bible stories.

**Circle the letter.**

142

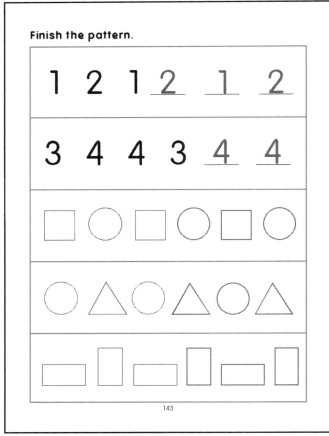

**Finish the pattern.**

| 1 | 2 | 1 | *2* | *1* | *2* |

| 3 | 4 | 4 | 3 | *4* | *4* |

143

## OBJECTIVES:

1. To review initial sounds: *m, p, qu,* and *n.*
2. To review initial consonant digraphs: *ch, th, wh,* and *sh.*

**MATERIALS:** pencils, charts and stories for *m, p, qu,* and *n,* charts and pictures for *ch, th, wh,* and *sh.*

## TEACHING PAGES 144 AND 145:

1. Instruct the children to look at the pictures in the boxes on page 144 and circle the picture that begins with the sound in the small box. Ask them to point to the *m* in the first box. Ask them which picture begins with the *m* sound (man). Have them circle the picture of the *man.* Have them complete the final three boxes on their own. Read the direction on the bottom of the page. Tell them to say the name of the picture slowly. Have them write the letter of the beginning sound on the lines. Check.

2. Review initial *ch, th, wh,* and *sh* as needed. Read the direction on page 145. Ask the children what is in the first box (cheese). Ask the children which set of letters they hear at the beginning of the word cheese. Have them circle the *ch.* Have the children name the other pictures and then allow them to work independently to complete the page. Check.

## EXTENDED ACTIVITIES:

1. Review any letters or digraphs that were missed.
2. Ask the children to give the ending sounds for the pictures on both pages.

## SUGGESTED READING/ STORY IDEAS:

1. Continue as in the previous lessons to review stories and prepare a class book.
2. Continue reading favorite library books and Bible stories.

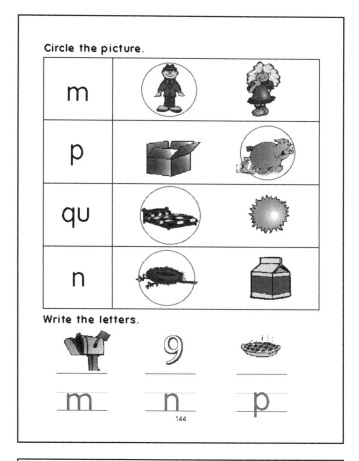

## OBJECTIVES:

1. To review capital letters.
2. To put the alphabet in order.
3. To match capital and small letters.
4. To recognize the same word in a group of words.

**MATERIALS:** pencils, alphabet charts and cards.

## TEACHING PAGES 146 AND 147:

1. Have the children say the alphabet or sing the alphabet song. Read the directions on page 146. Tell the children to print in the missing capital letters. Encourage them to work carefully and to use their best writing. Check for correctness and for letter formation.

2. Read the directions at the top of page 147. Have the children match the capital/small letters in the first box and the small/capital letters in the second box. Check.

3. The word recognition at the bottom of the page is more difficult because the words have many similarities. Tell the children to look at all the words very carefully before circling the one that matches. Let them work independently.

## EXTENDED ACTIVITIES:

1. Help children who are having difficulty with completing the alphabet.
2. Give extra letter practice for any letters not formed correctly.
3. Give additional practice and help to children who had difficulty matching the words on page 147.

## SUGGESTED READING/ STORY IDEAS:

1. Continue as in the previous lessons to review stories and prepare a class book.
2. Continue reading favorite library books and Bible stories.

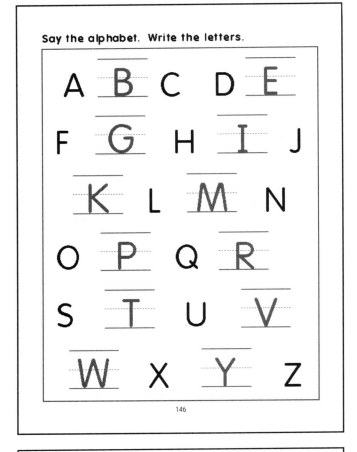

Say the alphabet. Write the letters.

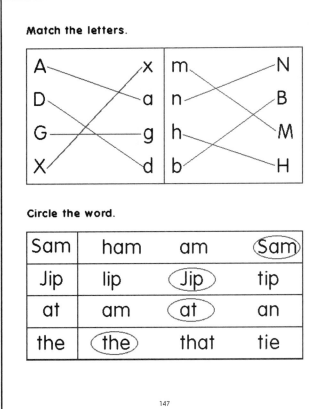

Match the letters.

Circle the word.

| Sam | ham | am | (Sam) |
| Jip | lip | (Jip) | tip |
| at | am | (at) | an |
| the | (the) | that | tie |

## OBJECTIVES:

1. To review the short vowel sounds.
2. To review basic shapes.
3. To listen carefully.
4. To follow directions given only once.

**MATERIALS:** pencils, crayons, short vowel charts and stories, basic shape cards and book.

## TEACHING PAGES 148 AND 149:

1. Briefly review the short vowel sounds with the children. Have the children say the letter names and the short sound for each of the letters in the box at the top of the page. Ask the children to point to the first picture (cup). Ask them which short vowel sound they hear (u). Have them write the letter u on the lines under the picture of the cup. Make sure the children know what each picture is. Have them complete the page on their own. Give help as needed.

2. Tell the children that they will listen carefully to your directions on page 149 and do what is asked. Remind them that you will read the directions only once.

*Read:*

Color the stars yellow.
Color the triangles blue.
Color the ovals red.
Color the circles green.
Color the squares orange.
Color the rectangles purple.
Finish pictures.

## EXTENDED ACTIVITIES:

1. Review short vowels as needed.
2. Ask the children to give beginning and ending sounds for the pictures on page 148.
3. Review shapes if needed.
4. Give additional listening directions to children who were not attentive.

## SUGGESTED READING/ STORY IDEAS:

1. Continue as in the previous lessons to review stories and prepare a class book.
2. Continue reading favorite library books and Bible stories.

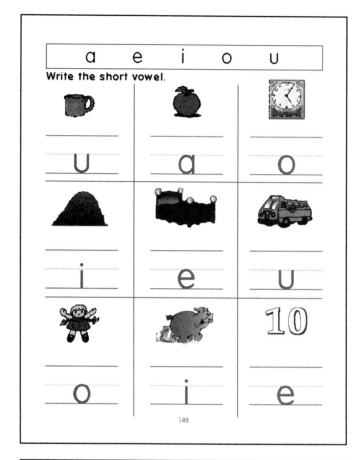

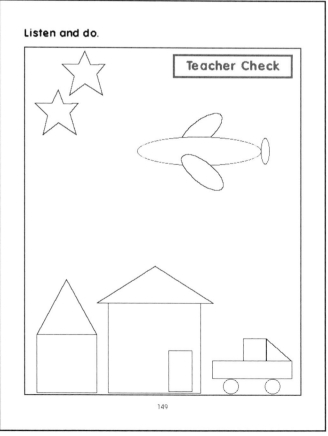

277

## OBJECTIVES:

1. To review initial consonants: *b, z, d, y, f, x, g,* and *w*.
2. To review color recognition.
3. To review color words.
4. To follow directions
5. To listen carefully.

**MATERIALS:** pencils and crayons, initial charts and stories for *b, z, d, y, f, x, g,* and *w*, color word cards.

## TEACHING PAGES 150 AND 151:

1. Review the initial sounds *b, z, d, y, f, x, g,* and *w*. Proceed with page 150 as in previous initial review lessons (Lesson 152, pages 144 – 145).

2. Review color words with the children. Read the directions on page 151. Ask the children to draw a line from the color word to the strip that shows the color for the word.

3. At the bottom of the page, ask the children to listen carefully. Have them circle the red square in the first box. Ask them to put an *X* on the blue circle in the second box. Finally ask them to draw a box around the green triangle in the last box. Check.

## EXTENDED ACTIVITIES:

1. Review any initial sounds that were missed.
2. Ask the children to give the ending sounds for the pictures on page 150.
3. Ask the more advanced students if they can give vowel sounds for most of the pictures on page 150.
4. Review color words as needed.

## SUGGESTED READING/ STORY IDEAS:

1. Continue as in the previous lessons to review stories and prepare a class book.
2. Continue reading favorite library books and Bible stories.

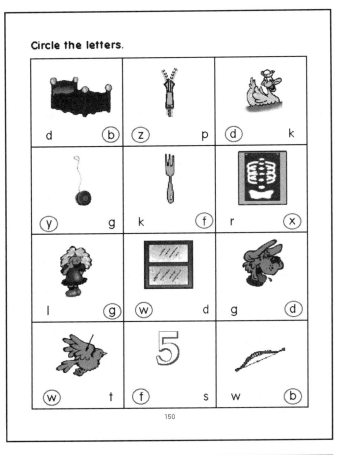

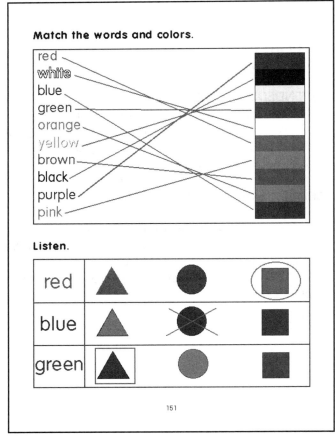

## OBJECTIVES:

1. To review numerical order from 1 through 10.
2. To match numerals to number words.
3. To review long vowel sounds.

**MATERIALS:** pencils, number word cards and charts, charts and stories for long vowels.

## TEACHING PAGES 152 AND 153:

1. Read the direction for the top of page 152. Ask the children to write in the missing numerals from 1 to 10. Check.

2. Review number words briefly. Read the direction at the bottom of page 152. Tell the children they are to match the numerals to the number word for each. Do the first one together (1 one). Let the children complete independently. Check.

3. Page 153 can be used as a review to check recognition of long vowel sounds. Review the vowel sounds briefly with the children. Read the direction on page 153. Have the children say the names of all the pictures to make sure they understand what they are. Do the first box with the children. Let them complete the page on their own. Check.

## EXTENDED ACTIVITIES:

1. Give extra practice with number sequence and recognition of number words as needed.

2. Give additional review on any long vowels missed.

3. Ask the children to give the beginning and ending sounds of the pictures on page 153.

## SUGGESTED READING/ STORY IDEAS:

1. Continue as in the previous lessons to review stories and prepare a class book.

2. Continue reading favorite library books and Bible stories.

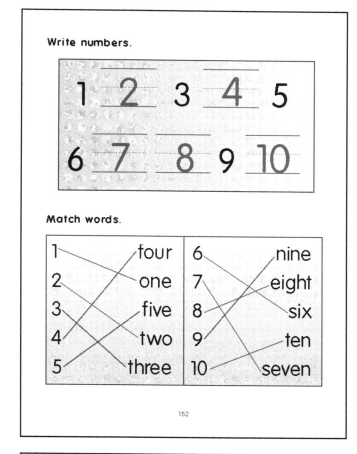

## OBJECTIVES:

1. To review initial consonants: *h, k, d, v, s, l, j,* and *r.*
2. To put pictures in order.
3. To put letters in order.
4. To put numerals in order.

**MATERIALS:** pencils, initial charts and stories for *h, k, d, v, s, l, j,* and *r,* number chart, alphabet chart, sequence cards.

## TEACHING PAGES 154 AND 155:

1. Review the initial sounds *h, k, d, v, s, l, j,* and *r.* Proceed with page 154 as in previous initial review lessons (Lesson 152, pages 144–145).

2. Review sequence cards, alphabet sequence, and numerical sequence briefly. Read the first direction on page 155. Ask the children what is happening in the pictures. Tell them they are to write a *1* under the picture that comes first, a *2* under the picture that shows what happened next, and a *3* under the picture that shows what happens last. (3, 1, 2)

3. Read the second direction. Ask the children to look carefully at the letters. Have them write the letters in the correct order on the lines. Check.

4. Read the third direction. Ask the children to look carefully at the numerals. Have them write them in order on the lines. Check.

## EXTENDED ACTIVITIES:

1. Review initial consonants as needed.
2. Ask the children to give the ending sounds for each picture on page 154.
3. Ask the children to give the vowel sounds that they know for the pictures on page 154.
4. Give further practice for any sequencing problems.

## SUGGESTED READING/ STORY IDEAS:

1. Continue as in the previous lessons to review stories and prepare a class book.
2. Continue reading favorite library books and Bible stories.

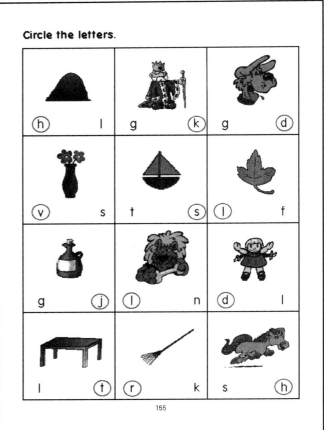

## OBJECTIVES:

1. To review initial consonant digraphs *th*, *wh*, *ch*, and *sh*.
2. To review initial sounds *m, p, n, qu, b,* and *f*.

**MATERIALS:** pencils, charts and stories for *th*, *wh*, *ch*, and *sh*; and for *m, p, n, qu, b,* and *f*.

## TEACHING PAGES 156 AND 157:

1. Review the initial sounds *th, wh, ch,* and *sh*. Proceed with page 156 as in previous initial review lessons (Lesson 152, pages 144–145).

2. Read the direction for page 157. Ask the children to name the first picture (mouse). Ask them what sound they hear at the beginning of the word mouse (*m*). Have them write the letter *m* on the lines under the picture. Have them name the other pictures on the page. Tell them to complete the page on their own. Check.

## EXTENDED ACTIVITIES:

1. Review any initial sounds missed on either pages 156 or 157.

2. Ask the children to give the ending sound for the pictures on both pages.

3. Check letter formation and practice any letters that need work.

## SUGGESTED READING/ STORY IDEAS:

1. Continue as in the previous lessons to review stories and prepare a class book.

2. Continue reading favorite library books and Bible stories.

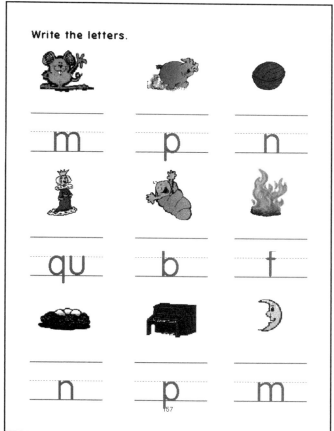

**OBJECTIVES:**

1. To listen carefully.
2. To follow directions given only once.
3. To demonstrate understanding of position and direction words.
4. To recognize ending sounds *b, m, p, ck, n, x, d, w, g, k,* and *l.*

**MATERIALS:** pencils and crayons, review pictures for ending sounds *b, m, p, ck, n, x, d, w, g, k,* and *l.*

**TEACHING PAGES 158 AND 159:**

1. Ask the children to look at page 158. What do they see? Tell the children that you will be directing them to draw things on the page. Tell them that they must listen carefully. Remind them that you will give a direction only once. Have them lay their crayons out where they are easy to reach. Read slowly and carefully.
*Read:*
Take a yellow crayon. (Pause while they find the crayon.) Draw the sun high up in the sky over the house.

Take a brown crayon. (Pause.) Draw a chimney on top of the roof.

Take a black crayon. (Pause.) Draw a door and two windows on the front of the house.

Take a green crayon. (Pause.) Draw a tree next to the house (either side is acceptable).

Take a blue crayon. (Pause.) Draw a bird sitting in the tree.

Take an orange crayon. (Pause.) Draw a table outside next to the tree.

Take a green crayon. (Pause.) Draw grass around the house.

Take a red crayon. (Pause.) Draw a red ball under the table.

Check. Note difficulties with colors, position, or listening.

2. Briefly review the ending sounds *b, m, p, ck, n, x, d, w, g, k,* and *l.* Read the direction on page 159. Ask the children what picture they see in the first box (knob). Ask them what sound they hear at the end of the word (b). Tell them to circle the *b* in the box.

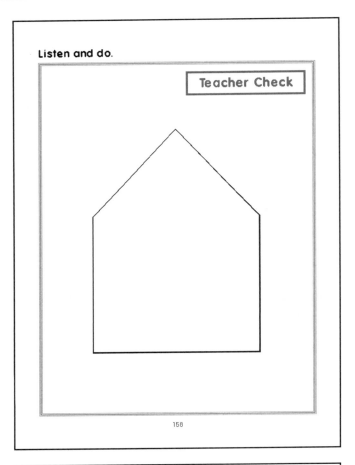

Listen and do.

Teacher Check

158

Circle the letters.

159

Have the children read all of the picture names. Then have them finish the page independently. Check.

## EXTENDED ACTIVITIES:

1. Give additional directions on page 158, if concepts need further reinforcement.

2. Have the children finish the picture and add more details.

3. Review ending sounds as needed.

4. Have the children give the beginning sounds and, if possible, the vowel sounds for the pictures on page 159.

## SUGGESTED READING/ STORY IDEAS:

1. Put the class book together. See how many stories the children can now read.

2. Make a list of favorite library books and Bible stories to send home.

**OBJECTIVES:**

1. To review the ending sounds *sh, v, t, th, s, r,* and *ch*.

2. To write name, age, and address.

**MATERIALS:** pencils, charts or stories for the ending sounds *sh, v, t, th, s, r,* and *ch*, name and address card.

**TEACHING PAGES 160 AND 161:**

1. Review the ending sounds *sh, v, t, th, s, r,* and *ch* briefly. Read the direction on page 160. Ask the children to look at the first ending sound on the page (*sh*). Have them trace the line from the letters to the picture of the *dish*. Review the other pictures to make sure the children know what they are. Have them complete the page independently. Check.

2. Read what Sam and Jip have to say on page 161. Ask the children to use their best writing to write their names (first and last), their ages, and their addresses on the lines marked. Help them to find the correct lines for each. They may use their name and address cards if necessary.

**EXTENDED ACTIVITIES:**

1. Review sounds if needed.

2. Have the children give the beginning sounds for the pictures on page 160.

**SUGGESTED READING/ STORY IDEAS:**

1. Distribute the class book.

2. Distribute the list of favorite library books and Bible stories.

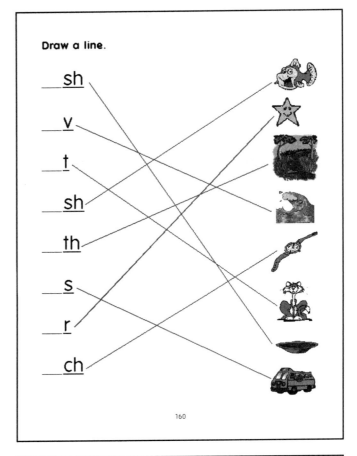

Draw a line.

_sh
_v
_t
_sh
_th
_s
_r
_ch

160

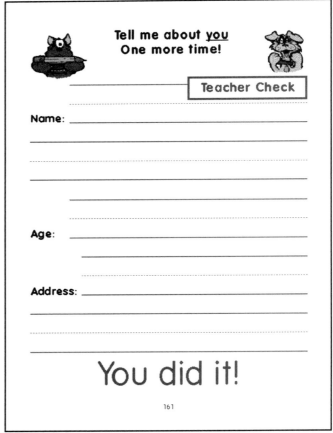

**Tell me about you
One more time!**

Teacher Check

**Name:** _____

**Age:** _____

**Address:** _____

You did it!

161

## STUDENT EVALUATION: LESSONS 1-40

**ALPHABET:**

Place a capital letter alphabet chart in front of the student. Have the student say as many letters of the alphabet as possible. Check all that are correctly identified.

| | | | | |
|---|---|---|---|---|
| ____ A | ____ F | ____ K | ____ P | ____ U |
| ____ B | ____ G | ____ L | ____ Q | ____ V |
| ____ C | ____ H | ____ M | ____ R | ____ W |
| ____ D | ____ I | ____ N | ____ S | ____ X |
| ____ E | ____ J | ____ O | ____ T | ____ Y |
| | | | | ____ Z |

Place a small letter alphabet chart in front of the student. Have the student say as many letters of the alphabet as possible. Check all that are correctly identified.

| | | | | |
|---|---|---|---|---|
| ____ a | ____ f | ____ k | ____ p | ____ u |
| ____ b | ____ g | ____ l | ____ q | ____ v |
| ____ c | ____ h | ____ m | ____ r | ____ w |
| ____ d | ____ i | ____ n | ____ s | ____ x |
| ____ e | ____ j | ____ o | ____ t | ____ y |
| | | | | ____ z |

**Colors:**

Place several objects of different colors in front of the student (crayons or pieces of construction paper are good). Have the student name the color as you point to it. Check the colors that are known.

| | | | |
|---|---|---|---|
| _____ red | _____ blue | _____ green | _____ yellow |
| _____ purple | _____ orange | _____ pink | _____ brown |

**Shapes:**

Have shape cards (or shapes cut from construction paper) available. Include different sizes for each shape and some shapes that the student does not know. Place them in front of the student. Ask the student to hand you all the examples of a shape that he sees. Check the shapes that are known.

| | | | |
|---|---|---|---|
| _____ circles | _____ squares | _____ triangles | _____ rectangles |

Have several objects that have obvious shapes in them (square or rectangular blocks or boxes, round wheels on toys, and so on). Ask the student to find an object for each shape as you name it. Have the student point out the shape in the object. Check those that are known.

| | | | |
|---|---|---|---|
| _____ circles | _____ squares | _____ triangles | _____ rectangles |

# Language Arts Kindergarten Student Evaluation

**Name Recognition:**
Place five first name cards (including the student's) in front of the student. Ask the student to find his/her name card.

_____ Recognized    _____ Did not recognize

Ask the student to write his/her first name.

_____Yes          _____ No

**Phonics:**
Have two or three pictures of short *a, e,* and *i* words available. Include a few short *o* and *u* pictures as well for distractors. Place the pictures in front of the student. Ask the student to name each picture. Repeat the name emphasizing the vowel sounds. Place a short *a* flash card on the desk or table. Ask the student to select the picture or pictures for short *a*.
Repeat for short *e* and *i*. Check those completed correctly.

_____ a              _____ e              _____ i

Review the initial consonants in the same manner using pictures or objects. Take the consonants in groups of three as follows:

First group:        _____ b      _____ t      _____ m

Second group:      _____ r      _____ s      _____ n

Third group:        _____ d      _____ p      _____ l

Include some pictures which begin with sounds other than those in the group in each set. Ask more advanced students to name these extra sounds if they can. Record which additional sounds are recognized.

**Writing:**
Have paper and pencils ready for the student and an alphabet chart which shows the correct formation of letters. Check the student on all letters learned in lessons 1 - 40.
Check all letters formed correctly.

| | | | | | |
|---|---|---|---|---|---|
| _____ A | _____ B | _____ I | _____ P | _____ S | _____ D |
| _____ R | _____ T | _____ E | _____ N | _____ L | _____ M |
| _____ a | _____ b | _____ i | _____ s | _____ m | _____ p |
| _____ d | _____ r | _____ t | _____ n | _____ e | _____ l |

**Left/ right:**
Check left/right progression in writing. Ask the student to look at a page in a large print book and show you where to begin reading and in what direction to read.

## STUDENT EVALUATION: LESSONS 41-80

**ALPHABET:**
Place a capital letter alphabet chart in front of the student. Have the student say as many letters of the alphabet as possible. Check all that are correctly identified.

| | | | | |
|---|---|---|---|---|
| ___ A | ___ F | ___ K | ___ P | ___ U |
| ___ B | ___ G | ___ L | ___ Q | ___ V |
| ___ C | ___ H | ___ M | ___ R | ___ W |
| ___ D | ___ I | ___ N | ___ S | ___ X |
| ___ E | ___ J | ___ O | ___ T | ___ Y |
| | | | | ___ Z |

Place a small letter alphabet chart in front of the student. Have the student say as many letters of the alphabet as possible. Check all that are correctly identified.

| | | | | |
|---|---|---|---|---|
| ___ a | ___ f | ___ k | ___ p | ___ u |
| ___ b | ___ g | ___ l | ___ q | ___ v |
| ___ c | ___ h | ___ m | ___ r | ___ w |
| ___ d | ___ i | ___ n | ___ s | ___ x |
| ___ e | ___ j | ___ o | ___ t | ___ y |
| | | | | ___ z |

**Colors:**
Place several objects of different colors in front of the student (crayons or pieces of construction paper are good). Have the student name the color as you point to it. Check the colors that are known.

| | | | | |
|---|---|---|---|---|
| _____ red | _____ blue | _____ green | _____ yellow | _____ purple |
| _____ orange | _____ pink | _____ brown | _____ black | _____ white |

**Shapes:**
Have shape cards (or shapes cut from construction paper) available. Include different sizes for each shape and some shapes that the student does not know. Place them in front of the student. Ask the student to hand you all the examples of a shape that he sees. Check the shapes that are known.

| | | | | |
|---|---|---|---|---|
| _____ circles | _____ square | _____ triangles | _____ rectangles | _____ ovals |

Have several objects that have obvious shapes in them (square or rectangular blocks or boxes, round wheels on toys, and so on). Ask the student to find an object for each shape as you name it. Have the student point out the shape in the object. Check those that are known.

| | | | | |
|---|---|---|---|---|
| _____ circles | _____ square | _____ triangles | _____ rectangles | _____ ovals |

# Language Arts Kindergarten Student Evaluation

**Name Recognition:**
Place five first name cards (including the student's) in front of the student. Ask the student to find his/her name card.

_____ Recognized                    _____ Did not recognize

Ask the student to write his/her first name.

_____ Yes                    _____ No

**Phonics:**
Have two or three pictures of short *a, e, i, o,* and *u* words available. Place the pictures in front of the student. Ask the student to name each picture. Repeat the name emphasizing the vowel sounds. Place a short *a* flash card on the desk or table. Ask the student to select the picture or pictures for short *a*. This may be done in two separate groups.
Repeat for other vowels. Check those completed correctly.

_____ a          _____ e          _____ i          _____ o          _____ u

Review the initial consonants in the same manner using pictures or objects. Take the consonants in groups of three as follows:

First group:          _____ k          _____ c          _____ f
Second group:          _____ j          _____ g          _____ h
Third group:          _____ v          _____ w          _____ y
Fourth group:          _____ z          _____ qu          _____ x

Review *b, d, l, m, n, p, r, s,* and *t* in two groups (one picture for each).

Include some pictures which begin with sounds other than those in the group in each set. Ask more advanced students to name these extra sounds if they can. Record which additional sounds are recognized.

**Writing:**
Have paper and pencils ready for the student and an alphabet chart which shows the correct formation of letters. Check the student on all letters learned in lessons 41 - 80 and any letters that were missed in the first evaluation.
Check all letters formed correctly.

_____ K     _____ C     _____ F     _____ H     _____ O     _____ G     _____ J
_____ Z     _____ Y     _____ V     _____ W     _____ Q     _____ U     _____ X
_____ k     _____ c     _____ f     _____ h     _____ o     _____ g     _____ j
_____ z     _____ y     _____ v     _____ w     _____ q     _____ u     _____ x

**Left/ right:**
Check left/right progression in writing. Ask the student to look at a page in a large print book and show you where to begin reading and in what direction to read.

**Position/ direction/ listening:**
Have several small objects available.  Tell the student that you will ask him to do certain activities.  You will give a direction only once.  Using the objects give simple directions which check the understanding of the following concepts:

_____ up          _____ down          _____ in          _____ out          _____ in front of

_____ behind          _____ open          _____ closed          _____ over          _____ under

Examples:   Put the ball under the table.
            Place the crayons in the box.

**Sequencing:**
Place three sets of story sequence cards on the desk or table in front of the student.
Ask the student to sort out the cards that go together.  Then ask the student to put the three cards that go together in order of what happened first, next, and last.

_____ Chose cards that fit together.
_____ Put sequence in order.
_____ Could not find cards that fit together.
_____ Could not put in sequence.

Place alphabet flash cards in front of the student.  Choose five letters that run in order, such as *d, e, f, g, h*.  Mix the cards and ask the student to put them in the correct alphabetical order.

_____ Completed                    _____ Not completed.

# Language Arts Kindergarten Student Evaluation

## STUDENT EVALUATION: LESSONS 81-120

**ALPHABET:**

Place a capital letter alphabet chart in front of the student. Have the student say as many letters of the alphabet as possible.  Check all that are correctly identified.

| | | | | |
|---|---|---|---|---|
| ____ A | ____ F | ____ K | ____ P | ____ U |
| ____ B | ____ G | ____ L | ____ Q | ____ V |
| ____ C | ____ H | ____ M | ____ R | ____ W |
| ____ D | ____ I | ____ N | ____ S | ____ X |
| ____ E | ____ J | ____ O | ____ T | ____ Y |
| | | | | ____ Z |

Place a small letter alphabet chart in front of the student. Have the student say as many letters of the alphabet as possible.  Check all that are correctly identified.

| | | | | |
|---|---|---|---|---|
| ____ a | ____ f | ____ k | ____ p | ____ u |
| ____ b | ____ g | ____ l | ____ q | ____ v |
| ____ c | ____ h | ____ m | ____ r | ____ w |
| ____ d | ____ i | ____ n | ____ s | ____ x |
| ____ e | ____ j | ____ o | ____ t | ____ y |
| | | | | ____ z |

## Colors:

Place several objects of different colors in front of the student (crayons or pieces of construction paper are good). Have the color word cards for each color.  Have the student select the color word for each object as you point to it. Check the colors that are known.

| | | | | |
|---|---|---|---|---|
| _____ red | _____ blue | _____ green | _____ yellow | _____ purple |
| _____ orange | _____ pink | _____ brown | _____ black | _____ white |

## Shapes:

Have shape cards (or shapes cut from construction paper) available.  Include different sizes for each shape and some shapes that the student does not know.  Have the shape word cards for circle, square, and triangle on the table in front of the student.  Ask the student to hand you the word card for the shape you choose and all the examples of a shape that he sees.  Check the shapes that are known (words for rectangle and oval are not yet covered, but the word cards may be included).

| | | | | |
|---|---|---|---|---|
| _____ circles | _____ squares | _____ triangles | _____ rectangles | _____ ovals |

Have several objects that have obvious shapes in them (square or rectangular blocks or boxes, round wheels on toys, and so on). Ask the student to find an object for each shape as you name it. Have the student point out the shape in the object. Check those that are known.

_____circles      _____squares      _____triangles      _____rectangles      _____ovals

**Name Recognition:**
Place five first name cards and five last name cards (including the student's) in front of the student. Ask the student to find his/her name cards.

_____ Recognized                _____ Did not recognize

Ask the student to write his/her first and last name.

_____ Yes                       _____ No

**Phonics:**
Have two or three pictures of short a, e, i, o, and u  words available. Place the pictures in front of the student. Ask the student to name each picture. Repeat the name emphasizing the vowel sounds. Place a *short a* flash card on the desk or table. Ask the student to select the picture or pictures for shor*t a*. This may be done in two separate groups.
Repeat for other vowels. Check those completed correctly.

_____ a        _____ e        _____ i        _____ o        _____ u

Review the initial consonant digraphs in the same manner using pictures or objects.

_____sh        _____ch        _____th (soft)      _____th (hard)

Review all initial consonant sounds using picture cards or objects. Use groups of 5 or 6:

| | | | | | | |
|---|---|---|---|---|---|---|
| First group: | _____ k | _____ c | _____ f | _____ b | _____ d | _____ l |
| Second group: | _____ j | _____ g | _____ h | _____ m | _____ n | |
| Third group: | _____ v | _____ w | _____ y | _____ r | _____ s | |
| Fourth group: | _____ z | _____ qu | _____ x | _____ t | _____ p | |

Include some pictures which begin with sounds other than those in the group in each set. Ask more advanced students to name these extra sounds if they can. Record which additional sounds are recognized.

Review long vowel sounds in the same manner.

_____ a        _____ e        _____ i        _____ o        _____ u

Review the final consonants covered to this point using pictures or objects.

_____ b        _____ ck        _____ d        _____ g        _____ k        _____ l

# Language Arts Kindergarten Student Evaluation

**Writing:**
Have paper and pencils ready for the student and an alphabet chart which shows the correct formation of letters. Check the student on all letters of the alphabet.
Check off all letters formed correctly.

| | | | | |
|---|---|---|---|---|
| ____ A | ____ F | ____ K | ____ P | ____ U |
| ____ B | ____ G | ____ L | ____ Q | ____ V |
| ____ C | ____ H | ____ M | ____ R | ____ W |
| ____ D | ____ I | ____ N | ____ S | ____ X |
| ____ E | ____ J | ____ O | ____ T | ____ Y |
| | | | | ____ Z |

| | | | | |
|---|---|---|---|---|
| ____ a | ____ f | ____ k | ____ p | ____ u |
| ____ b | ____ g | ____ l | ____ q | ____ v |
| ____ c | ____ h | ____ m | ____ r | ____ w |
| ____ d | ____ i | ____ n | ____ s | ____ x |
| ____ e | ____ j | ____ o | ____ t | ____ y |
| | | | | ____ z |

**Left/ right:**
Check left/right progression in writing. Ask the student to look at a page in a large print book and show you where to begin reading and in what direction to read.

**Position/ direction/ listening:**
Have several small objects available. Tell the student that you will ask him to do certain activities. You will give a direction only once. Using the objects give simple directions which check the understanding of the following concepts:

_____ up       _____ down     _____ in      _____ out       _____ in front of

_____ behind    _____ open     _____ closed    _____ over      _____ under

Examples:  Put the ball under the table.
                   Place the crayons in the box.

**Sequencing:**
Place three sets of story sequence cards on the desk or table in front of the student.
Ask the student to sort out the cards that go together. Then ask the student to put the three cards that go together in order of what happened first, next, and last.

_____ Chose cards that fit together.

_____ Put sequence in order.

_____ Could not find cards that fit together.

_____ Could not put in sequence.

Place alphabet flash cards in front of the student. Choose five letters that run in order, such as d, e, f, g, h. Mix the cards and ask the student to put them in the correct alphabetical order.

_____ Completed                    _____ Not completed

Repeat the same procedure using numerals from 1 through 6.

_____ Completed          _____ Not completed

## Patterns

Use some simple pattern cards of basic shapes and colors with the student.  Have basic shapes cut from construction paper available for the student to use to copy the pattern.  Ask the student:

1. To identify the pattern and tell what shape and color will come next.
2. To use basic color shapes to duplicate the pattern.
3. To create a pattern of his own.

_____ Student can identify the pattern on the card.
_____ Student can duplicate the pattern.
_____ Student can create a new pattern.

## Rhyming and Word Formation:

Make a set of cards with some of the more common rhyme endings on them:
 -it, -an, -am, -ake, -ike, -in.  Have available a set of alphabet cards which the student can use to form new words with these endings.  Ask the student to sound out the ending.  Ask the student to see how many new words can be made using the ending.  Record the student's efforts.

_____-it      _____-an      _____-am      _____-ake      _____-ike      _____-in

## STUDENT EVALUATION: LESSONS 121-160

**ALPHABET:**
Place a capital letter alphabet chart in front of the student. Have the student say as many letters of the alphabet as possible.  Check all that are correctly identified.

| | | | | |
|---|---|---|---|---|
| ____ A | ____ F | ____ K | ____ P | ____ U |
| ____ B | ____ G | ____ L | ____ Q | ____ V |
| ____ C | ____ H | ____ M | ____ R | ____ W |
| ____ D | ____ I | ____ N | ____ S | ____ X |
| ____ E | ____ J | ____ O | ____ T | ____ Y |
| | | | | ____ Z |

Place a small letter alphabet chart in front of the student. Have the student say as many letters of the alphabet as possible.  Check all that are correctly identified.

| | | | | |
|---|---|---|---|---|
| ____ a | ____ f | ____ k | ____ p | ____ u |
| ____ b | ____ g | ____ l | ____ q | ____ v |
| ____ c | ____ h | ____ m | ____ r | ____ w |
| ____ d | ____ i | ____ n | ____ s | ____ x |
| ____ e | ____ j | ____ o | ____ t | ____ y |
| | | | | ____ z |

**Colors:**
Place several objects of different colors in front of the student (crayons or pieces of construction paper are good).  Have the color word cards for each color.  Have the student select the color word for each object as you point to it.  Check the colors that are known.

| | | | | |
|---|---|---|---|---|
| _____ red | _____ blue | _____ green | _____ yellow | _____ purple |
| _____ orange | _____ pink | _____ brown | _____ black | _____ white |

**Shapes:**
Have shape cards (or shapes cut from construction paper) available.  Include different sizes for each shape and some shapes that the student does not know.  Have the shape word cards for circle, square, rectangle, oval, star,  and triangle on the table in front of the student.  Ask the student to hand you the word card for the shape you choose and all the examples of a shape that he sees.

_____ circles _____ squares _____ triangles _____ rectangles _____ ovals _____ stars

Have several objects that have obvious shapes in them (square or rectangular blocks or boxes, round wheels on toys, and so on). Ask the student to find an object for each shape as you name it.  Have the student point out the shape in the object.  Check those that are known.

_____ circles _____ squares _____ triangles _____ rectangles _____ ovals _____ stars

**Name Recognition:**
Ask the student to write his/her first and last name.

_____Yes                _____No

**Age:**
Ask the student how old he is.

_____Yes                _____No

**Address:**
Ask the student to tell you his address.

_____Yes                _____ No

**Phonics:**
Have  pictures or objects that have short a, e, i, o, and u vowels in their names available.  Ask the children to select a picture or object for each short vowel sound as you give it.  Place a *short a* flash card on the desk or table.  Ask the student to group the pictures or objects for short *a*.  This may be done in two separate groups.
Repeat for other vowels.  Check those completed correctly.

_____ a        _____ e        _____ i        _____ o        _____ u

Review the initial consonant digraphs in the same manner using pictures or objects.

_____ sh        _____ ch        _____ th(soft)        _____ th(hard)

Review all initial consonant sounds using picture cards or objects. Use groups of 5 or 6:

| | | | | | | |
|---|---|---|---|---|---|---|
| First group: | _____ k | _____ c | _____ f | _____ b | _____ d | _____ l |
| Second group: | _____ j | _____ g | _____ h | _____ m | _____ n | |
| Third group: | _____ v | _____ w | _____ y | _____ r | _____ s | |
| Fourth group: | _____ z | _____ qu | _____ x | _____ t | _____ p | |

Include some pictures which begin with sounds other than those in the group in each set.
Ask more advanced students to name these extra sounds if they can.  Record which additional sounds are recognized.

Review long vowel sounds in the same manner.

_____ a        _____ e        _____ i        _____ o        _____ u

# Language Arts Kindergarten Student Evaluation

Review all final consonants covered to this point using pictures or objects. Take them in groups of 4 or 5.

| | | | |
|---|---|---|---|
| _____ b | _____ m | _____ ck | _____ d |
| _____ g | _____ k | _____ l | _____ p |
| _____ n | _____ r | _____ s | _____ t |
| _____ v | _____ w | _____ x | _____ z |

Review all final consonant digraphs either using pictures and objects as above or by reading words which end in the digraphs and asking the student to select the card for the correct digraph. Lay cards for __ch, __th, __sh.

_____ ch  _____ th  _____ sh

## Writing:
Have paper and pencils ready for the student and an alphabet chart which shows the correct formation of letters. Check the student on all letters of the alphabet.
Check off all letters formed correctly.

| | | | | |
|---|---|---|---|---|
| ___ A | ___ F | ___ K | ___ P | ___ U |
| ___ B | ___ G | ___ L | ___ Q | ___ V |
| ___ C | ___ H | ___ M | ___ R | ___ W |
| ___ D | ___ I | ___ N | ___ S | ___ X |
| ___ E | ___ J | ___ O | ___ T | ___ Y |
| | | | | ___ Z |

| | | | | |
|---|---|---|---|---|
| ___ a | ___ f | ___ k | ___ p | ___ u |
| ___ b | ___ g | ___ l | ___ q | ___ v |
| ___ c | ___ h | ___ m | ___ r | ___ w |
| ___ d | ___ i | ___ n | ___ s | ___ x |
| ___ e | ___ j | ___ o | ___ t | ___ y |
| | | | | ___ z |

## Left/right:
Check left/right progression in writing. Ask the student to look at a page in a large print book and show you where to begin reading and in what direction to read.

## Position/ direction/ listening:
Have several small objects available. Tell the student that you will ask him to do certain activities. You will give a direction only once. Using the objects give simple directions which check the understanding of the following concepts:

| | | | | |
|---|---|---|---|---|
| _____ up | _____ down | _____ in | _____ out | _____ in front of |
| _____ behind | _____ open | _____ closed | _____ over | _____ under |
| _____ high | _____ low | _____ inside | _____ outside | _____ top |
| _____ bottom | | | | |

Examples: Put the ball under the table.
Place the crayons in the box.

Give the student a blank sheet of paper.  Give directions such as the following suggested.
Read the direction once.

Examples:

_____ Write your name at the top of the paper.
_____ Draw some grass at the bottom of the paper.
_____ Draw a line across the middle of the paper.
_____ Draw a house on the line.
_____ Draw a door on the front of the house.
_____ Draw a tree behind the house.
_____ Draw a bird on top of the tree.
_____ Draw the sun high up in the sky.
_____ Draw a blue ball in the grass.
_____ Draw a table next to the house.
_____ Draw a cat under the table.
_____ Draw a cloud in front of the sun.

Continue this process checking the concepts for position and direction.

| _____ up | _____ down | _____ in | _____ out | _____ in front of |
|---|---|---|---|---|
| _____ behind | _____ open | _____ closed | _____ over | _____ under |
| _____ high | _____ low | _____ inside | _____ outside | _____ top |
| _____ bottom | _____ middle | | | |

## Size:

Have several objects of varying sizes available and pictures of things which can be compared on
the basis of size.  Check the knowledge of size by asking the student to find one object or picture
for each.  Be specific.  For example: If you have a picture of several buildings, ask the student to
find the tallest building, or the biggest building, or the smallest building, and so on.   If you have
three different sizes of balls, cars, dolls, ask for the big ball, or the little doll.

| _____ big | _____ little | _____ large | _____ small | _____ tall |
|---|---|---|---|---|
| _____ biggest | _____ smallest | _____ largest | _____ tallest | |

## Sequencing:

Place three or more sets of story sequence cards on the desk or table in front of the student.
Ask the student to sort out the cards that go together.  Then ask the student to put the three
cards that go together in order of what happened first, next, and last.

_____ Chose cards that fit together.
_____ Put sequence in order.
_____ Could not find cards that fit together.
_____ Could not put in sequence.

Place alphabet flash cards in front of the student. Choose five letters that run in order, such as d, e, f, g, h. Mix the cards and ask the student to put them in the correct alphabetical order.

\_\_\_\_\_ Completed          \_\_\_\_\_ Not completed

Repeat the same procedure using numerals from 1 through 6.

\_\_\_\_\_ Completed          \_\_\_\_\_ Not completed

## Patterns

Use some simple pattern cards of basic shapes and colors with the student. Have basic shapes cut from construction paper available for the student to use to copy the pattern. Ask the student:

1. To identify the pattern and tell what shape and color will come next.
2. To use basic color shapes to duplicate the pattern.
3. To create a pattern of his own.

\_\_\_\_\_ Student can identify the pattern on the card.

\_\_\_\_\_ Student can duplicate the pattern.

\_\_\_\_\_ Student can create a new pattern.

## Rhyming and Word Formation:

Make a set of cards with some of the more common rhyme endings on them: -un, -ing, -ee (e), -ar, -ip, -all. Have available a set of alphabet cards which the student can use to form new words with these endings. Ask the student to sound out the ending. Ask the student to see how many new words can be made using the ending. Record the students efforts.

\_\_\_\_\_ -un     \_\_\_\_\_ -ing     \_\_\_\_\_ -ee(e)     \_\_\_\_\_ -ar     \_\_\_\_\_ -ip     \_\_\_\_\_ -all

## Sentence formation:

\_\_\_\_\_ The student speaks in complete sentences.

\_\_\_\_\_ The student can describe things in complete sentences.

\_\_\_\_\_ The student can recognize a complete sentence in a story.

\_\_\_\_\_ The student knows that a complete sentence begins with a capital letter and ends with a period.